Boxing

An Illustrated History

BOXING
An Illustrated History

HARRY CARPENTER

CRESCENT BOOKS
New York

Preceding page: Carpentier
begins well against Battling
Siki, from Senegal, at the
Velodrome Buffalo in Paris in
1922. But he was counted out
in the end after a left swing
from Siki, who became world
light-heavyweight champion

© 1982, 1975 Harry Carpenter

Designed and produced by London Editions Limited
70 Old Compton Street, London WIV 5PA

First English edition published in 1975 by William Collins

This 1982 edition is published by Crescent Books, a division of
Crown Plublishers Inc.

Library of Congress Cataloging in Publication Data

Carpenter, Harry
  Boxing, an illustrated history.

1. Boxing - History. I. Title.
GV1121.C36   796.8'309   82-7472
ISBN 0-517-37855-8   AACR2
hgfedcba

Printed in Belgium

Contents

Introduction by Harry Carpenter

Boxing has always been the big sport in my life, since that summer of 1937 in a London suburb when I was allowed to get up in the middle of the night, creep downstairs in my dressing-gown, sit in front of the wireless, and listen to the American radio commentary of the Joe Louis-Tommy Farr fight. Twenty years later I was able to claim both Joe and Tommy as my friends and even now that appears to me to be some sort of miracle. I am one of those lucky people in life whose work involves the very thing they enjoy most.

A history of boxing is nothing new, but this one, if I may be allowed to say so, does go about it differently from the rest. Instead of dividing the sport weight by weight and telling the story that way, I have divided it decade by decade and tried to tell the story of each 10 years as a separate essay. Whether it works well enough is for you to judge.

Undeniably, the book has one enormous advantage over many others. Thanks to the untiring efforts of my publishing colleagues who specialise in picture research, I believe we do offer between these covers many of the finest boxing photographs ever taken. In fact, the reason you are reading these preliminary words may well be that you were tempted to reach for the book simply because of the remarkable photo on the cover: Muhammad Ali, with an immodest fist and a vengeful snarl, towering over the pitiable figure of Sonny Liston in Lewiston, Maine. I was there at the time and can vouch that the photo perpetuates the drama.

Enough of this. May you enjoy what lies ahead – as true a wish for a book as it is for life.

London, 1982

BC-AD: Where would we be without Mr Figg?

FIGG, MENDOZA, CRIBB, SAYERS, SULLIVAN

The English invented boxing as we know it: a fair fight, hands only, no aid to the fist other than a protection of horsehair in leather. The glove is there to guard the hand from damage, not add to its power. Therein lies the demarcation line between boxing today and boxing yesterday.

Yesterday is a long time ago – back, back, back into the thick mists of ancient time. Homer, around 1100BC, was the first fight reporter. In the 23rd book of the *Iliad*, he describes Epeus *v.* Euryalus, promoted by Achilles at the funeral games of Patroclus. For the winner: a mule. The loser: a drinking cup:

> Amid the circle now each champion stands,
> And poises high in air his iron hands,
> With clashing gauntlets now they fiercely close,
> Their crackling jaws re-echo to the blows,
> And painful sweat from all their members flows.
> At length Epeus dealt a weighty blow
> Full on the cheek of his unwary foe.
> Beneath that ponderous arm's resistless sway.
> Down dropped he, nerveless, and extended lay.
> As a large fish, when winds and waters roar,
> By some huge billow dash'd against the shore
> Lies panting: not less batter'd with his wound
> The bleeding hero pants upon the ground.
> (translation by Alexander Pope)

Epeus, builder of the wooden horse, winner by KO. Pierce Egan, noted chronicler of fights in Georgian times, could not have etched that final blow more graphically. The very word, boxing, is from the ancient Greek 'puxos', a box, itself derived from 'pugme', a fist doubled for fighting. The clenched fist, you see, resembles the shape of a box, and all else follows. In Latin it becomes 'pugilatus', fighting with the fist, hence pugilism. Classical Greek and Latin are studded with references to boxing: and studded is an apt word. Our barbarous ancestors 'studded' the fist with rawhide and spikes, salving their consciences with pious rules forbidding one man to kill another on pain of losing the prize!

One look at the *caestus*, the knuckleduster these gladiators wore, is enough to convince us that Baroness Summerskill, the British

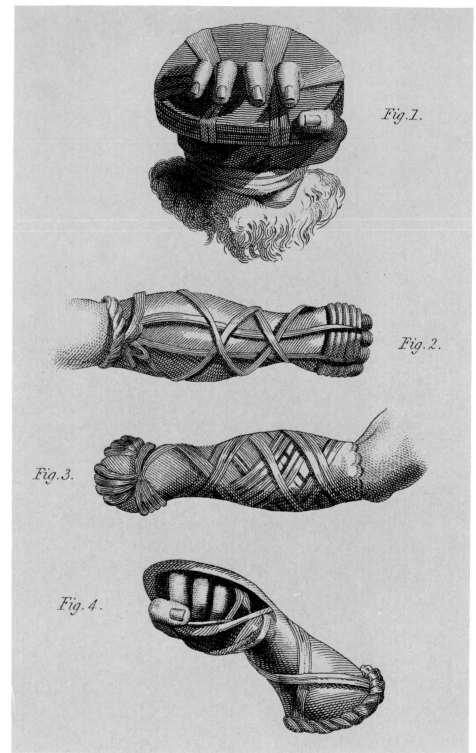

Types of caesti (above): 1. Rawhide, cut circular, with fingers thrust through holes. 2. Leather binding, tops of fingers protruding. 3. Fist completely bound. Greek poets write of iron and lead studs being inserted. 4. Not so deadly. Knuckles and back of hand protected with leather only.
Boxing BC (right): ancient pugilists wearing the heavy caesti. Arms were swung up and brought crashing down in hammer blows

Ant. Sal. exc.

This Dutch engraving (above) from a sketch dated 1674 clearly shows that boxing flourished to some extent in Europe before its official 'birth' in England in the 18th century. Broughton's Rules (right), as displayed at his Soho amphitheatre in front of the Duke of Cumberland. Note the gloves in the surrounding pictures. Broughton called them 'mufflers'. His aristocratic pupils wore them, but not the lower-class prizefighters

scourge of modern boxing, would have been better employed 2000 years ago. Layers of bull's hide, cut circular with holes for the fingers, were bound to the wrist with thongs. The *de luxe* model came with iron teeth or lumps of lead embedded in the hide. To be fair, the warriors were allowed to don the 'amphotides', a leather helmet not so different from the headguard today's professional boxers wear in training and which the US Armed Forces insist on their amateurs using in competition. One day prudence may compel all boxers to wear one at all times. As usual, the Greeks will have had a word for it.

They bred them tough, as though training for war. Eurydamus swallowed his broken teeth, rather than spit them out and show he was hurt. In the 23rd Olympiad of the ancient Games, Onomastos was boxing's first gold-medallist, fighting nude, body gleaming with oil. The weight of the *caesti* prevented hitting horizontally from the shoulder. The fist was swung up and crashed down like a hammer-blow. In the 38th Olympiad, *caesti* were discarded and a new event, the pancratium (all-round contest), devised. Wrestling, kicking, hair-pulling, eye-gouging, even strangling, were permitted. Biting, however,

was not. When boxing revived in England, it was much like this for 150 years.

Lucilius, satirical Latin poet of the second century BC, jibes tartly at the 'sport', mocking all Olympic pugilists with faces battered out of shape: 'Having such a face, Olympicus, go not to a fountain nor look into any transparent water, for you, like Narcissus, seeing your face clearly, will die, hating yourself to death.' (translation by W. R. Paton)

The later Romans, in their debauched circuses, dragged the sport down deeper still, and when their Empire fell, so did boxing. A thousand years pass with almost no reference, just an occasional glimmer in the dark. King Alfred's soldiers box for recreation. The city fathers of Tuscany's Siena encourage it in the thirteenth century as a safety-valve for young Italians, who much prefer killing other Italians. Richard III is alleged to be handy with his fists.

In 1681, when Charles II is king, the *Protestant Mercury* reports a match between a footman and a butcher, and a few years later is born, in the Oxfordshire village of Thame, the man destined to start a boom which has lasted for the best part of 300 years. James Figg (or Fig) was an itinerant, illiterate roustabout who could wield cudgel, backsword, quarterstaff *and* his fists. He worked the rowdy fairgrounds in village and town through the reign of Queen Anne into that of George I and by 1719, when he was twenty-four, had clobbered enough other rough gentlemen to establish himself as the first recorded champion of England.

Figg, his pate shaven so rivals couldn't grab him by the hair, was lionized. He was friendly with Jonathan Swift and Alexander Pope. William Hogarth painted him and designed his trade-card. The Earl of Peterborough set him up in an amphitheatre in London's Tottenham Court Road, a wooden arena seating 1000 at ground level, hundreds more in the gallery. A circular stage, 40ft across, set in the centre of the floor, was guarded with wooden rails and here 'Professor' Figg, master of ye noble science of defence, exhibited his skills for 'money, love or a bellyful'. Figg was not all goodness. Sometimes a promised show was called off and no money returned. Sad that such a scallywag should be The Founder, but in remission he's had many successors who have done worse things.

Salute James Figg! His prowess prompted imitation, which bred rivalry and led to a succession of champions. He died young, only thirty-nine, but not before he had dis-

THE RING.

RULES

TO BE OBSERVED IN ALL BATTLES ON THE STAGE

I. THAT a square of a Yard be chalked in the middle of the Stage; and on every fresh set-to after a fall, or being parted from the rails, each Second is to bring his Man to the side of the square, and place him opposite to the other, and till they are fairly set-to at the Lines, it shall not be lawful for one to strike at the other.

II. That, in order to prevent any Disputes, the time a Man lies after a fall, if the Second does not bring his Man to the side of the square, within the space of half a minute, he shall be deemed a beaten Man.

III. That in every main Battle, no person whatever shall be upon the Stage, except the Principals and their Seconds; the same rule to be observed in bye-battles, except that in the latter, Mr. Broughton is allowed to be upon the Stage to keep decorum, and to assist Gentlemen in getting to their places, provided always he does not interfere in the Battle; and whoever pretends to infringe these Rules to be turned immediately out of the house. Every body is to quit the Stage as soon as the Champions are stripped, before the set-to.

IV. That no Champion be deemed beaten, unless he fails coming up to the line in the limited time, or that his own Second declares him beaten. No Second is to be allowed to ask his man's Adversary any questions, or advise him to give out.

V. That in bye-battles, the winning man to have two-thirds of the Money given, which shall be publicly divided upon the Stage, notwithstanding any private agreements to the contrary.

VI. That to prevent Disputes, in every main Battle the Principals shall, on coming on the Stage, choose from among the gentlemen present two Umpires, who shall absolutely decide all Disputes that may arise about the Battle; and if the two Umpires cannot agree, the said Umpires to choose a third, who is to determine it.

VII. That no person is to hit his Adversary when he is down, or seize him by the ham, the breeches, or any part below the waist: a man on his knees to be reckoned down.

As agreed by several Gentlemen at Broughton's Amphitheatre,
Tottenham Court Road, August 16, 1743.

Will. Hogarth fᵗ

James Figg

Master of yᵉ Noble Science of Defence
on yᵉ right hand in Oxford Road
near Adam & Eve court. teaches Gentle-
-men yᵉ use of yᵉ small. backsword. &
Quarterstaff. at home & abroad

covered a young waterman from Cirencester who forsook Figg's rougher arts of eye-gouging and grappling to concentrate on a form of barefist fighting closer to modern boxing. Jack Broughton, born 1704, lived eighty-four years and was master of blocking, parrying, slipping and hitting on the retreat. He beat George Taylor to become champion, then killed a challenger, George Stevenson. He thought at first of retiring, but instead in 1743 drew up a code of conduct, boxing's first rules, so basic and intelligent that today's regulations are closely related. Briefly, they prescribe:

A square of one yard drawn in the centre of the stage, to which boxers are brought to face one another at the start and after each fall.

A man has 30 seconds after a fall to return to the square; otherwise, he is beaten.

Each boxer to choose an umpire to settle disputes. If they cannot agree, a third is picked and his word final.

No hitting a man who is down (on the knees is considered down).

These rules of Broughton's lasted almost 100 years. His patron, the Duke of Cumberland, brought him other noblemen who wished to learn, so Broughton invented gloves for them. He called them 'mufflers', worn in sparring by the aristocrats to save them, as Broughton put it, 'the inconveniency of black eyes, broken jaws and bloody noses'. But gloves in earnest combat are at least 100 years away and the cross-buttock throw will remain a part of boxing almost into the twentieth century. It's described in *Fistiana*, published 1868: '... the most fatal of all falls ... get your arm firmly over your adversary's neck, grasping his loose arm with the other hand ... get his crutch upon your hip or buttock, give him a cant over your shoulder: .. he goes over with tremendous violence, and you fall upon his abdomen.'

We hurry on through the eighteenth century, sullied by ruffians such as butcher Jack Slack of the East Anglian city of Norwich, who 'threw' fights and with his dreaded

James Figg, first champion of England, was illiterate, but had artistic admirers. This business card (left) was designed and drawn by William Hogarth

Above: Jack Broughton (on the left) sparring with Figg, his patron. Broughton came to London from Gloucestershire and drew up boxing's first humane rules in 1743. Some are not so different from today's.
A street fight (below), painted in oils by Andreas Moller around 1750. It hangs in the Town Library of Kassel, Germany

Top: Mendoza (on the left), the first Jewish champion. Modern scientific boxing is traced back to Mendoza, a small man who beat hefty ones with skill and agility. First black man to make a mark in prizefighting: Bill Richmond (below). British general, Earl Percy, brought him to England from America in 1777. Richmond's losing fight with Cribb in 1805 was the first Anglo-American championship

THE CLOSE OF THE BATTLE or the

Englishman Cribb pulled a fast one on Molineaux, the plantation slave, in 1810 (above). Cribb was all in after 28 rounds, but his seconds accused the American of loading his fists with lead. The row gave Cribb breathing space and he won after another five rounds. Cribb beat him again in 1811

Gentleman John Jackson (above), friend of Byron, was not so friendly with Mendoza, whose long hair he grabbed

PION TRIUMPHANT. *1 Round. Sparring for one minute, Crib made play right & left a right handed blow let slightly on the brow of [...] down by a hit on the throat 2 Crib shewed first blood from the mouth, a dreadful rally Crib put in a good [...] received by the Moor on the head [...] rally the Black deficient in wind, requires a number in the body, Crib damaged in both eyes & [...] 4 rally his exertions Crib [...] with a light [...] blow & received either in falling. 6 Black fatigued by want of wind, a blow in the body mark'd settles him up 7 a [...] & that of great length. 7 Black [...] [...] falls from weakness 8 Black rallies Crib made him gets his head under his left arm & fall'd [...] 9 Black runs in [...] with a left handed [...] made an unsuccessful effort & fall from weakness, it [...] [...] of the fight Black received another knock [...] unable again to come up [...]*

cleaver punch blinded Jack Broughton and brought him to his knees in fourteen minutes. Boxing fell into disrepute, to the dismay of Dr Samuel Johnson, who wrote: 'I should be sorry to see prizefighting go out. Every art should be preserved, and the art of defence is surely important.'

When the Doctor penned that, the man to lift boxing out of the gutter was growing up in Aldgate in London's East End. Daniel Mendoza, first Jew to illumine the sport (he was called the Light of Israel), improved on Broughton's arts. At 5ft 7ins and about 160lbs, he showed how a small man could fend off the bully-boys' clumsy rushes, starting in the 1780s by taming Harry the Coalheaver. He became champion roughly at the time Marie Antoinette lost her head and was not deposed until 1795, when Gentleman John Jackson belied his name by grabbing Mendoza's long black locks with one hand and pummelling him in the face with the other (nothing in Broughton's Rules to say he shouldn't – hadn't Mendoza heard of Figg's shaven head or was he vain?). Mendoza's hit-and-hop-it artistry didn't please all. Some thought him cowardly, but clever boxers suffer this through the ages. Jack Johnson was similarly accused. Mendoza led the way for Jewish fighters, of whom Dutch Sam, inventor of the uppercut, and his son, Young Dutch Sam, first welterweight champion of England in 1825, were early examples.

Artist's impression of how Deaf Burke (above) escaped from his New Orleans fight with Irish Sam O'Rourke in 1836. When O'Rourke was in trouble, his mob cut the ropes and invaded the ring with cudgels. Some reports say Burke 'ran for his life'. Others that a friend just happened to have a horse handy.
Deaf Burke (left), son of a Thames waterman, was the Muhammad Ali of his day. He talked to opponents during battle. But could he hear their replies? He died of tuberculosis at the age of 35

As the eighteenth gives way to the nineteenth century, we are in Napoleonic times and one-eyed Jem Belcher, grandson of the crooked Slack, knots his yellow kerchief to a cornerpost and starts a fashion. Soon everyone flaunts his colours and in Britain today amateurs still sport coloured sashes for identification. Belcher gives way to Hen Pearce, the Game Chicken, first unbeaten

champion since Figg. It's also the era of John Gully, rescued from a debtors' jail by Pearce, then thrashed by him in a fight lasting 1hr 17min. Gully becomes Liberal MP for Pontefract in Yorkshire, a colliery owner, wins the Derby and St Leger with his horses, and sires twenty-four children. The heroes and villains parade; we have come a hundred years since Figg. England still has her monopoly of boxing, soon to end. America is stirring after the Declaration of Independence and in 1777 a British general sails home from New York with Bill Richmond, fourteen-year-old son of a slave. Richmond is the first negro and first native-born American to make a mark in prizefighting, all of it in England.

In 1805 Richmond, now forty-two, fought Tom Cribb, respected champion of England, and lost after ninety minutes, but in America another negro, Tom Molineaux, born on a Virginia plantation, heard of the heroic battle and set sail for England. With Richmond's help, Molineaux fought Cribb twice for the championship, at Copthall Common, Sussex, in 1810, and Thistleton Gap, Leicester, in 1811. He lost both, but the second fight drew the biggest crowd yet – 25,000 – and Anglo-American rivalry was established. The term

'ring', from the ring of people who surrounded these early fighters in the fields, has lived on as a synonym for the sport.

In London, Gentleman John Jackson, who so roughly seized Mendoza by the hair, formed the Pugilistic Society in 1814 in a bid to control English prizefighting. George IV, at his coronation in 1820, had a bodyguard headed by Jackson, with Belcher, Cribb and Tom Spring, Cribb's protégé, as members. Despite all this, prizefighting was still a hole-and-corner pursuit, certainly in America, where it flourished illegally on the eastern seaboard in the backrooms of sailors' taverns. In 1816 Jacob Hyer and Tom Beasley had fought the first public contest on American soil, but it was not until 1849, when Hyer's son Tom beat Yankee Sullivan in Baltimore for 5000 dollars, that America's first heavyweight champion was proclaimed.

First English champion to fight in America was James (Deaf) Burke, who in 1833 at St Albans had taken part in the longest heavyweight fight of all time: ninety-nine rounds, lasting 3hr 16min, with Irishman Simon Byrne, a bloody, brutal encounter from which Byrne died. This enraged another Irish fighter, Sam O'Rourke, who bellowed for

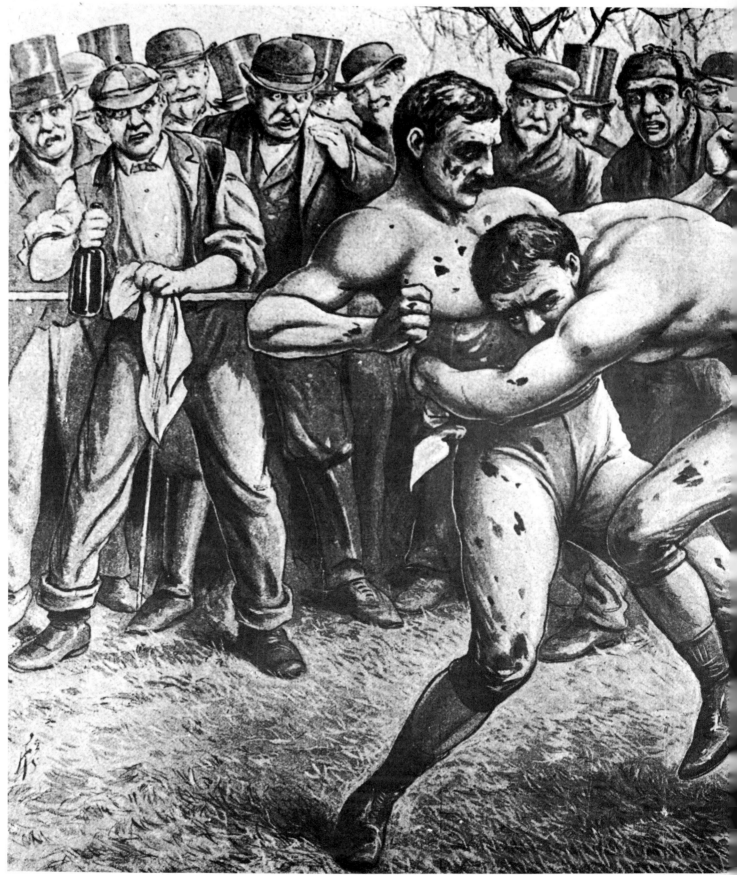

The first southpaw? — William Abednego Thompson (above), whose middle name was corrupted to Bendigo. He beat Deaf Burke to become England's champion in 1839. After going to jail 28 times for fighting illegally, he turned evangelist.

England's champion Tom King (left) struggles to stay upright as 6ft 2ins American, John C. Heenan, tries to throw him in their 35-minute, £1000-a-side fight at Wadhurst, Kent, in 1863. Heenan's seconds threw in the sponge at the start of the 24th round

Overpage: history here in every way — the last of the bare-knuckle championships. John L. Sullivan is beating challenger Jake Kilrain at Richburg, Mississippi, in 1889. It's Sullivan's last win as champion (75 rounds, 2hr 16mins). And it's the only bare-fist fight ever photographed

revenge from across the Atlantic. So Burke set sail and in New Orleans, 1836, fought O'Rourke and had the Irishman in such trouble that O'Rourke's cronies cut the ropes and attacked Burke, who ran for his life. British boxers have seldom done well in America since.

Note how the Irish, driven from their own land by famine, dominate early American ring history. John Morrissey and Paddy Ryan, two of the earliest champions, came from Tipperary.

Remember Broughton's Rules in 1743? In 1838, as Victoria settles into her long reign, they are revised and renamed the London Prize Ring Rules. The square yard is out. Now we have a single line called the scratch. 'Coming up to scratch' works its way into the language as a cliché for being on time and in good order. Kicking, gouging, butting are outlawed and so is that old bugbear of going down (and getting a rest) without being hit, which made so many of the old fights long and tedious. Now a complete thirty-second rest is allowed after a fall, plus another eight seconds in which to come up to scratch, *alone*. This was vital. Many fighters had died after being carried back to the square by their seconds and made to fight when totally exhausted.

Deaf Burke, back in England safe from O'Rourke's cut-throats, lost his title to Bold Bendigo of Nottingham in the first championship under the new Rules. But now we move on to 1860 and the most remarkable fight in 150 years since Figg. Tom Sayers of Brighton, England's champion, and John Camel Heenan of California, America's champion, are to meet in the first world title fight, and all England and all America know about it, illegal though it may be. Special trains are hired and pull out of London Bridge station in the early hours of 17 April, fans and fighters aboard, bound for a dawn rendezvous in a rural field. Metropolitan Police line the track for fifteen miles to ensure the fight doesn't take place on their 'manor'.

The patrol peters out and the train steams on to Farnborough, Hampshire, where Sayers, 5ft 8 ins, weighs in at 149lbs, and Heenan, 6ft 2 ins, at 195lbs. The American uses this weight in round after round to cross-buttock the little Englishman to the turf, while Sayers prods and pokes the big American in the eyes. Sayers has the breath knocked out of him, Heenan is half-blinded with blood, and in the thirty-seventh round, when the American has Sayers bent back across the ropes and his two hands at the Englishman's throat, some-

one cuts the ropes and the mob storms into the ring. The referee runs, but the fighters stay and grapple, until in the forty-second round police at last burst through. The two men, who have fought for 2hr 20min, break and run, and a draw is declared.

Thackeray and Dickens were there, and so were American newspapermen, but what with the midnight exodus, thuggery of the crowd, tardy action by police, and brutality of the fight itself, sharp questions are asked in the House of Commons, and prizefighting is doomed.

Prizefighting, yes. Boxing, no. A new code of conduct was needed and it came from John Graham Chambers, a member of the London Amateur Athletic Club, in 1865 (often confused with Arthur Chambers, the famous lightweight champion of the time). He wrote out twelve rules, designed to govern amateur boxing but which came to be accepted on all sides. In essence they are the rules we understand today: a 3-minute round, with a minute's interval; no cross-buttock throwing; a 10-second count after a knockdown; and, most important of all, gloves to be worn. John Sholto Douglas, the 8th Marquess of Queensberry, agreed to sponsor the new rules and they came to bear his name. But the rules were not accepted quickly, as we shall see.

As Queen Victoria celebrates her Golden Jubilee in 1887, who is this beefy American with the fine mustachios stepping off the boat in England and getting a mighty hello from the Liverpool Irish? It's John L. Sullivan, the Boston Strong Boy, whose father came from Tralee and mother from Athlone. He's already a legend on both sides of the Atlantic, having beaten Paddy Ryan with his bare hands in 1882. Now as America's champion, and a roaring, hard-drinking man of the world, he wants another fight with little Charley Mitchell of England, a middleweight who once knocked him down in a New York fight. Sullivan likes to thump his big fist on the bar and bellow: 'I can lick any son-of-a-bitch in the world!' He probably can, but he's drowning his health in whisky.

Sullivan and Mitchell can't fight in England because the law won't let them, so off they go to Baron Rothschild's estate in Chantilly, France, behind the stables, ankle deep in mud, battling for thirty-nine rounds and over three hours, at which point the referee calls a draw and the gendarmes move in, locking both men up for several hours. Mitchell has upheld British honour, but America is rapidly taking over. Fate has picked on big John

Lawrence Sullivan to usher boxing from its bareknuckle days to the new glove era.

On 8 July 1889, Sullivan, miraculously fit again having survived typhoid, jaundice and whisky, fights Jake Kilrain at Richburg, Mississippi, under a blazing sun, his title at stake plus a 10,000-dollar side bet. During the long scorching fight Sullivan is sick, but when Kilrain asks if he'd like to quit, John L. knocks him down. Charley Mitchell, in Kilrain's corner, takes a message round to Sullivan: if Kilrain retires, will big John give him 2000 dollars? Sullivan nods yes, but before the deal is complete, referee Fitzpatrick declares Sullivan the winner, after 75 rounds, 2hr 16min.

It is the last bareknuckle championship, last under the old London Prize Ring Rules. Charley Mitchell reckons he can still beat Sullivan. He won't get the chance, but he will fight Corbett. By then it's Queensberry Rules.

Not bad. We've come from the murderous *caestus* to civilized padding of the hands – and it's taken only 3000 years.

Norfolk-born Jem Mace, one of the last of England's bare-fist champions and a defensive genius. Like Mendoza, he handed down scientific principles on which today's boxing is based. On a New Zealand tour, he discovered Bob Fitzsimmons

Gentleman Jim and those other swells in gloves 1890-9

HEAVY: SULLIVAN,   CORBETT,   FITZSIMMONS,   JEFFRIES

LIGHT: MCAULIFFE,   CARNEY,   BURGE

FEATHER: DIXON

BANTAM: DIXON

Big John L. was not THAT big. His 5ft 10½ins puts him eyeball to eyeball with Rocky Marciano, the smallest recent champion, and he is dwarfed by Muhammad Ali and George Foreman, both 5ins taller and a stone and a half heavier. But Sullivan was a BIG character and left his mark on the sport for years. We must leave him for the moment in his ten-year stint as champion, challenging all-comers to stand up for four rounds with gloves and 1000 dollars as bait while we look around at this crucial closing decade of the nineteenth century.

Jem Mace, England's great bareknuckle champion who quit competing only in 1890 at the age of fifty-eight is, like Sullivan, famous the world over and has taken his skills to America, where they have been absorbed and reproduced, with improvements, ever since. Just as we gave soccer to the world, then lost our way, so it is in boxing. Mace also spread the gospel in Australasia, a matter of vital importance for Britain, as we shall see.

In 1890 fights with gloves are common-place, although the heavyweights have held out to the bitter end. A rudimentary scale of weights exists, but champions tend to nominate the weight they can fight best at, and make THAT the limit. The Queensberry Rules are slowly being adopted and adapted; the sport is feeling its way into a new era. We must just glance back at an extraordinary international lightweight battle in 1887 between Irish-born Jack McAuliffe of America and Jem Carney of England in a Massachusetts barn at 1am by lantern-light. Each fighter was permitted to take fourteen friends, so with the referee a total of thirty-one persons trooped silently out to the barn after midnight. All this to keep the police away!

For more than three hours they battled; it was well past 4am and into the seventy-fourth round when Carney had McAuliffe on the floor for the second time. The American was saved by his fourteen pals rushing the ring, at which point referee Frank Stevenson hastily called a draw. They wore skin-tight gloves without padding. The draw saved McAuliffe's amazing record. He fought for thirteen years and was never beaten. As if to prove it wouldn't lie down easily, the old prize-ring produced its longest fight of all in 1893 when lightweights Andy Bowen and Jack Burke fought 110 rounds in New Orleans, from 9.15pm to 4.34am, a matter of 7hr 19min, about the time it takes to fly from New York to London.

A fighter without a flaw? George Dixon (above), of Nova Scotia, knew it all, from more than 800 fights. Late in his career, he fought in Britain, beating Pedlar Palmer and Digger Stanley, but losing to Jim Driscoll.
The great John L. (right), ready for anyone. But that paunch gives the game away. Sullivan has finished with fighting. And with whisky. He preaches temperance from now on

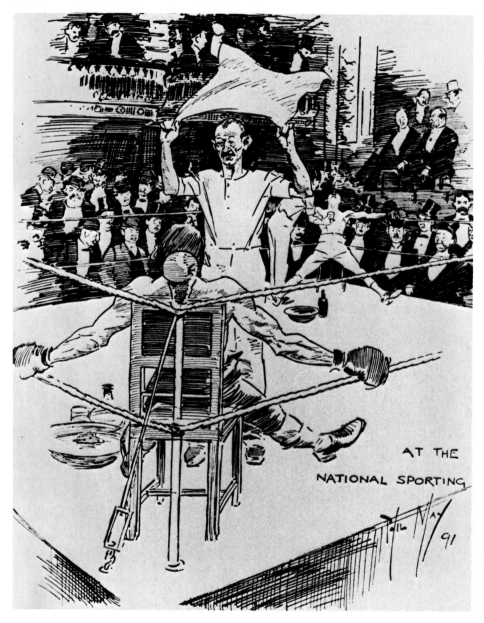

AT THE
NATIONAL SPORTING

Renowned sporting artist Phil
May captures the atmosphere of
the National Sporting Club

Australia, under Mace's influence, begins to figure prominently, notably with one of the finest featherweights of all time: Young Griffo (Albert Griffiths), never beaten at his weight, who had to chase bigger men like McAuliffe, one of the few who outpointed him. Griffo sailed from Sydney in 1893 and had three draws in the States with George Dixon, the superb Little Chocolate, who may well be the greatest pound-for-pound fighter of all.

A quadroon (his grandfather was white) Dixon was The Fighter Without a Flaw. He could box, punch, had dazzling footwork and brilliant defence. Born in Nova Scotia, he appeared at London's aristocratic Pelican Club in 1890, where he won the world bantam title by beating Nunc Wallace, the English champion, in eighteen rounds, wearing 4oz gloves. He gave up that title and in 1891 in San Francisco won the featherweight crown by stopping Abe Willis of Australia in five rounds. With one break he held it until 1900.

In twenty years, Dixon had more than 800 bouts, at one time averaging FIFTEEN A WEEK! Even more remarkable, he was only a flyweight (112lbs), a division which didn't exist at the time. Had it done so he might have joined Henry Armstrong and Bob Fitzsimmons as a triple world champion. Out of the ring he drank heavily, chased girls and gambled away a fortune, dying a pauper at thirty-nine.

Focus your attention closely now on London's Covent Garden, particularly on No 43 King Street where on the night of 5 March 1891 hansom cabs are disgorging sporty gentlemen of prosperity (stockbrokers, shopkeepers, bookmakers) privileged to attend the opening night of the National Sporting Club. The sporting earl, Lord Lonsdale, he of the fat cigar and even fatter income, £130,000 a year, is president and it is run autocratically, for the future good of boxing, by John Fleming and A. F. (Peggy) Bettinson, ex-amateur lightweight champion of England. Bear in mind, a prizefight is still illegal. If police get wind of one they jump on the fighters beforehand and bind them over to keep the peace. Those caught fighting are treated as felons. Prizefighting reeks of ruffians fixing contests for betting coups. Bernard Shaw has written: 'It isn't boxers who bring disrepute to boxing, but betting men.'

The National Sporting Club, fighting its legal battles from a bastion of respectability, will change all that. The Club lasted almost into the 1930s in its original form and in those thirty-eight years enforced the Queensberry Rules, regularized title fights, conducted its bouts with a decorum horribly close to reverence. When it closed, it left behind the British Boxing Board of Control (1929) which continues to govern professional boxing in Britain today.

The supreme irony of the NSC is that it existed for betting. Because large sums were being put up by its middle-class members in wagers and patronage of fighters, strict control was essential. Evening dress was encouraged, but not compulsory. The referee sat outside the ring wearing a top hat. Members, men only, descended from the grill-room, where they dined on lamb chops and steaks, to a basement theatre. Privileged members sat on the stage, others in the stalls. The ring was in the centre of the stalls under electric chandeliers. Co-owner Fleming's creed was: 'Every boxer should try to overcome his adversary in a fair, manly and generous spirit, and bear in mind that there is more honour in losing like a gentleman than in winning like a blackguard.' Some patrons, not so high-minded, in dull bouts would shout 'More gore!' not during the rounds, of course, when silence was enforced.

Prime importance of the NSC is that it took on and beat the courts. A series of test cases began the year before it was founded, 1890, when Jack McAuliffe was in London to fight Frank Slavin of Australia. Both were arrested beforehand and bound over in the sum of £1000 apiece, the first time a fight under Queensberry Rules had fallen foul of the law. Lord Lonsdale summoned support and decided to go ahead with the fight at the Ormonde Club, Walworth, where McAuliffe, in a miserable showing, collapsed in the second round. The fighters were arrested, but the charges withdrawn. The case led, however, to a change in the rules: a referee was empowered for the first time to stop a fight when a man had no chance.

Legal action – and the NSC saw plenty in the next few years – was based on the assumption that sparring with gloves as a test of skill was not illegal, but to fight with the express purpose of knocking the other man unconscious WAS. In 1897 America's Jimmy Barry, successor of George Dixon as bantam champion, knocked out Walter Croot of Leytonstone at the NSC in the twentieth and final round. Croot died of brain damage a few days later. Barry and NSC officials were summoned to Bow Street to see if they should be committed for trial at the Old Bailey, but were discharged.

A bastion of fair play at the National Sporting Club: top-hatted referee John H. Douglas, a timber-merchant described in the 'Daily Telegraph' as 'calm, cool, courageous, and as fair-minded as it is possible for a human being to be'. His timekeeper is Mr E. Zerega

In 1901, after another boxer died at the NSC, Club officials were charged with manslaughter but found not guilty. These cases are landmarks in boxing, whose legality has seldom been challenged since, although the British Board even today is careful never to mention a knockout in its regulations. Fighters are counted out of time.

Secure in the knowledge that boxing is changing its ruffian image, we press on. Skill, not endurance, is the essence. Those who take boxing forward are always the scientific exponents, from Broughton down through Corbett to Muhammad Ali, while the sluggers, like Dempsey and Marciano, splash on the colour.

This year of 1891 not only brought the NSC into being, but exactly fifty days before it opened an Englishman won the world middleweight title in New Orleans – Bob Fitzsimmons, of course, and Britain has not produced another like him. Born in Helston, Cornwall (a plaque marks the house), he was taken to New Zealand as a boy, where he learned the blacksmith's trade and by some incredible stroke of good fortune came across old Jem Mace out there in 1880, when Fitz was eighteen. Mace took this 140lbs stripling and entered him for the New Zealand amateur HEAVYWEIGHT championship. Using the ramrod lefts Mace had taught him, saving his big right for the finisher, Fitzsimmons toppled four big fellows in one night. Mace packed him off to Australia, to a gypsy protégé of his named Larry Foley, who rounded off the Englishman's fighting education. In 1890 Fitz sailed for San Francisco.

He was quickly dubbed Ruby Robert, because of his flaming red hair and freckles, and other less complimentary names. Fitzsimmons didn't look like an athlete. There was nothing of him from the waist down. He was knock-kneed, skinny, going bald and had a long nose. Billy McCarthy, an Australian he later KO'd, called him a bald-headed kangaroo, and John L. Sullivan described him as a fighting machine on stilts. But he had blacksmith's shoulders which produced a big punch for his weight (never more than 168lbs) and Mace and Foley had given him technique.

Boxing's new look: the first heavyweight championship with gloves. Sullivan, last of the bare-knuckle kings, falls to Corbett, a suave ex-bank clerk helping to fashion boxing's changing image

The Ex-Champion.

ROUND 21
SULLIVAN'S VAIN ATTEMPT TO RISE.

Gentleman Jim whips the Boston Strong Boy at New Orleans on September 7, 1892.

To win that middleweight crown he stopped Nonpareil Jack Dempsey, no relation of the future heavyweight king. This Dempsey is an Irish immigrant who's held the title nearly seven years, but in thirteen rounds Fitz has him down thirteen times and in the end is begging him to quit. Dempsey won't, so Fitz has to finish him, after which he helps carry him back to the corner, where Jack McAuliffe is one of his seconds.

Fitzsimmons is already twenty-nine, but this is only the first of his three world titles. He's just beginning, but old John L. Sullivan is near the end of HIS reign. The signs are there to see: a paunch, bags under the eyes, shortness of breath, all the classic symptoms of excessive lifting of the elbow.

Sullivan hasn't fought, apart from exhibitions, for three years and yet his world-wide army of supporters cannot believe that John L. is anything but invincible. Hasn't he been telling them so for ten years? How laughable that this dude, this ex-bank clerk, this Californian dandy called Corbett should think he can beat the Boston Strong Boy! Here's our first meeting with Gentleman Jim Corbett, whose very elegance and suavity epitomize boxing's new look. The fight with Sullivan in New Orleans is to be the first legal heavyweight championship with 5oz gloves and Queensberry Rules. Corbett fits the cleaned-up image to perfection. He's learned his boxing from an imported English coach, Professor Watson.

John L.'s jaunty backers will lay you 4–1 against Corbett this night of 7 September 1892: but surely there's a feeling in the air of something spectacular about to happen? Why, for example, should the Olympic Club of New Orleans make it a three-night orgy of boxing called the Carnival of Champions? On Monday, Jack McAuliffe puts his light-weight title up against Billy Myer, and wins. On Tuesday, George Dixon defends the feather crown against Jack Skelly, success-fully. Now, on Wednesday, the great climax, and Corbett comes stepping to the Club in a light summer suit, straw hat and bamboo cane. Billy Delaney, his handler, can't believe it: 'You're not going dressed like that?' says Corbett. 'Why not? I'm not going to fight in them!' So the dude, Pompadour Jim as he's known, with that carefully brushed-up quiff of hair, saunters through the crowds to·the fight, hearing nothing but 'Sullivan, Sullivan!' Corbett said later he didn't hear one soul calling HIS name.

When they strip, they even look like men of different eras: Sullivan in the old familiar

prize-ring breeches, Corbett wearing shorts. Poor John L. It's no match. Gentleman Jim, only 178lbs, nearly 35lbs lighter, dances rings round Sullivan, who's almost thirty-four. Corbett is twenty-six and this young Cali-fornian has left nothing to chance. He's even had a gym fitted up in the baggage car of the train from San Francisco to New Orleans, so he can work out on the trip.

The downfall of a great champion is never pleasant to watch (men cried at this one), so let's draw a veil over John L.'s knockout in the twenty-first round. It took Corbett 1hr 20min, a tribute to the old man's bravery. Sullivan did nothing of note in the ring again, but he did turn teetotal – too late.

In case the picture of Corbett the fop is overdrawn, a reminder that he was also a tough egg. The year before, he'd engaged in a bitter sixty-one round draw with black Peter Jackson, whom Sullivan would never fight. 'I don't defend against niggers.' Jackson, yet another pupil of Larry Foley, worked his passage from the West Indies to Australia as a stoker and was one of the great fighters of the time, but never got the championship crack he deserved against Corbett.

Gentleman Jim reigned for five years. During this time the NSC staged its first world championship between Dick Burge, the English lightweight champion who later promoted at the Blackfriars Ring, and Kid Lavigne, a French-Canadian known as the Saginaw Kid, a muscled attacker who stacked a ton of power into a 5ft 3½ins frame. Burge had to sweat off a stone in the Turkish baths, so it's not surprising that Lavigne hammered him in seventeen rounds to become the first recognized world lightweight champion of modern times.

That zany character Charley Mitchell, the sawn-off Birmingham middleweight who, you recall, went thirty-nine rounds with Sullivan in the Chantilly mud, slung abuse and chal-lenges at Corbett until, in 1894, Corbett agreed to fight him for the title in Jackson-ville, Florida (which didn't impress itself again on the British public until, seventy-four years later, Tony Jacklin won a golf tournament there). Mitchell, thirty-two, weighing a mere 158lbs, swore so violently at Corbett before the first bell that the champion lost his temper, abandoned his boxing style, and smashed little Charley into defeat in three rounds, the last seen of Mitchell in the ring.

Corbett after this was a reluctant warrior who, in 1895, announced his retirement, naming Irish Peter Maher as his successor,

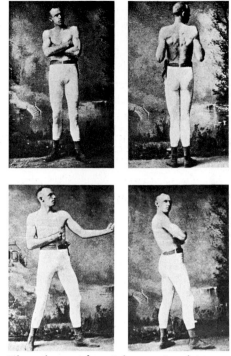

Fitzsimmons's skinny physique (above): a shade under 6ft, he weighed less than 12 stone (168lbs). He conceded 16lbs to Corbett when he won the title, and 39lbs to Jeffries when he lost it.

Peter Jackson (below), the West Indian heavyweight against whom Sullivan drew the colour bar. At London's National Sporting Club in 1892, Jackson knocked out Australian Frank Slavin and was acclaimed 'British Empire Champion'. He died in Queensland, aged 40

Historic strip of
Fitzsimmons beating Corbett
clearly shows the name of the
company — Veriscope — which
filmed the fight, the first
big-fight movie for public
display

the cue for Bob Fitzsimmons to knock out Maher inside a round and so force Corbett's hand. We come now to that moment in history cherished and lingered over in Britain as our finest boxing hour: the day Fitzsimmons, an Englishman, became heavyweight champion of the world. England's one and only.

How splendid it should happen in, of all years, 1897, when Victoria is celebrating her Diamond Jubilee. Corbett and Fitzsimmons came together 4270ft above sea-level in Carson City, brand-new capital of the gold-digging state of Nevada, where an open-air arena was built specially for the fight, the first time this had happened, and movie cameras filmed it, another first.

Fitzsimmons, almost thirty-five, still weighing only 167lbs, conceded 16lbs. Early rounds were cautious, then in the sixth a jolting left-hook to the jaw laid Fitz on the floor. He claimed a slip, but stayed there all the same, clutched Corbett's legs and waited nine seconds. Corbett, who believed Fitz didn't want the fight and was scared, must have been shattered in the eighth when the Englishman operated his celebrated 'shift', where he changed quickly to a southpaw stance and rammed a left hook to the pit of the stomach: the solar-plexus punch. No one except doctors had heard of the solar-plexus before (it had always been 'one up the belly'), but the term went into the language. The blow achieved two things. It deprived Corbett of his strength so that he was never in the fight again. It also placed Rose, Bob's wife, in history because she is said to have browbeaten Fitz into throwing the punch by yelling, 'Hit him in the slats, Bob, hit him in the slats!' Probably fictionäl; a pity the lady should be commemorated by such unladylike language.

In the fourteenth, Fitzsimmons worked the shift again and this time crowned the solar-plexus blow with a left to the chin. Corbett fell on his handsome face, groping in the dust of Carson City, but finding no gold there, not even the tooth Fitz had knocked out of

Cornishman Bob Fitzsimmons on the way to victory over Gentleman Jim Corbett at Carson City, Nevada, in 1897. The gold-miners in the 'bleachers' saw Britain's one-and-only world heavyweight champion take over with a 14th-round KO. In this fight, the solar-plexus punch was born

his mouth. The referee counted him out while Corbett retched and gagged in vain for the breath he'd had smashed out of him.

These nineteenth-century heroes, Sullivan, Corbett, Fitzsimmons, all had flings at acting. They spent more time on the stage in melodrama than training in the gym, and Fitzsimmons lasted as champion only two years. He lost the title in his next fight. The man who took it learned what science he had from Corbett. While training for the Fitzsimmons fight, Corbett had employed as a sparring partner a thick-waisted bull of a man called James Jackson Jeffries, a boilermaker in the Californian iron foundries.

Massive Jim Jeffries, 6ft 2 ins, traded on strength and was easy to nail, despite a defensive crouch taught him by middleweight Tommy Ryan. Fitz picked him for his first defence because he thought he would be easy. Jeffries had had only thirteen fights. The night before the fight in New York's Coney Island, Fitz stayed up late drinking, prematurely celebrating victory. This contempt irked Jeffries, who hadn't really believed he could win, although at 260lbs was nearly 42lbs heavier. But now brute strength allied with an angry determination not to be beaten too easily got him through against the thirty-seven-year-old champion. A savage fight ended in the eleventh round with two lefts and a right, all to the jaw, leaving the Englishman trembling on his back for the full count. The defeat was stunning, not merely for Fitzsimmons; all boxing had confidently expected him to win.

Most of Jeffries's fights were bloodbaths. His next, a defence against tattooed sailor Tom Sharkey, went to a twenty-five-round decision, leaving Sharkey with two busted ribs and a face cut to pieces. Although boxing had entered a new age, typified by the dapper Corbett, Jeffries proved there was still a place for the slugger. There always would be. Somewhere in Colorado at this time was a ragged toddler, born 24 June 1895. When he grew up he would prove the point again. His name was Dempsey.

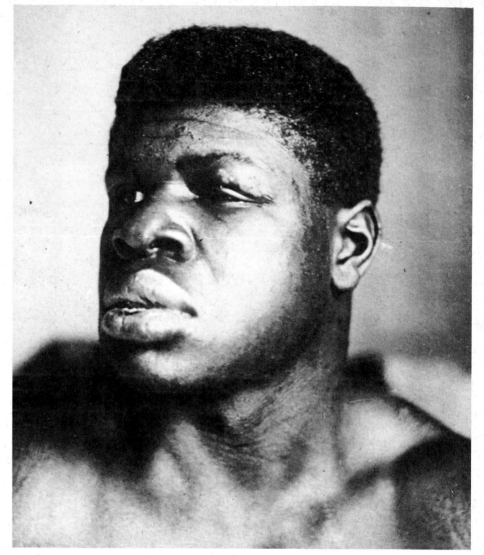

A great black heavyweight who never got a sniff of the world title: Sam McVey (above) of California. He and Sam Langford, another side-tracked black boxer, met 15 times. McVey's first recorded fight, at 17, was over 20 rounds - against Jack Johnson! But he went the distance. James J. Jeffries (The Boilermaker) was 35 and had just been called out of retirement to fight Jack Johnson when this picture was taken(left). Note the cauliflower ear. Yet Jeffries had only 23 fights in all, fewer than any other world heavyweight champion

The 20th century-and Black isn't Beautiful!

1900-9

HEAVY: BURNS, JOHNSON

LIGHT-HEAVY: FITZSIMMONS

MIDDLE: KETCHEL

LIGHT: GANS

FEATHER: ATTELL, DIXON

BANTAM: PALMER, WALSH

Anew century. The old lady on the British throne is close to death. Boxing, not yet socially respectable, flourishes in North America, Europe and Australia. In the port of Galveston, Texas, a skinny negro whose mother calls him a rank coward wins a few fights for very few dollars. His name is John Arthur Johnson – Jack Johnson. He doesn't yet have the money to buy big cars and dazzle his white girl friends. He will do. Before this decade ends, Johnson will be the most hated man in America, because he's black, and a winner. The same racial bitterness will be resurrected and poured on another champion half a century later. His name: Muhammad Ali. He, too, was saucy enough to thumb his nose at the white boss.

The twentieth century is only nine days old when a new champion is crowned. At New York's Broadway Athletic Club (members only: Manhattan forbids public prizefighting) Terry McGovern, the Brooklyn Terror, brings masterly George Dixon's featherweight reign to an end. Only four months ealier McGovern had won the bantam title and abandoned it because he couldn't make weight. What a good fighter. Six months after beating Dixon, he tempted the world lightweight champion, Frank Erne, into the ring. Erne agreed to take the thin end of the purse if he couldn't knock McGovern out within ten rounds. McGovern, one of the best body-punchers ever, hammered Erne until, in the third round, the lightweight champion's handlers threw in the towel. Luckily for Erne, his title wasn't at stake. We'll meet Erne again later.

The US and Great Britain had a monopoly of the best small men. Among the most gifted was Jim Driscoll of Wales, where he was, and is, regarded as the perfect boxer. In 1909, when he was twenty-eight, Driscoll sailed to America for a series of fights, culminating in a match which ranks as one of the finest performances by a British boxer on foreign soil. His opponent was Abe Attell, the Jewish world champion from San Francisco, whose claim to the featherweight crown was established in 1901 and was still valid.

Driscoll's fame lay in his classic straight left. He so ably outboxed Attell that an American sportswriter immediately dubbed him Peerless Jim, a name which stuck. The writer was Bat Masterson, one-time marshal of Dodge City, who had swapped his gun for a pencil. The fight went the full ten rounds and as this was the age of the no-decision bout (some States forbade officials to give verdicts) the title was only yours if you stopped or

In four months at the turn of the century, Terry McGovern (above), born in Pennsylvania, but known as the Brooklyn Terror, won the bantam crown against Britain's Pedlar Palmer and the featherweight title from superb George Dixon. McGovern's style was dubbed 'whirlwind'.
Jewish Abe Attell (right), of San Francisco, whose 1909 fight with Jim Driscoll of Wales led to Driscoll's nickname 'Peerless'. Attell's claim on the world featherweight title lasted from 1901 to 1912. He lived to be 85

knocked out the champion.

So Driscoll never did become world champion, although he deserved to. When you realize he was in the early stages of tuberculosis, which killed him at forty-five, his achievement against Attell, who was a good fighter, is the more remarkable.

British triumphs at world level are rare enough: let's lift our hats, then, to Salford-born Joe Bowker. In 1904, at London's famous National Sporting Club in Covent Garden, Bowker won the world bantam title when he outpointed America's Frankie Neil over twenty rounds. Bowker, 5ft 3½ins, was smart, not only in boxing style. He had the brains to give up the title, undefended, when he knew he couldn't make the weight. Seventy years on from Bowker's win, Britain had not produced another undisputed holder of the title, although John Caldwell of Belfast won a part-recognized version, and game little Alan Rudkin of Liverpool made three attempts in the 1960s.

Now that we are clear of the nineteenth century, you might expect to hear no more of Bob Fitzsimmons, who is in his forties. Not a bit of it. Ruby Robert was almost as permanent as his freckles. In 1902 he climbed back in with James J. Jeffries, imbued with that fond belief of all ex-champions that they are as good as ever. Fitz almost was. He gave Jeffries a lot of trouble, before age and the Iron Man caught up with him.

The following year, 1903, a Chicago newspaperman, Lou Houseman, who managed on the side a fighter called Jack Root, had a brainwave. Root was a middleweight who had outgrown the division, but wasn't big enough to be a heavyweight. Why not an in-between class? thought Houseman. Thus, the light-heavyweights were born. In Britain, naval tradition prompted the thought that if these in-between chaps weren't battleships, they were at least battle-cruisers. Hence the term cruiserweight, which still lives.

This new class suited Fitzsimmons to a T, and seven months after it was formed he outpointed George Gardner over twenty rounds in San Francisco to win his third world crown: middle, light-heavy and heavy had all been his. Fitz is one of boxing's super-champs. He and Henry Armstrong, the whirlwind fighter of the 1930s and 1940s, are the only men to win world championships at three different weights, and likely to remain so. With increased tightening of control, fighting out of your weight is frowned upon. Medically, correct; but it is hypocritical to stifle a secret longing for the barbarous days.

How pleasant it would be now to record that Fitzsimmons quietly removed himself from the scene at this historic moment. Not he. Bald, tired, forty-three, and lacking the punch of his youth, the Cornishman staked the light-heavy crown in 1905 against the scientific boxing of Philadelphia Jack O'Brien. Pity was O'Brien hadn't the punch to dispatch him, clean and quick. Over thirteen brutal rounds, Fitz absorbed all the punishment, until the referee called it off when Fitzsimmons twice slumped off his stool with exhaustion in the interval.

At about the time Houseman was dreaming up the cruiserweight division, a fifteen-year-old farm boy from Michigan had wandered way out west to Butte, Montana, living like a hobo and taking fights for money. His parents were Polish. His name was Stanislaus Kiecal. He called himself Stanley Ketchel and was to become one of the truly great fighters. His nickname was the Michigan Assassin, which tells you all you need to know about his fighting style. He was 5ft 9ins, usually weighed around 154lbs, barely big enough to make a middleweight, but fought anyone up to heavyweight. He won the world middleweight title in 1908, smashing Mike Twin Sullivan inside a round, and in his next fight, eleven weeks later, created some sort of record by stopping Mike's twin brother Jack in twenty rounds.

Ketchel was as ruthless and exciting in his time as Marciano in his. Consider his title fights with the German-American, Billy Papke of Illinois, in 1908. In the first, Papke roused a Los Angeles crowd to hysteria, savaging and stopping Ketchel in twelve rounds. Wasting little time on recovery, Ketchel was back two months later in San Francisco. Like a human version of the threshing machines he'd seen in action down on the farm, Ketchel flung punches at Papke for eleven rounds, until he landed one from which Papke couldn't beat the count.

There was the astounding battle with Philadelphia Jack O'Brien. In a New York club, O'Brien trotted out the skills that had befuddled Fitzsimmons, defying Ketchel to land a KO (another no-decision bout). If O'Brien thought he had coasted home, the shock came just before the final bell, when Ketchel smashed home a right to the chin. O'Brien was unconscious before he hit the floor. His head, in fact, crashed into his own resin box. When the referee reached 'eight' the bell rang, and O'Brien was saved. Even this was not Ketchel's finest bout. How about the one with Jack Johnson? But we are ahead of

Nelson-Gans Contest. Goldfield. Nevada. Won By Gans. 42 Rounds. Sept

The year is 1906. In Goldfield, Nevada, a shanty town full of panhandlers, black Joe Gans, past 30, defends his lightweight title against Battling Nelson. It is Tex Rickard's first big promotion.
Brilliant bantams: Joe Bowker (above left), of Salford, England, beat Frankie Neil for the world title in 1904; Harry Harris (below left), of Chicago, was known as the Human Scissors. He was 5ft 7½ins, and in 1901 won the vacant title by beating Pedlar Palmer in London. Palmer, five inches shorter, was down four times, but went the distance

ourselves. Jim Jeffries is still the heavyweight champion.

Before we see how Jeffries made out, one more look at the smaller men in these baby years of the twentieth century, as electric light replaces gas and the motor car, jerky and noisy, is hard-pressed to keep up with horse-drawn vans. In the lightweight class, two men stand out: Joe Gans, born Joseph Gaines, from Baltimore, and Battling Nelson, born Oscar Nielsen, from Copenhagen.

In 1902, at Fort Erie, Gans punched himself into boxing history in a fight with Frank Erne, the Swiss immigrant who, you recall, came to grief against Terry McGovern. Gans and Erne had met before, in 1900, and Gans had taken so much stick from Erne he asked the referee to stop the fight. Gans's action had been a talking-point ever since, but the return fight was even more notorious. Later in this book we shall come to the bizarre victory of Muhammad Ali over Sonny Liston in Lewiston, Maine, a one-round fiasco so extraordinary that those who saw it doubted the evidence of their eyes. The Gans-Erne fight was much the same. The first punch of the fight, thrown by Gans, laid Erne flat and

he was counted out. No one had ever won a world title with just one blow. Erne, like Liston, was accused, at the very least, of faint-heartedness.

Now we move ahead to 1906, and a lusty gold-mining camp in Nevada. The town, which hadn't even existed the year before, was called Goldfield and here was staged one of the most spectacularly successful open-air promotions in history. Gans, now known as the Old Master, defended the lightweight crown against Battling Nelson, the Durable Dane, and they split a bulging purse of 34,000 dollars (£8500), a huge sum for lightweights at the time.

It came about because a young citizen of Goldfield, a gambler by profession and nature, shrewdly assessed the hunger for thrills of a crowd of gold-fevered panhandlers. The gambler was Tex Rickard, later to become America's most famous fight promoter. At this time he was still a minor figure in a shanty town, but he knew what he was doing. Skinny Gans won the fight on a foul – Nelson hit him low in the forty-second round! Rickard's 34,000-dollar gamble paid off. He took close to 70,000 dollars at the gate. Later

This is how Nelson lost. Gans is down and wins on a foul. It's the 42nd round

The first black heavyweight champion: Jack Johnson (left), brilliant defensive artist with a KO punch. America couldn't stomach his affairs with white girls, any more than she could take Muhammad Ali's stand on Vietnam 60 years later.
On the shores of Sydney Harbour, Johnson plays cat-and-mouse with Tommy Burns in 1908 (right). Johnson smiled, spoke and smashed his way through 14 rounds before police rescued Burns. 'Where's mah yellow streak now, Tahmmy?' crooned Johnson.
The end is nigh for Burns (right, below)

he built the third and most famous Madison Square Garden at Forty-ninth Street and Eighth Avenue, in 1925.

So what IS James J. Jeffries, the Boilermaker, up to in this brand new century? Doing what most heavyweight champions do after winning the title – cashing in with exhibitions and easy fights? Exhibitions, yes. Easy fights, no. Jeffries might have thought that Gentleman Jim Corbett was over the hill at thirty-three, but their 1900 fight at the Seaside Athletic Club, Coney Island, convinced him otherwise. Corbett, the shrewd master-boxer, had lost none of his guile in the three years since Fitzsimmons had dethroned him. His style was the perfect foil for Jeffries's blood-and-guts method. It almost beat Jeffries. Corbett couldn't miss him with a left and in the early rounds, James J. looked exactly like the shambling bear he was sup-

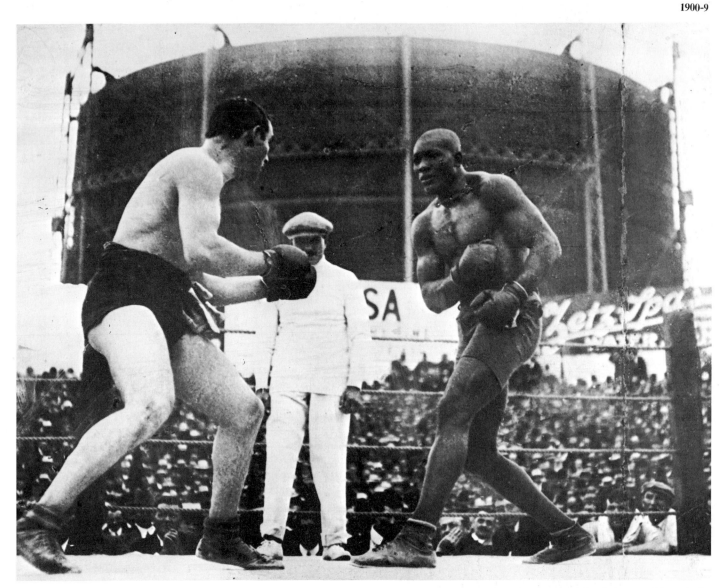

posed to resemble. One good right hurt Corbett in the fifteenth, but that was about all. Before the twentieth round, Billy Brady, Jeffries's manager, yelled at him: 'You either knock him out, or lose the title. Which is it?'

Sturdy Jeffries, eight years younger, got the message and Corbett wilted under pressure, until in the twenty-third round a left-hook to the stomach and a right to the jaw sent Corbett slithering down, his head lolling on the bottom rope, and he was counted out. Jeffries looked even worse when Fitzsimmons, the man he'd beaten for the title, came back for it in 1902 in San Francisco. Fitz was forty, but he broke Jeff's nose, cut his eyes and gashed both cheeks open. Jeffries was once more at the brink of defeat, blind with blood and pain, when he summoned two punches in the eighth round, a right to the stomach and a left-hook to the jaw, to get rid

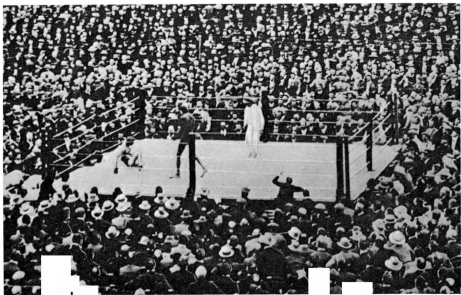

Johnson going down in the 12th against middleweight champion Stanley Ketchel at Colma, California, in 1909. Johnson, 35lbs heavier, got up and immediately threw an upper-cut which stretched Ketchel for the count and allegedly broke all his front teeth off at the gums

of the old man. No wonder Jeffries was known as the Iron Man, a Boilermaker who was himself steel-plated. Fights such as these could not be maintained and after beating Corbett again, more easily this time, Jeffries wisely announced his retirement in 1904.

Now the situation was confused until a squat Canadian, Noah Brusso, alias Tommy Burns, only 5ft 7ins (no other man this short ever won the modern title) established himself in 1906–8 as champion with a barnstorming tour of fights in London (Gunner Moir, Jack Palmer), Dublin (Jem Roche), Paris (Jewie Smith, Bill Squires) and Australia (Squires, Bill Lang). All wins. But Burns's days as champion are numbered. The man from Galveston, Texas, who was knocking over bum rivals in 1900 for mere dimes and cents, is seeking him. Jack Johnson. He's come a long way. Sleek, smiling, soft of voice and proud, Johnson has now won enough to afford fat cigars, slim white women and flashy cars.

He knows he has the God-given ability to be champion. But he's black – and no white man is rushing to help him win the title. He must run Burns to earth.

Black was not beautiful in 1908. A black man who could whip whites and take their women could expect only revilement. Johnson was not afraid to answer back. He was the Muhammad Ali of his time, with a super-ego, boxing wizardry to back it up and a taste for the high life. It took Johnson more than ten years to fight to the top. He was thirty when he cornered Burns, chasing him from capital to capital, including London, where Johnson was made to wait on the doorstep of the National Sporting Club. America was not alone in racial bigotry. In 1906 Sam Langford, the finest boxer (black, of course) never to get a shot at a world title, conceded nearly two stone to Johnson, put him on the floor, but lost the decision. Johnson had beaten the best of his time, including Sam McVey, Joe Jeannette, Bob Fitzsimmons and Jim Flynn before the showdown with Burns.

When it came the manner of his triumph only exacerbated American feelings. The lasting image of Johnson as an uppity negro forever taunting the white man goes back to this fight, at Rushcutters Bay, Sydney, on Boxing Day, 1908. An Australian, Hugh D. McIntosh, promoted and refereed the contest – refereeing at Johnson's request. The black man said: 'For every point I'm given, I'll have earned two, because I'm a negro. But I want to be sure I get my one point, anyway. There's only one man I know I can trust to give it me, and that's you.'

McIntosh guaranteed Burns 30,000 dollars (£7500), the most ever paid to a fighter at that time. Burns earned it the hard way. Johnson had him down twice in the first round, but didn't finish it until the fourteenth, which is how the story that he played a malicious cat-and-mouse game with Burns became accepted. Johnson certainly talked to Burns throughout the fight and is believed to have said: 'Who's yellow now, Tahmmy?', a reference to Burns's alleged remarks before the fight that Johnson had a yellow streak. This allusion to cowardice is a constant thread through the Johnson story. It's hard to swallow when you remember he was beaten only seven times in a long career. But it started with his mother (he's a rank coward) and it stuck. Hadn't the same been said of the Jew Mendoza, another crafty boxer, in the eighteenth century?

Johnson's win unleashed a torrent of white spite. Blacks had not long been out of slavery and their role in life was still menial. Little education and no good jobs were open to them. The heavyweight title had been exclusively white property, but here was a grinning gold-toothed negro who had chased Burns halfway round the world to thrash him in front of an almost all-white crowd. There was no radio or TV, only cabled dispatches to newspapers printed days later, from white reporters who may or may not have been experts. Plenty of scope for rumour and gossip, and it would be weeks before the shaky silent film of the fight arrived in the local picture-house.

How much truth is there in the story that Johnson toyed with Burns to make him suffer? Nat Fleischer, foremost authority on boxing in America, who saw Johnson fight, ranked him as the finest defensive boxer he ever saw, but said that he was inclined to loaf. Johnson was not by nature an attacker, but a master of the counter-punch, who seldom took chances and never pounced until the victim was ripe. Johnson's own comment: 'If I were a bullfighter I'd make the public think I was within inches of death, but I'd keep my margin of safety. I did in the ring. My God, against the men I beat when I was at my best, I was padding backwards round the ring for three rounds out of four. Defence always wins in the end, if it's good enough.'

Johnson relished his superiority. No doubt of that. His liaisons with white girls led to exile and a frantic hunt for a white giant to destroy him. The bigots would have a long wait. This hatred of Johnson poisoned boxing for more than a quarter of a century. After him no black man was allowed to fight for the

L'ÉVOLUTION DE LA GARDE DE GEORGES CARPENTIER

Carpentier à ses débuts (12 ans). *Carpentier en 1908, en boxe française.* *Georges Carpentier à ses débuts de professionnel.* *Carpentier à son premier championnat de France.*

Carpentier à 17 ans, champion d'Europe des poids mi-moyens. *Carpentier à 20 ans, champion d'Europe des poids lourds.* *Carpentier, en 1921, quand il rencontra Jack Dempsey.* *L'une des gardes les plus récentes de Georges Carpentier.*

heavyweight title (there were plenty good enough, notably Harry Wills in the Dempsey era) until Joe Louis came along in the 1930s.

Meanwhile, Johnson returned home from Australia. The full storm had not yet broken. Within a year he put up the title at Colma, California, against the farm boy Ketchel: yes, the Michigan Assassin, the middleweight who fought anyone. Ketchel conceded 35lbs in weight and in the twelfth round put Johnson on the floor. For a second or two, it seemed as if the white man's prayers had been answered. But the 'coward' jumped up and with one punch spreadeagled Ketchel for the knockout.

French guide to Georges Carpentier's evolving defence, from the age of 12 to late in his career

Almost exactly one year later, Walter Dipley, a hired hand on Ketchel's Missouri ranch, fired a bullet into his boss in a squabble over a girl. Ketchel died. Joe Gans was already dead of pneumonia. George Dixon had gone in 1909.

Jack Johnson was alive – and detested.

Never mind the war— get on with the fight 1910-19

HEAVY: WILLARD, DEMPSEY

LIGHT-HEAVY: LEVINSKY

WELTER: LEWIS

LIGHT: WELSH, LEONARD

BANTAM: WILLIAMS

FLY: WILDE

Where had all the young men gone? To the bloodletting of 1914–18, but there was no shutdown of civilian life under bombing as in the Second World War. Boxing flourished. There were new faces: Jimmy Wilde, Freddie Welsh, Ted Kid Lewis, all British, all world champions. Here's handsome Georges Carpentier, whose face and fists haunt us at every turn. With so many good young men coming up, how strange that America turns to an old man in their detestation of a black one. Author Jack London, watching Jack Johnson half-murder Tommy Burns, wrote: 'Jim Jeffries must now emerge from his alfalfa farm and remove that golden smile from Johnson's face. Jeff, it's up to you. The White Man must be rescued.'

So they dragged the flabby Boilermaker from retirement at thirty-five. Jeffries hadn't fought for six years. Gambler Tex Rickard promoted and refereed this White Man's hate fight in Reno, Nevada, in July 1910. Reno was not the quick-divorce roulette wheel of today, but a Western farm community living down its Gunsmoke past. Thousands poured into town, choking hotels and bars. They ran the place out of food. Sullivan, Corbett, Fitzsimmons and Burns were there. Strangers with guns had to check them in at the turnstiles before Rickard would let them in. Jim Jeffries could have done with a gun.

The trust placed in him by all those white onlookers was pathetic. They even made him a 10–7 favourite. Jack Johnson, always cautious, took his time (taunting, it was called) while old Jim did little. The execution came in the fifteenth. Five punches in a row, Jeffries on his back. He clambered up, and Johnson knocked him down. Rickard didn't stop it, so Jeffries got up and Johnson knocked him down a third time. The towel came in to save the old man who had licked Fitz and Corbett and who, until this moment, had never lost a fight. Exit White Man from Reno, quietly.

What else goes on in 1910? Dick Burge converts the Surrey Chapel (built circular so the devil couldn't hide in a corner) into the Blackfriars Ring, London's first working man's boxing arena, which survived thirty years until the bombs KO'd it in 1940. Georges Carpentier, aged sixteen and a pro boxer for three years already, is beaten in Paris by Kid Snowball, alias Ted Broadribb, who later managed Tommy Farr and Freddie Mills.

Poor Jim Jeffries (top), dragged from retirement as the white man's avenger, slogs at his roadwork alongside Jack Johnson in Reno. His manager, Sam Berger, is on Jeffries' right. Note the name 'White' on the cars. Coincidence? No.
Johnson (above), evading arrest, quits the USA with wife Lucille in 1912. They sailed to Paris.
Jeffries' corner retired him in the 15th round against Johnson (right). It was his last fight and his only defeat

Britain invents the flyweight class and the smallest men now have a place to call their own. The weight eventually is fixed at 112lbs (8st.), or 1cwt. Wales, from its Rhondda coalmines, brings to the surface a skinny, flat-chested, will-o'-the-wisp who weighs much less than a hundredweight sack of coal. Jimmy Wilde seldom went more than 102lbs and was the greatest flyweight who ever lived. He had the secret of timing and he was known as the Ghost with a Hammer in his Hand. Starting at five shillings a fight, he was given a bag of diamonds worth about £7000 for beating Joe Conn, a featherweight, in 1918. How many men did he beat? No one knows for sure. Hundreds, most of them in fairground boxing booths. He once KO'd fifteen men, one after the other, each trying to earn £1 by staying three rounds. 'The sixteenth managed it,' said Jimmy, 'but he was 8ins taller, 2 stone heavier and, besides, I was getting tired.'

While German Zeppelins dropped bombs on Britain, Wilde became the world's first flyweight champion, beating Young Zulu Kid (alias Joe de Melfi of Brooklyn) in eleven rounds at Holborn Stadium in 1916. In thirteen years' fighting, Wilde was beaten just four times, once in 1915 at the National Sporting Club by Scotsman Tancy Lee. Apart from giving Lee a stone in weight, Wilde had been down with flu for three weeks. Badly knocked about, he was dragged protesting to his corner by his seconds in the seventeenth. 'Don't ever do that again,' he yelled. 'If the other man can knock me out, let him have the credit.'

In 1909 the first Lonsdale Belt was put up at the NSC for a very good reason. The Club did not have big money to tempt top men, so the Belt was invented to distinguish the British champion. If a man wanted to be the accepted champion he had to come to the NSC to fight. The first Belt was won by Freddie Welsh (real name Thomas, but he didn't want his mother to know he was a boxer) who came from Pontypridd, but learned his boxing in Philadelphia, and he took the British lightweight title from Johnny Summers. Welsh was a fine boxer who had good wins in America over men such as Abe Attell and Ad Wolgast. In July 1914, C. B. Cochran, theatrical impresario and one of Britain's first big promoters, tempted America's Willie Ritchie to defend his world lightweight title in London against Welsh, who won on points. Ritchie got all the money: 20,000 dollars. Welsh was out of pocket, but had the championship and kept it

almost three years until the superb Benny Leonard beat him. Welsh was such a crafty technician he once frustrated the classic left of Jim Driscoll to such effect that Driscoll blew his top, butted Welsh and was disqualified for the only time in his life.

Here's a nice little note sent by the Ku Klux Klan to Jack Johnson in 1912, just before his fight with white Jim Flynn in New Mexico: 'Lie down tomorrow or we string you up.' Johnson smashed Flynn so hard the police stopped the fight, but he was on the run now. In the course of his tempestuous life, Johnson married two white girls and lived with a third: Belle Schreiber. This injudicious liaison brought indictment under the Mann Act for abducting Belle across a State line for immoral purposes. Sentence: a year and a day. Johnson fled, and from 1913 to 1920 wandered, self-exiled, through Canada, South America and Europe. In Paris he fought on stage against wrestlers, and at the London Palladium, his bald black pate gleaming under the lights, he did a knock-about turn with comedian George Robey. He is alleged to have offered Lord Lonsdale half his fee if the noble Earl would announce the act.

With Johnson away, the manic hunt for a white champion began. In America, Luther McCarty was proclaimed, only to die of a brain hemorrhage against Arthur Pelkey in a Calgary fight promoted by Tommy Burns. Europe was not free of racial taint. Cochran wanted Johnson to fight British champion Bombardier Billy Wells at Olympia, but the Home Office stamped on it 'for fear of racial trouble'.

In her undaunted search for a world heavyweight champion, Britain truly believed for a time she had one in Billy Wells, born in Mile End, who had gone off to be a soldier long before the First World War and had won the Army championship in India. He was 6ft 3ins, a natural athlete who boxed like a dream and could hit, but whose chin and belly couldn't take it from the best of men. At the domestic level he was unbeatable for almost eight years, beating off challengers like Pat O'Keefe, Gunner Moir, Bandsman Rice and Dick Smith. From 1911 until 1919, when Joe Beckett beat him, Bombardier Wells made thirteen successful defences and

What, still around? Bob Fitzsimmons, now 48, sparring with US negro Joe Jeannette in Paris in 1910. He didn't finish boxing until he was 51

was Britain's longest-reigning heavyweight champion until Henry Cooper beat his record in 1966. A few months later Wells died, just short of eighty.

The truth about Wells took a long time to dawn. In 1912 he went to America to fight Al Palzer for the 'white championship'. Palzer, an Iowa farmer, weighed 209lbs and Wells was beaten in three rounds. But back he went to New York in 1913, this time to be knocked out in two by Gunboat Smith of Philadelphia.

Britain still wasn't convinced: in 1913 Wells went to Ghent to defend his European title against nineteen-year-old Carpentier and this time almost pulled it off. Four inches taller, 17lbs heavier than the lissom, Frenchman, Wells had him on the floor in the first round, but, ever the gentle giant, didn't follow up and was KO'd in the fourth. That same year at the NSC he had another go with Carpentier, which proved to be the most wretched few minutes of the Bombardier's life. He was a long time coming to the ring, which upset members, and when he did get there Carpentier knocked him out in 73 seconds. Jim Driscoll ran to the ringside shouting 'coward' at Wells as the big man lay on the floor humiliated.

This left the slim teenage Carpentier, no heftier than a middleweight, as Europe's best heavyweight and in 1914, when he stopped America's Gunboat Smith on a foul in London, he was the world's white hope. Could *he* beat Jack Johnson? Let's pause here to savour the extraordinary glamour of Georges Carpentier, Gorgeous Georges, the Orchid Man, idolized at this time as much in London as in Paris. He took tea with the Prince of Wales at St James's Palace and when he arrived in London for the Gunboat Smith fight, a band played the Marseillaise and a carriage drawn by two white horses awaited him. An adoring crowd yanked the horses out of the shafts and pulled the carriage themselves. Georges was friend of royalty and theatrical folk; he hobnobbed with Maurice Chevalier and Mistinguett. But this was July 1914, and a few days later Europe was at war. Typically, Georges became a flying ace, winning the Croix de Guerre, Médaille Militaire and Légion d'Honneur. Jack Johnson had to be ignored while Carpentier faced the Hun. America, not yet in the war, looked elsewhere. They sorted out a raw-boned giant from Kansas, a cowhand, a near-novice fighter called Jess Willard, 6ft 6¼ins, who never had a glove on until he was twenty-

eight. Willard was appointed the White Man's rescuer.

At this time America was cheering a young Briton born in Aldgate who like Mendoza brought lasting fame to the Jewish race. Ted Kid Lewis was one of the great *fighters* of all time, hence his immortal tag-line: the Smashing, Bashing, Crashing, Dashing Kid. Lewis (born Gershon Mendeloff) was British champion at nineteen, European champion at twenty and world welterweight champion at twenty-one. He fought most of his great fights in the States, where he stayed from 1914 to 1919.

When he left England Lewis was an orthodox, left-lead boxer; when he came back he was the tigerish assailant the world remembers. In 1915 he won a decision over the Irish-American Jack Britton in Boston to be recognized as world champion; lost the title to Britton in 1916; won it back in 1917; lost it to Britton finally in 1919. These two fought one another twenty times in twelve different US cities, a series beaten only by Sam Langford and Harry Wills. The achievements of Kid Lewis in America are underlined when you remember that not until the 1970s, when Ken Buchanan came along, did Britain have another man good enough to

One of 22 gold-and-enamel
Lonsdale Belts issued by
London's National Sporting Club
between 1909 and 1929 (above).
This one, for the light-
heavyweight division, was
never won outright and
eventually went to the winner
of a heavyweight competition
when the NSC was revived in
the 1930s. Today's belts are
issued by Britain's Boxing
Board of Control and sport a
plaque of Lord Lonsdale at the
front.
Freddie Welsh (right), of
Pontypridd, learned to box in
Philadelphia. He won boxing's
first Lonsdale Belt in 1909
and later, the world lightweight championship from Willie
Ritchie. He also provoked Jim
Driscoll into losing his cool.
Greatest flyweight of them all:
Jimmy Wilde (left), with wife
Elizabeth Anne, a fighter's
daughter herself, and their
son. From his early purses
Jimmy would buy Elizabeth a box
of her favourite chocolate
almonds

become world champion on US soil. Lewis earned £150,000 in twenty years and gave most of it away. He was a favourite of rich and poor; a close acquaintance of Charlie Chaplin in Hollywood. When he returned to humble Aldgate as a world celebrity, Lewis scattered silver on the streets for the kids, recalling his own ragged start as the son of a cabinetmaker. He had his first fight at fourteen, for sixpence and a cup of coffee (actually fivepence – a penny back for the coffee!).

Jack Johnson's landlady in Paddington has had to throw him out for smashing her crockery and by the time he gets to Cuba the black champion has been living a wild life in Europe for two years. Cuba? Yes. If he takes on Jess Willard in America the Government will slap him in jail. So here they are face to face in a ring staked out on the Oriente race-track in Havana on a broiling April day in 1915 and the doubts must be fluttering in Johnson as he sees the massive man opposite. Willard is 6ins taller and at 211lbs nearly 25lbs heavier. Although Willard is thirty-three, Johnson is now a portly thirty-seven and looks it. Yet in the early rounds Johnson

Gorgeous Georges (right): idol of the boulevards.
Welshman Jim Driscoll (left), master of the straight left. He was 28 when this was taken in 1910.
Driscoll's tragic last fight (below). One report said he won 14 of the first 15 rounds against French pastrycook, Charles Ledoux, but a right to the body finished him and the towel came in during the 16th round. He died less than six years later

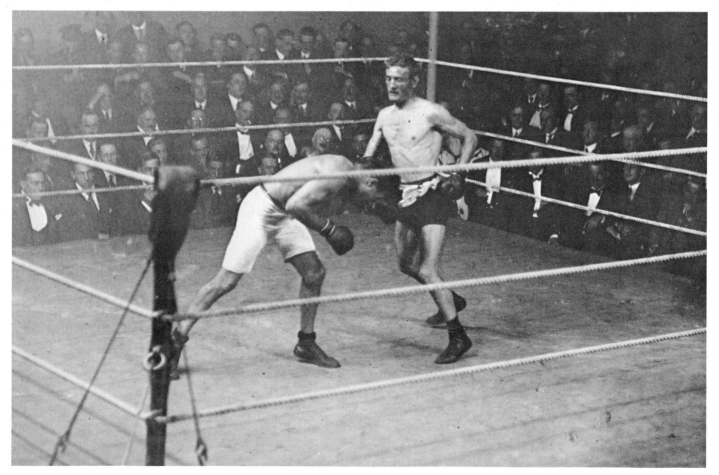

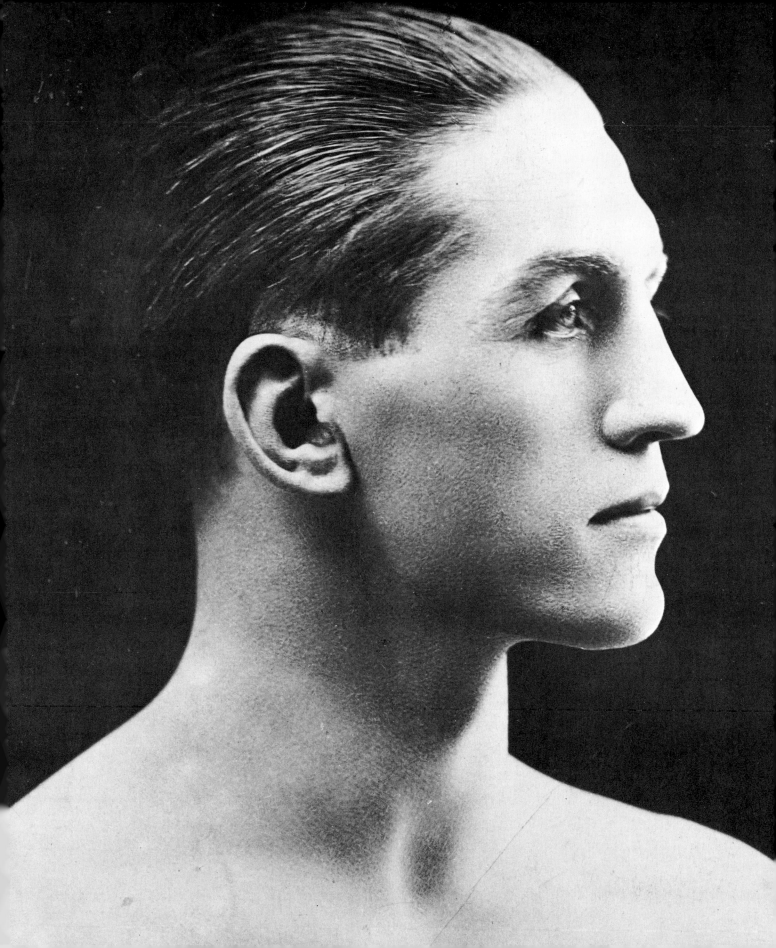

Sunday afternoon, June 1913.
In Ghent, Belgium, Georges
Carpentier (left) is about to
win the European heavyweight
title from Britain's Bombardier
Billy Wells (right) in four
rounds. Wells had him down,
then let him off the hook.
Six months later, they fight
again, the worst night of
Wells's life. He was KO'd in
73 seconds at the National
Sporting Club in London.
(Top) The French camp
celebrate. (Centre) Lord
Lonsdale congratulates
Carpentier. (Bottom)
Forlorn Wells tries to
apologize and just makes
matters worse

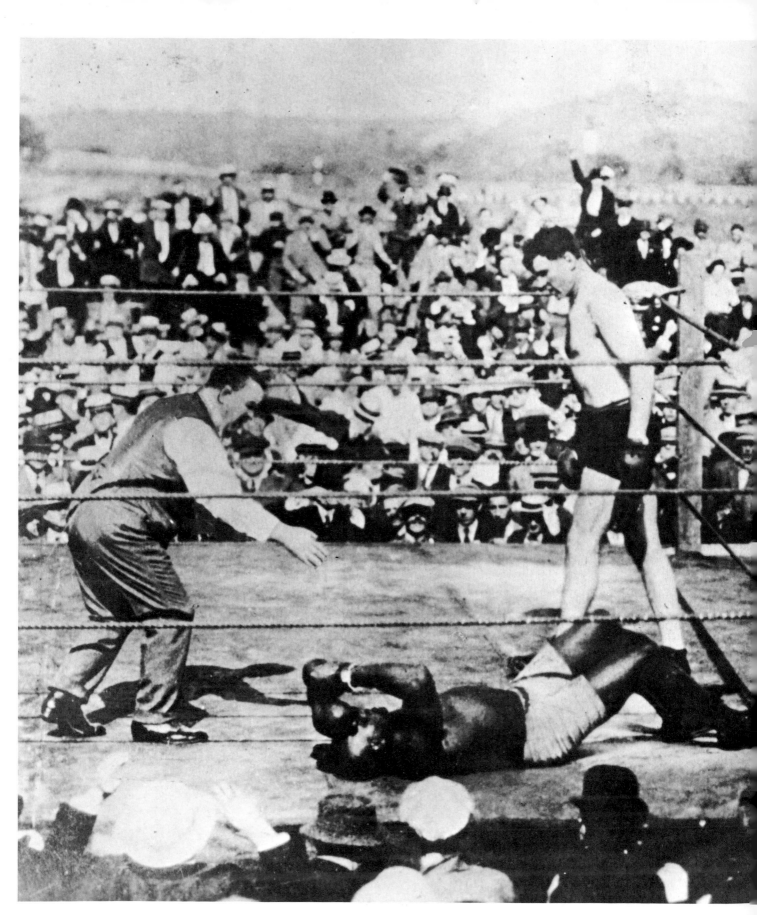

displays the old skills and shows up Willard for the bumbling giant he is. Over twenty rounds, the distance Johnson requested, he would have walked it. But he was talked (forced?) into a forty-five-rounder. The red-hot cinder sun is grilling the sap out of Johnson. From the corner he sends a message to his white wife, who gets up and leaves – 'I didn't want her to see what was going to happen.'

In the twenty-sixth round Johnson wilted into a corner where Willard hit him with a big slow left to the body. The crowd sensed it quickly. 'Kill the black bear!' they screeched. Creased in half, Johnson lowered his arms to guard his ribs and Willard caught him a right to the chin. Down went Johnson, rolled on to his back and lay with knees up, right arm crooked across the black face as if he were consciously shielding his eyes from the sun, which of course is just what people said he WAS doing.

The accusation still rings out down the years: he could have got up, but lay there and 'sold' the title to Willard. Some said he was yellow and couldn't face the licking he was sure to get. Johnson himself wrote a 'confession', sold for considerable money to America's *Ring* magazine, saying he'd done it in return for a US pardon. If so, he was rooked. He served the jail sentence later. His trainer claimed he couldn't admit the simple truth: Willard had beaten him fair and square. Whatever the reason, Johnson's 6½-year reign was over. The White Man breathed again, and made sure no uppity black challenged for the title again for nearly a quarter of a century. Johnson faded into a strange twilight, fighting on unimportantly for another thirteen years. How macabre that this negro who roused white envy by flaunting himself in fast cars should die in one in

1946.

Now Willard. One look at the famous photo which men have studied for over half a century, the one showing Johnson 'shielding his eyes', tells you more about Willard than whether Johnson was faking. That stiff, statuesque pose of Willard's, even as he stands over the prostrate Johnson, is a give-away. He was no boxer and not much of a fighter. Gunboat Smith had beaten him. Willard was a hired hand, big and strong, brought in to do a job against Johnson and the reality of this was brutally exposed four years later when he had to face Jack Dempsey.

Meanwhile, a tribute to Johnny Kilbane, the Cleveland, Ohio, featherweight who in 1912 surprisingly closed the ten-year reign of Abe Attell and began one himself that lasted eleven years. This division is memorable for its succession of fine champions from 1891 – George Dixon, Attell, then Kilbane; while in England there are Ben Jordan, Jim Driscoll, Ted Kid Lewis (he was British featherweight champion at first) and Tancy Lee. What a vintage era for the 126lbs class.

The Great War is ending. America has

Britain's finest fighting machine (above): Ted Kid Lewis, of Aldgate, had 253 fights, won titles from feather to middle-weight, and even fought Carpentier for the European heavyweight championship, weighing 150lbs. He got through £1000 a week, when money was money.
The white man's revenge – at last. Giant Jess Willard towers over the stricken Johnson under Havana's broiling sun in 1915 (left). Here is the most controversial photo in boxing. Is Johnson deliberately shielding his eyes from the sun – and therefore faking the KO ? We shall never know
Overpage: the moment Jack Dempsey thought he was champion. Willard, down for the seventh time in round one, has been counted out by referee Ollie Pecord. But no-one heard the bell. Willard struggled on to the third round and never went down again. But he was only postponing the inevitable. The date: 4 July 1919, in Toledo, Ohio

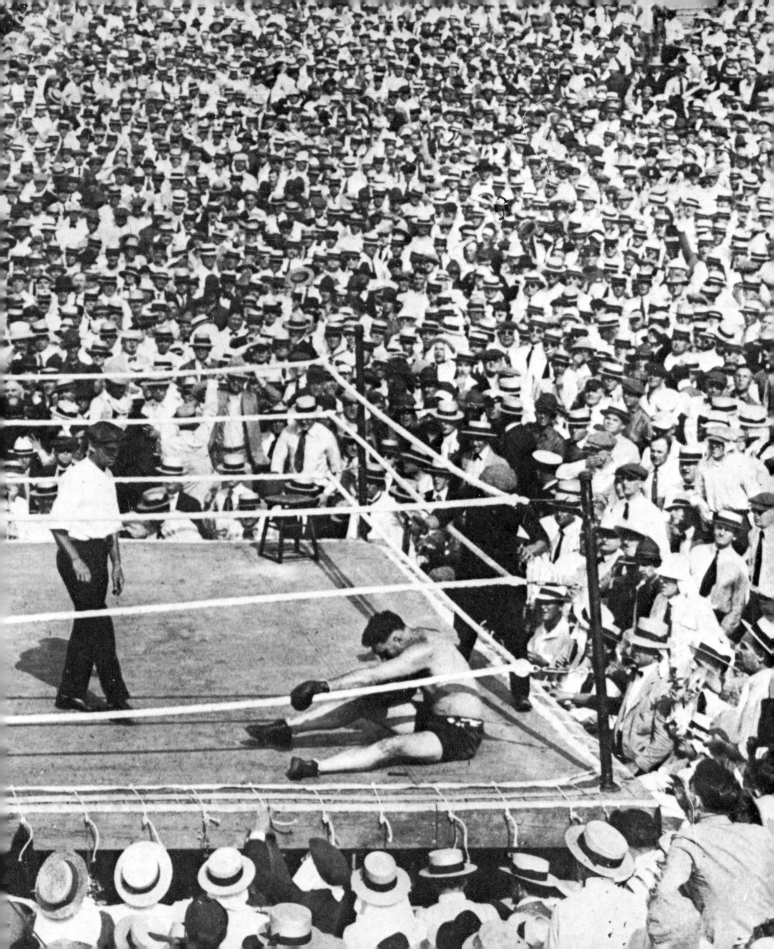

plonked her might down on the side of the Allies, and who on earth persuaded Jack Dempsey to have that picture taken in 1918? He's on his way up, aged twenty-three, hungry and hard from years of deprivation way out West. He's about to explode on Willard. There is just one sensitive spot in public opinion. Dempsey is not in the Forces and America is on a patriotic splurge. Some genius hauls Dempsey into the nearest ship-yard, shoves a riveting tool in his hands and tells him to look patriotic while the camera clicks. So here is honest Jack smiling at us from the newspapers, doing his bit for the war effort, only someone has forgotten to tells him to look patriotic while the camera Oh, the uproar! Not until 1920 was he for-mally cleared of draft evasion.

Now it's 4 July 1919. The war is over. The sun is scorching down on a ring in Toledo, Ohio, where a most savage annihilation is about to take place. Dempsey is dwarfed by Willard, who is 5ins taller and outweighs him by 53lbs, but none of this matters. There is a maniacal fury in Dempsey's fighting and on this day no man could stop him, let alone the aging, inept Willard. In the final minute of the first round the giant is smashed down seven times until the massive legs will lift him no longer. He sits there, this White Man's rescuer, head bowed between his

knees while the referee counts him out. The ecstatic Dempsey leaps the ropes and rushes headlong into the hysterical mob, convinced he's champion of the world. But no, Willard is not beaten . . . yet. The din was so great no one, including the referee, heard the bell at 'seven'. Poor Jess is not KO'd. My God, he must be wishing he were as they drag him back to the corner to revive him. Jack Kearns, Dempsey's manager, yells to his man to get back in the ring. Round Two. Willard, feeble pawn in the game, now brands himself a king for courage. In this round, and the next, he stands, a human wreck, under a remorseless battering from Dempsey who can't finish him. After three rounds Willard has both eyes swollen shut and two teeth missing. He collapses on his stool and admits defeat. Someone should have saved him long before.

Out there under the Ohio sun boxing has swerved on to a new course. Dempsey will ride out in front in headlong pursuit of riches. Others will shelter in his slipstream, grabbing the golden haul of dollars as they fly by. The sobbing, shaking hulk of Willard on the stool cuts all links with the past, which is cold in the grave now like Mace, Sullivan and Fitzsimmons.

Georges Carpentier, back from the war bemedalled, is as elegant and worldly as

Champion Dempsey in Utah, as president, believe it or not, of the Great Western Coal Mines Company. Was this a board meeting? Left to right: Bernard Dempsey, Jack's brother; Jack 'Doc' Kearns, his crafty manager; Wild Bill Lyons, a rodeo champion; Mrs Lyons; Dempsey. Plus the Lyons children

Dempsey is stark and gauche, and looks a million dollars. Why not? He and Dempsey are about to open up the Million Dollar Era.

Long Count? You try counting a million dollars quickly 1920-9

HEAVY: DEMPSEY, TUNNEY, CARPENTIER

LIGHT-HEAVY: CARPENTIER, GREB

MIDDLE: GREB, WALKER

WELTER: WALKER

LIGHT: LEONARD

FEATHER: CANZONERI

BANTAM: BROWN

FLY: WILDE

The day Willard stretched Johnson on his back in Cuba, Jack Dempsey, whose early fighting was in the name of Kid Blackie, lost a four-rounder to Jack Downey in Salt Lake City. Jim Flynn once knocked him out inside a round. In 1916 John Lester Johnson broke two of his ribs – the best way, said Dempsey, to understand the value of body punching.

Born in Manassa, Colorado, Dempsey was the ninth child of Mormon farmers, Hiram and Celia Dempsey, who were almost destitute. Hiram had Irish and Scottish blood; Celia a strain of Cherokee. The ninth child was christened William Harrison (at home he was called Harry). He pinched 'Jack' from the nineteenth-century middleweight champion, Nonpareil Jack Dempsey. That was after he'd run away from home in his teens to bum a living as best he could – lumberjack, copper-miner, saloon bouncer, and fighter.

He would fight anybody, anywhere, for a couple of dollars. He said: 'They could hit me on the chin with a sledgehammer for five dollars. When you haven't eaten for two days you'll understand.' The day that transformed Dempsey's life was when he got a letter in Salt Lake City. Inside was five dollars, a train ticket to Oakland, California, and a note from a young West Coast fight manager, Jack Kearns, which said: 'Come and join me. I'll make you a champion.' What did Dempsey have to lose? Dempsey took the five dollars and the train: the journey led him to a fortune. The truest thing Dempsey ever said was: 'My big gates did more to commercialize fighting than anything else in pugilistic history.'

At first Dempsey was anything but popular. There had been the patent leather shoe affair. The savage victory over Willard raised an unfair accusation heard even today: that the gloves were 'loaded'. The usual theory is that his bandages were sprinkled with plaster of Paris and then water, so that they set like concrete. Men who saw the bandages put on deny it. From personal experience, I know that Willard, a bitter old man, went to his death in 1968, not far short of ninety, still convinced Dempsey had *something* in those gloves, other than his hands. Yet there is evidence enough from Dempsey's other fights that he could tear the guts and heart

The first million-dollar gate:
Dempsey v. Carpentier, 1921.
A crows-nest for movie cameras
amid the 80,183 crowd. A
record 700 pressmen covered
the action

out of a man with hands alone. The years of hunger out West gave him the killer instinct in the ring. Outside it, he was gentle and courteous.

Why should we look down on Joe Beckett's prostrate body in London's Holborn Stadium on 4 December 1919? Because Georges Carpentier put it there. When they were introduced, Beckett, the British champion, said: 'I'm not a Bombardier Wells, you know.' Beckett lasted just one second longer than Wells: when he met Carpentier a second time, he lasted even less time than Wells.

In America, Tex Rickard was looking for a sure-fire box-office winner to put against Dempsey. Carpentier, the war hero, idol of Europe, must be the man. Rickard paid for Carpentier and his bride Georgette, with her maid and fifteen trunks full of clothes, to visit America on a publicity tour. But as Rickard mentioned to François Descamps, Carpentier's manager, this was not enough.

Georges must first win on US soil. He was matched for the world light-heavyweight title in Jersey City with Battling Levinsky, alias Barney Lebrowitz, who in more than 200 fights had been knocked out once only, by Dempsey. Carpentier knocked him out in four rounds. Rickard had his sure-fire winner.

What of Britain's idol, flyweight Jimmy Wilde, who is still the world champion? On a January night in 1921 he sits in his dressing-room at the Royal Albert Hall refusing to come out and fight the American, Pete Herman, whom he believes has pulled a fast one on him. Herman is a bantamweight (in fact, a few weeks earlier he had been the world champion) and Wilde wants him to weigh in just before the fight, so he can keep Herman down to the stipulated 118lbs. But Herman weighed in at two o'clock, has since eaten, and now weighs anything up to 122lbs. Wilde won't fight. The crowd is angry, because Battling Levinsky has also pulled out at the last moment from a fight with Bombar-

Boyle's Thirty Acres (above) seen from a plane, 2000 feet up, 'an octagon of teeming humanity', as one paper put it. A white canvas screen, bottom left, foils pirate cameramen on a hospital roof. Note the many empty seats. Promoter Tex Rickard put in 117,000, and failed to fill nearly 37,000 of them.
Slim and light (172lbs), Carpentier folds under Dempsey's hammer blows (left). He tries to get off his knees, but the count beats him. As recompense, the Frenchman pocketed $200,000 (£54,000); Dempsey $300,000 (£81,000).
Harry Greb (above right), world middleweight champion, only man ever to beat Tunney. He was 5ft 8ins, blind in one eye, reputed to entertain girls in his dressing-room before fights and died under a surgeon's knife at 32, having his battered nose prettified

dier Wells. Lord Lonsdale enters Wilde's room: 'The Prince of Wales is waiting to see you fight,' he says. Wilde relents, but in the seventeenth round Herman has him down three times and because Wilde won't quit, referee Jack Smith tucks an arm round him and drags him protesting to his corner.

In Jersey City, Rickard builds a wooden bowl on a site known as Boyle's Thirty Acres and guarantees Dempsey 300,000 dollars, Carpentier 200,000. George Bernard Shaw predicts that Carpentier ('a reincarnation of Charles XII') will win. Shaw doesn't realize that Dempsey is not a fragile European heavyweight. Carpentier understands. At

As good a lightweight as the world has seen: Benny Leonard (right), conqueror of Freddie Welsh. He retired as undefeated world champion in 1925, having held the title nearly eight years. He almost won the welter crown. He was ruled out for striking Jack Britton when the champion was down.

Left: Jimmy Wilde (on the right) in his ill-starred encounter with America's Pete Herman at the Royal Albert Hall, London, in 1921. Wilde, furious that Herman tricked him over a weight agreement, refused to leave his dressing-room. But when he was told the Prince of Wales was waiting to see the fight, Wilde relented and was badly beaten in the 17th round

only 172lbs, conceding 16lbs, he won't have the strength for a long fight. He works on his right hand for a quick KO. Gorgeous Georges v. Killer Jack. It's Beauty and the Beast and the biggest crowd yet, more than 80,000, pack Rickard's rickety stands, contributing for the first time in boxing a million-dollar gate (closer to two million, when Rickard got around to counting it). Major Andrew White, picking up a microphone, goes into history as the first man to broadcast a commentary on a world title fight, and in the second round babbles merrily about the marvellous right hand with which Carpentier hits Dempsey on the chin. Bombardier Wells and Joe Beckett know all about that right. So does Dempsey. But he doesn't go down, just wobbles a little. The impact breaks Carpentier's thumb in two places. And that is that. In the fourth, Carpentier is KO'd and Lloyd George sends him a cable: 'I admire you more than ever.' Watching the fight closely is an ex-Marine who earlier in the evening beat Soldier Jones. His name is Gene Tunney. He criticizes Carpentier's tactics: 'He should have boxed on the retreat.' Five years later Tunney proved his point.

Next year, 1922, Tunney relieved Battling Levinsky of the American light-heavyweight title, and Carpentier came to Britain once more to defend the world cruiser crown (and the European heavyweight title) against the indomitable Ted Kid Lewis, who weighed a mere 152lbs fully clothed. Lewis believed he could take the heavyweight title from Dempsey and wanted to make his point by stopping Carpentier in faster time than Dempsey. One interested observer at Olympia that night was Dempsey himself, signed to write a story for a newspaper. Jimmy Wilde and Lord Lonsdale were also present. One thing all were sure about: Lewis would be no one-round victim like Wells and Beckett. Yet he was. Attacking furiously, working inside like a madman, Lewis was told not to hold. He turned to the referee to protest his innocence, holding his hands out in resignation, and Carpentier hit him with a right. Lewis, giving away nearly two stone, was counted out and such fury erupted that someone swung a bottle at François Descamps' head. Major Arnold Wilson, the promoter, counted £27,000 in the till that night, a British indoor-receipts record which stood for twenty-five years.

It was the end, and a bitter end, of Lewis's world title ambitions, although in this decade he won British, European and Empire titles at both welter and middleweight, beating fighters like Jack Bloomfield, Johnny Basham and Roland Todd. He went on until 1929.

LE PETIT JOURNAL
ILLUSTRÉ

LA DERNIÈRE AVENTURE DU BOXEUR SIKI

In 1922, Carpentier suffers
again (right), this time at the
black hands of Battling Siki.
At the Velodrome Buffalo in
Paris, a wild left swing drops
Carpentier. He's counted out;
then Siki is disqualified;
finally, it's ruled that
Carpentier's seconds tossed in
the towel. Siki is world
light-heavyweight champion.
A French magazine illustrator
imagines the dying moments of
Siki's bizarre life (above).
The Senegalese was shot in a
brawl in Hell's Kitchen, New
York, in 1925

Britain will not produce his like again. A
testimonial in 1950 raised £3000 and before
he died in 1970 he made a remark that sums
up all the wisdom men have learned about
fighting in 3000 years: 'The best boys are
those who can take a punch, but are smart
enough not to have to.'

Lewis's old rival Jack Britton came close
to losing the world welter title in 1922 to the
lightweight champion, Benny Leonard, who
having put Britton on the floor, hit him
while he was there and got disqualified. It
was one of only two defeats for Leonard
(real name: Benjamin Leiner) in a career
lasting from 1914 to 1932. He retired undefeated lightweight champion after wins
over Rocky Kansas and Lew Tendler and the
argument will always be: was Leonard a
better lightweight than Joe Gans? Benny
found the best answer: 'If you have to go

Action all the way (above): Dempsey v. Firpo in New York's Polo Grounds, 1923. Top: Dempsey smashed out of the ring in round one. Bottom: shoved back by reporters. But Firpo dropped seven times in the first round and was KO'd in the second

back that far to find someone who can beat me, I'm not worried.' Leonard was managed by Billy Gibson, a wealthy racehorse owner who clearly had a good eye for talent, equine and human, because he also managed Gene Tunney.

Tunney, throughout his professional life, lost once only, to a middleweight called Harry Greb, of Pittsburgh, whose rough behaviour in the ring and amatory exploits outside it are legendary. Two stories make both points.

Dempsey once used Greb as a sparring partner and when a fight between them was hinted, Doc Kearns said: 'No thanks. We want no traffic with that son-of-a-bitch.' Greb was asked why his hotel and dressing-room doors were always unlocked, when other famous fighters barred the way to almost everyone. Greb replied: 'What, and have some skirt try to get me and can't?' Despite being blind in the right eye and later almost blind in the other, Greb won the world

Boxing's most celebrated count (this page and opposite): referee Dave Barry tries to pull Dempsey away from Tunney and send him to a neutral corner. He won't start counting until Dempsey goes. By then, five seconds have elapsed and Tunney takes another nine, to save his title. The Long Count of 1927, at Soldier's Field, Chicago, in front of 104,000 hysterical fans

middleweight title.

In 1922 Greb and Tunney fought for the US light-heavyweight title in New York city. In the opening round Greb broke Tunney's nose in two places and cut his left eye. Tunney somehow got through the fifteen rounds (to lose) but collapsed and was carried to the dressing-room. Greb showered, dressed and within the hour was on his night-clubbing rounds. They met four times more; Tunney won every time.

Boxing at this time was crammed with extraordinary fighters. Four months after he'd hit Lewis while Ted was talking to the referee, Carpentier defended his light-heavy crown in Paris against Louis Phal of Senegal, otherwise known as Battling Siki, or the Singular Senegalese. Few believed Siki had any right in the ring with Georges and among these was Siki himself who at the start was going down from mere taps, until something inside him snapped and he turned from tame tabby into fighting wildcat. The fight became a shambles with Carpentier sliding and slithering under Siki's berserk attacks. In the sixth a left swing sent Carpentier down in a tangle of arms and legs. He was counted out. Sensation! A minute later came the announcement: 'Siki is disqualified for tripping Carpentier.'

François Descamps, whose head had been a target for a bottle in London after the Lewis fight, now had more problems. Angry spectators rushed at Carpentier and spat in his face. Siki cried, flustered officials met, and an hour later changed the result. Siki had won, they said, because Descamps threw in the towel just before the tripping incident. There never was a more bizarre finish to a

major fight. Siki's fame was short-lived, and so was he. He lost the title in 1923 to Mike McTigue of America on St Patrick's Day in Dublin as rebel guns fired in the streets. Another gun fired in 1925 in Hell's Kitchen, New York, and Siki, who had taken to leading a lion cub on a leash, dropped dead, murdered. He came from nowhere to a world title and disappeared almost as quickly.

Jimmy Wilde's days as champion were also numbered. Now thirty-one, the little Welshman placed his flyweight title on the line in June 1923, at New York's Polo Grounds baseball park against Pancho Villa, the Filipino, in front of 23,000 people. He hadn't fought since the Pete Herman disaster. He was KO'd in the seventh and once more he refused to let the towel come in (remember his anger in 1915 during the Tancy Lee fight?). He let Pancho Villa have full credit. It was Wilde's last fight and the only time he was ever KO'd. Pancho Villa died of blood poisoning from an infected tooth following his losing fight with Jimmy McLarnin in 1925. Siki . . . Villa . . . strange deaths . . . but not so weird as Harry Greb's. In 1926 he died on the operating table under a surgeon's knife which was attempting to restore a semblance of shape to his battered nose.

Such hectic years these, as boxing at all weights thrives. Dempsey and Kearns went to Shelby, Montana, a hick town where oil had been struck and the citizenry gushed at the thought of promoting the world heavyweight championship. The situation was made to measure for Kearns's shrewd bargaining. As it happened, Dempsey turned in one of his worst fights against Tommy Gibbons of Minnesota. His eye was cut and he had to go the distance. But Kearns conned almost 300,000 dollars out of the tiny community; four Shelby banks went bust and Gibbons got nothing.

Kearns (full name John Leo McKiernan) had another good fighter: Mickey Walker, admittedly a victim of the ubiquitous Greb, but who in 1922 beat Jack Britton to win the welterweight title and in 1926 beat Tiger Flowers, conqueror of Greb, to win the middleweight crown.

Walker, squat and blunt-nosed, known as the Toy Bulldog, came to Britain in 1927 to defend his middleweight title against Tommy Milligan, the Scot who held the British championship. Once again we see Kearns's astute bargaining. He forced C. B. Cochran, the promoter, to pay Walker £22,000, while

Milligan had to be content with £3000. It was the biggest purse so far in Britain and Cochran had to charge £11 ringside at Olympia. He lost £15,000. Milligan also lost, counted out in the tenth. But Kearns and Walker won. Walker deserved to; he was a middleweight who could KO heavyweights.

Who would believe that Jess Willard is still around? And yet here he is, aged forty-one and hard up, trying to make a comeback in 1923. Rickard has matched him with 6ft 3ins Luis Firpo of Argentina. One of them will be Dempsey's next rival. It turns out to be young Firpo, who stops Willard in eight rounds. Rickard reckoned he now had a good fight, but just *how* good he could not have foreseen, even though Firpo had won nine fights in succession in the US and at 216lbs with a potent right hand was sure to be a box-office attraction. Damon Runyon tagged Firpo the Wild Bull of the Pampas and the name stuck. Rickard once more had a million-dollar gate as 82,000 people shrieked themselves hoarse in the Polo Grounds: can you blame them?

Firpo was on the floor seven times in the first round. But he was on his feet long enough to throw one punch that smashed Dempsey clean through the ropes, feet in the air, to come crashing down on the Press tables where several pairs of hands heaved him off typewriters and back into the ring. Those journalistic shoves saved Dempsey's title. He never would have made it on his own. The amazing thing about this fight is that Firpo didn't come out of it world champion. He failed to follow up when Dempsey came back through the ropes, dazed and tottery, and in the second round Firpo was knocked out. The action lasted only 3min 57sec. Dempsey never won another title fight.

Gene Tunney studied Dempsey throughout these turbulent years ('I put him in a test-tube' was erudite Tunney's comment) and in 1924 stopped Georges Carpentier in fifteen rounds. The Frenchman was now close to the end of his twenty-year career; when Tommy Loughran beat him in 1926 Carpentier's days in the big-time ring were over. Only one man now had a better claim than Tunney to a fight with Dempsey and that was black Harry Wills, whose name actually got on a contract, even on to tickets, for a fight with Dempsey, but it fell through. Wills couldn't quite overcome the antipathy that remained from Jack Johnson's days.

Harry Greb had forecast in 1924 that Tunney would beat Dempsey. Tunney *knew* he would. Hadn't he slated Carpentier for

doing all the wrong things with Dempsey? The public was unconvinced. Dempsey was made a 4–1 favourite although he was now thirty-one and hadn't fought anyone since the narrow squeak with Firpo three years earlier. Even by Rickard's standards, this was a mammoth production in Philadelphia's Sesquicentennial Stadium. More than 120,000 people. Receipts: almost 1,900,000

dollars. Dempsey's share: 711,868 dollars. Rain poured throughout, as if the skies were weeping for Dempsey's downfall, for that's what it was. The first side step of Tunney's and the exact right hand that jerked Dempsey's rush to a standstill pointed the way. Although a left-hook jolted Tunney badly in the fourth, he cut Dempsey in the fifth and continued to box precisely and

scientifically. There was nothing the tiring champion could do. In a nationwide surge of disbelief, Tunney won on points over ten rounds.

Tunney, the son of an Irish docker in New York's Greenwich Village, had a taste for booklearning, a severe, dry talent for boxing, and remains the most clinically clever heavyweight of all time. Dempsey thought of retiring. He fell out with Kearns, but Rickard dangled bait and insisted he could come back. Mind you, he made Dempsey prove himself by first taking on Jack Sharkey at Yankee Stadium. Sharkey had beaten Wills and if he'd had Tunney's consistency of mind might have licked Dempsey. He certainly outboxed him at first, until confidence got the better of him and he decided to mix it with the best in-fighter of the lot. Result: Sharkey counted out. He made the same mistake as Kid Lewis, turning to talk to the referee when he should have been watching his opponent.

So the Dempsey-Tunney show was on again, this time at Soldier's Field, the vast football stadium in Chicago. More than 104,000 people turned up, paying 2,658,660 dollars, the only time gate receipts have ever topped the two-million mark. Tunney got the lion's share: 990,445 dollars. He wrote Rickard a cheque for 9555 dollars, so he could get one back (which he framed) for a million dollars. The betting this time was even and the opening rounds were just like Philadelphia.

The seventh round placed both men in history, when they became associated with what has always been known as the Long Count. How long it was nobody has discovered or ever will. The point was this: Dempsey at last landed a left-hook and down went James Joseph Tunney, proving he was after all human and that books can't teach you everything. Dempsey, naturally excited at the prospect of getting his title back, stood over Tunney waiting for him to rise.

Referee Dave Barry, in retrospect the coolest man on Soldier's Field, refused to start the count until Dempsey obeyed the rules and retired to the furthest neutral corner. Tunney, meanwhile, lifted himself off the seat of his pants by clutching with his left hand at the middle rope and waited, squatting. By the time Barry forced Dempsey away, five seconds (or more) had elapsed. The count started – and Tunney took nine seconds, as much as he could. In all he was down at least 14 seconds. Could he have

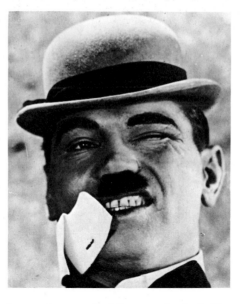

beaten the count had Dempsey backed off at once? Yes, said Tunney. Ah, but if he *had* beaten the count, would his head have been as clear as it was after fourteen seconds? Yes, said Tunney. What else would you expect him to say?

After this Tunney backpedalled, put Dempsey briefly down in the eighth, cut him on both eyes and at the end of ten rounds had his arm lifted again as the winner. Lucky Tunney, said Dempsey's army of fans. But in a sense it was lucky Dempsey. The incident and the controversy it aroused turned Jack into the most popular champion there had ever been. His reputation was intact as the man who MIGHT have got the title back, if only . . .

Tunney fought once more, beating New Zealand's Tom Heeney, for which he prised half a million dollars out of Rickard, who wound up 150,000 dollars in the red, said to be his first loss on a fight for twenty-two years. What was that Dempsey said about 'my big gates did more to commercialize fighting . . .' etc? How right. In their two fights Dempsey and Tunney were paid close to 2½ million dollars. The total recepts were more than 4½ million dollars, over £1 million . . . and this nearly fifty years ago!

From Willard to Tunney, Dempsey's earnings from fights alone came to 2½ million dollars and he is estimated to have pushed his income over the years to 10 million dollars. It all came about from a train ticket and a five-dollar bill. Jack Kearns knew what he was doing.

Jack Dempsey didn't fight for three years, between Firpo and Tunney. This is why. He was too busy making films. Disguised as Charlie Chaplin, Dempsey didn't realize he would never win another title fight

It took only 200 years to produce Joe Louis

1930-9

HEAVY: BAER, BRADDOCK, LOUIS

LIGHT-HEAVY: CONN

MIDDLE: THIL

WELTER: ROSS, ARMSTRONG

LIGHT: CANZONERI, ROSS, ARMSTRONG

FEATHER: MILLER, ARMSTRONG

BANTAM: BROWN

FLY: LYNCH

Who was Max Marek? Good question. A VIP, as it happens. In 1934 he was America's amateur heavyweight champion. Runner-up? Joseph Louis Barrow. That's right. Joe Louis. He dropped the 'Barrow' when he turned pro, which was right after Marek beat him. Boxing should be indebted to Marek for hastening Joe's entry to the paid ranks. Louis became the greatest of all champions. His mother had hoped he'd be a violinist.

Early in 1930 there was no heavyweight champion. Tunney had retired, married his Carnegie heiress and withdrawn to a life of well-heeled business and leisure. Tex Rickard was dead. In Britain the newly formed Boxing Board of Control, abolished twenty-round fights. America rocked from the Wall Street crash and in Britain the unemployed went on hunger marches. Boxing did well. That hackneyed term 'hungry fighter' is founded in reality. Boxing booms when men starve. At this time Britain had thousands of professional fighters, queuing for the dole AND for fights. Nostalgic simpletons tell you these were the 'good old days'. Ask Len Harvey if they were. He boxed for money when he was twelve and on his first trip to London at sixteen, already an experienced pro, he was glad to get fifteen shillings for six rounds. Fighters were ten a penny; promoters could throw them a crust as they pleased. Harvey calls them 'the bad old days' but believes such intolerable conditions spawn the best fighters. Britain in the thirties had a score of men at every weight good enough to fight for the national title. No one got to the top quickly. Harvey, Jock McAvoy, Cast Iron Casey, Jack Hood, Harry Mason, Johnny Cuthbert – they had more fights *before* reaching title status than today's boxers have in an entire career.

Harvey is the father-figure of this time; we shall not see his like again. A Cornishman (like Fitzsimmons) he held titles at three weights, the same three weights, oddly enough, as Fitz: middle, light-heavy and heavy. But Harvey's were British, not world, championships and yet, in some ways, his career was more exceptional than Fitzsimmons's. It spanned well over twenty years, more than 400 fights, twenty-one major title fights from welter to heavy. There was scarcely a big fight at Wembley, White City, Harringay or the Albert Hall in which Harvey, the master, was not involved. He fought twice for a world championship: in 1932 at middleweight against the bald,

Nel Tarleton (above) had one lung, but fought his way to two Lonsdale Belts. Here he is on his way back to Liverpool from London after beating Dave Crowley in a British featherweight title fight in 1934. Eleven years later, Tarleton, in his last fight, beat Al Phillips to win a second Belt outright

Low point of Carnera's chequered career: losing the world
heavyweight championship to Max Baer in 1934 (above). Carnera
was down 11 times and Baer, the Clown Prince of the ring,
taunted him all the way. Had Baer taken the game more
seriously, he might have been a great champion.
Giant Italian Primo Carnera (left) in Windsor, England, in 1929,
training to fight Jack Stanley. He wasn't quite 6ft 6ins (Jess
Willard was taller), but the gimmick was to surround him with
tiny men to make him look bigger. Clutching Carnera's right
fist is American Frankie Genaro, then the NBA flyweight
champion. He fought England's Ernie Jarvis on the same bill

durable Frenchman, Marcel Thil; and in 1936 at cruiserweight against the slim US negro, John Henry Lewis. It seems unfair that he won neither, but Harvey lacked the stunning punch that would have made him greater still.

His rival was the well-educated, impetuous Welshman, Jack Petersen, looking remarkably like Carpentier. Had he stayed at his natural weight he might have succeeded Carpentier as a world cruiserweight champion. Instead, he chose to test his potent right hand on heavyweights with outstanding domestic success. He is the only man to win British light-heavy and heavyweight titles in successive fights. He beat every leading British heavy of the time: Harvey, Reggie Meen, Jack Pettifer, the laughable Jack Doyle (a sort of Irish Harry Greb, but unfortunately never as good at fighting as wenching), George Cook of Australia, and Jock McAvoy. Now *there* was a fighter. Only 5ft 9½ins, McAvoy, a middleweight, took on all-comers, destroying men stones heavier, inches taller. He won the British middleweight crown from Harvey in 1933 and held it more than eleven years. In America he knocked out Babe Risko inside a round and went the distance with John Henry Lewis for the world cruiserweight title. Biting the thumb of his glove as he fought, McAvoy, the Rochdale Thunderbolt, brought excitement to British and foreign rings for almost twenty years and it was cruelly sad later to see him crippled by polio.

None of these – Harvey, Petersen, McAvoy, or indeed Larry Gains, the coloured Canadian who won the Empire heavyweight crown – was able to win world titles, a strong tribute to the general quality of boxing at the time. But Jack Kid Berg, from Whitechapel, natural successor to Ted Kid Lewis, thrust himself to the forefront with a whirlwind style which foreshadowed the remarkable Henry Armstrong. Berg, who beat America's Mushy Callahan in London in 1930 to win the junior-welterweight title, took America by storm at the age of nineteen. He beat the superb lightweight champion Tony Canzoneri over ten rounds (yet lost to him twice in title fights) and just as Lewis had done some fifteen years earlier adopted a two-fisted, care-for-nobody style which seized US fans' imagination long before he won a British title. That came in 1934 when he took the lightweight championship from the astute Harry Mizler.

If Berg was all smash-bang, then Nel Tarleton of Liverpool was his opposite: a

Above: Marcel Thil (right), most accomplished French boxer of the 1930s, beating America's Al Diamond in Paris, 1935. Thil, generally acclaimed at this time as world middleweight champion, beat Jock McAvoy of England this same year to retain the European cruiserweight crown.
The night New York had its first look at Joe Louis (right): 25 June 1935. Topping the bill at Yankee Stadium, Louis rips Carnera to pieces, despite conceding him 65lbs. A knock-out in the sixth round began the Golden Era for Louis ... and for boxing

supreme defensive artist, almost a second Driscoll. He boxed a draw with the physical freak, Panama Al Brown, an elongated bantam champion who stood a fraction under 6ft and whose reach exceeded his height by 5ins. Tarleton made two plucky efforts to win the world featherweight crown from Freddie Miller, the Cincinnati southpaw who fought so regularly he seldom needed to train. In 1935, for example, Miller had thirty-five fights, which today would be regarded as a full career. Tarleton ran him so close on a Liverpool dog track, angry fans, unable to accept the decision, clawed clods of turf from the ground and hurled them at the ring. The reedy Tarleton won two Lonsdale Belts – this with only one lung!

Britain had a good crop of lightweights. Dave Crowley, of Clerkenwell, fought well in America, notably against Mike Belloise. He was managed by Harry Levene, who some

thirty years later became Britain's principal promoter. By coincidence, Crowley's successor was Eric Boon, managed by Levene's great rival, Jack Solomons. The muscular Boon, a blacksmith from Chatteris in Cambridgeshire, cycled all the way to London on a Sunday morning to fight at Solomons's famous Devonshire Club, where patrons enjoyed kippers and boxing for breakfast. Boon's fight at Harringay with the elegant young Arthur Danahar in 1939 roused national excitement seldom surpassed: a classic match between slugger Boon and artist Danahar who, although not long out of the amateurs, defied the stronger Boon for fourteen rounds.

Anglo-American battles were restricted by the time it took to sail the Atlantic (no plane was capable of the journey) and European boxing was isolated from British. Few Continental fighters made much impression in

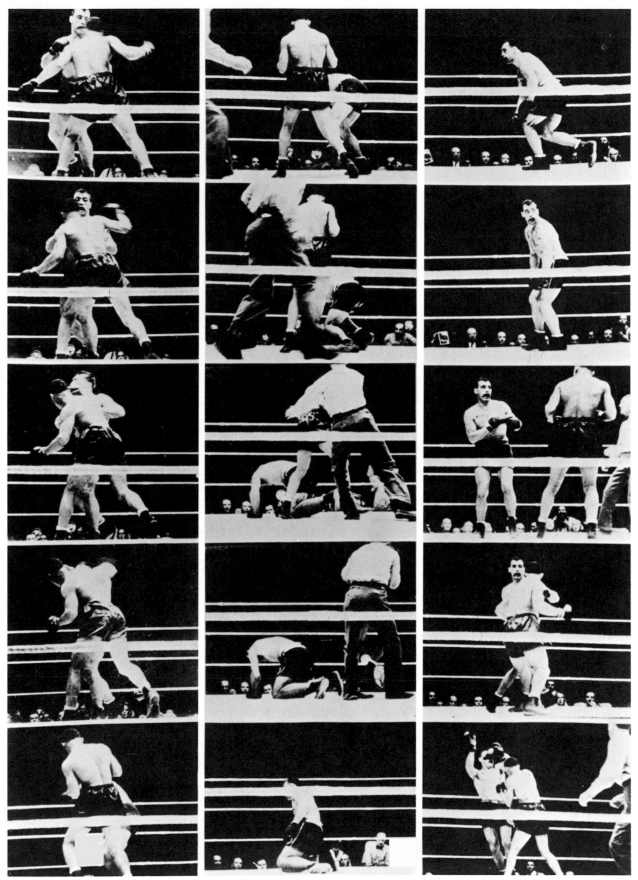

America, yet two achieved the ultimate: the world heavyweight championship. Schmeling of Germany and Carnera of Italy made the most of what I call the Seven-Year Famine, that period when the title went from hand to hand after Tunney's retirement. Max Schmeling lost it to Jack Sharkey; Sharkey lost it to Primo Carnera; Carnera lost it to Max Baer; and Baer lost it to Jim Braddock. These five formed a Caretaker Government.

Sharkey, of Lithuanian descent, was capable, but had a flawed temperament. He was chosen, you recall, to test Dempsey in 1927 and his victims included Harry Wills, Mike McTigue, Young Stribling and Tommy Loughran. But too many of his important fights ended unsatisfactorily. England's much maligned Phil Scott ('Phainting Phil' to the Americans) had a point in 1930 when he complained from an undignified posture on the seat of his pants that Sharkey hit him low. Scott was ignored, but a few months later when the same fate befell Max Schmeling, the German was declared winner on a foul and so became the first man to win the world heavyweight championship while being carried semi-conscious to his corner. Sharkey hit him with a low left – the incident and uproar led directly to the adoption in America of the no-foul rule – and when Sharkey later took the title from Schmeling, things weren't much better. This time it was a dubious verdict. Still later, when Sharkey lost to the giant Carnera, he was counted out after one right-hand punch in the sixth round of a fight he was apparently winning. The crowd were as stunned as Sharkey seemed to be. However, he had a redeeming dry wit and in 1973 on his seventieth birthday he said from New Hampshire: 'I'm in good shape and I've got all I need. The doctor lives across the street, the druggist is on the corner, I can see the funeral parlour from here, and the cemetery's just down the road.'

Primo Carnera, the Ambling Alp, a circus strongman fashioned into a fighter, has been derided as a freak foistered on the public purely on his size. His boxing was not as crude as all that and probably a good deal better than Jess Willard's, the other 6½ft champion. Carnera's left jab was good enough to beat the former world light-heavyweight champion Tommy Loughran,

In 1936, Louis's first setback: Arthur Donovan counts him out in the 12th and Germany's Max Schmeling, former world champion, is jubilant

Henry Armstrong (above) ducks under the right hand of Barney Ross. Armstrong, nearest human equivalent of perpetual motion, is already world featherweight champion. Now, at Long Island City, in May 1938, he seizes Ross's welter crown.

Two years after Schmeling's victory over Louis, a terrible revenge (above left). The Brown Bomber's fists draw an agonized shriek from Schmeling as they pierce his side. The same referee who counted over Louis does the same for Schmeling. The act of vengeance lasts 124 seconds.

Cinderella man James J. Braddock finds a way through Louis's defence at Comiskey Park, Chicago, in 1937 (left). A short right drops Louis in the opening round. Will Braddock hold on to his title after all ?

No. In the eighth round, Louis throws a right, and Braddock is down ... and out. The world has a new heavyweight champion. He will defend the title a record 25 times in the next 11 years

one of the cleverest boxers of his time, who had beaten Jim Braddock. The tragedy of Carnera lies not in his lack of craft, but in his exploitation by unscrupulous managers, who left him without a cent and forced him into wrestling where at length he made a good living. Carnera's credibility was destroyed by his successor, Max Baer, as over-rated as Carnera was under-rated. Baer had a good right and a personality as big as Carnera, but he was a playboy whose skill and dedication failed to match his exuberance. His humour was grossly misplaced in the hideous fight with Carnera. Baer guyed his rival and when they sprawled together called out: 'Last one up's a cissy.' By the time the referee came to Carnera's aid in the eleventh round, the massive Italian had been down ten times, but Baer couldn't keep him there. Carnera was never short of courage.

Baer's frailty was exposed in 1935 by the

Panama Al Brown (right), nearly 6ft tall, yet only a bantamweight (118lbs) ... but what a good one. He held the world title from 1929-35. This is when he lost it, to Spain's Baltazar Sangchilli, in Valencia. Sangchilli was 8ins shorter. But Brown was nudging 33.

After Ross, Armstrong's next fight is for the lightweight title (top left). In the fifth round, champion Lew Ambers is on the floor. Armstrong wins on points, despite bad injuries, to become the only man with three world titles simultaneously.

The finest flyweights Britain ever had: Scotsman Benny Lynch (left) and Welshman Jimmy Wilde. Jimmy lived to be 76, but Benny died of drink at 33. Drained of strength by incessant battles with the scales, Lynch (below) is flattened in three rounds at Earl's Court, London, by Rumania's Aurel Toma in 1938. He never fought again, except in the booths

longshoreman James J. Braddock, thought to be washed-up, but who was only twenty-nine and had recently beaten John Henry Lewis. He had too much experience for Baer, easily outpointing him, upsetting odds of 10–1 which reflect serious misjudgment of both Baer and Braddock. The best of the Caretaker Champions was probably Schmeling. He was the only one who beat Joe Louis, at a time when the young negro was smashing everyone out of his way, including Baer, Sharkey and Carnera. Let's study this upset closely, because it is one of only three defeats suffered by Louis in his seventeen-year career.

It happened on 19 June 1936, in New York's Yankee Stadium in front of 40,000 people. Braddock is the champion and Louis his likely challenger. But first he must beat Schmeling, who is close to thirty-one. Louis, twenty-two, sprains both thumbs in futile punching, and the left side of his face swells under the German's bludgeoning until it is twice its normal size. Dazed, uncomprehending, Louis flings punches anywhere. Several hit Schmeling low. Louis's left eye shuts and his lips bleed. He is down in the fourth. In the twelfth round a final attack puts him on his knees at the ropes as if praying for salvation. None comes and he is counted out. It's Schmeling's finest win. Of course, Louis had revenge of such savage and stunning proportions the defeat was wiped from

Britain's master-boxer, Len Harvey (above), in a 1939 tussle with brilliant coloured Canadian, Larry Gains, at Harringay, London. In this fight, Harvey won the British Empire heavyweight crown. His career lasted more than 20 years and he fought at every weight, fly to heavy.
Surprise for Louis in his first defence (right): Britain's Tommy Farr, thought to be easy meat, goes the full 15 rounds. It will be another 2½ years before anyone else does as well ... Arturo Godoy, as a matter of fact

memory. But that night in 1936 Schmeling was the world's greatest heavyweight, even if Braddock *was* champion.

Louis had powerful moneyed backing from his wealthy Chicago managers and from Rickard's successor, Mike Jacobs, the new czar. If justice meant anything, Schmeling should have been Braddock's next opponent, but money talked and Braddock was persuaded to meet Louis, who had picked himself up to win eight more fights. Almost exactly a year after the Schmeling setback, Louis emerged from the tunnel under the stands of the White Sox baseball park in

Chicago to take his place in the ring with Braddock, who had been sitting on the title for two years without defending it. Braddock now had the payday of a lifetime: 50 per cent of the receipts (that alone gained Braddock almost 300,000 dollars) but more importantly, he had a deal, if he lost, guaranteeing him 10 per cent of Mike Jacobs's share in all future Joe Louis championships. In the light of Louis's long supremacy, this stands as one of the shrewdest deals ever struck.

Louis, sleek, quick, punching home the short blows which were his trademark, subdued game Braddock in eight rounds. The Cinderella Man spoke his own epitaph: 'I fought as well as I'd ever done, but that Louis . . . oh, he was *good*! In the eighth I had nothing left and when he hit me with that right. I just lay there. I couldn't have got up if they'd offered me a million dollars.' His 10 per cent investment in Louis's future wouldn't net a million, but it paid off well. How would Braddock know, as he lay stricken in Comiskey Park, that Louis would be around as champion for the next ten years?

A sharecropper's cabin in the Deep South was where Louis first saw the light of day. Henry Armstrong, the other superb negro fighter of this time, had the same background. Louis's huge ability dominated the sport for years, but Armstrong came and went like the whirlwind he was: Homicide Hank, the Human Buzz-Saw . . . the titles speak for themselves. He achieved immortality in ten months, by winning world titles at three weights! Fitzsimmons had done this . . . but Armstrong held them *simultaneously*. He won them in a strange order.

In October 1937, the featherweight crown fell with a looping right hand that knocked out Petey Sarron (Sarron had never been KO'd before or even knocked down). Armstrong was having trouble making the weight and should have gone next for the lightweight title held by Lou Ambers, but Ambers's manager, Al Weill, blocked the fight, probably suspecting what might happen. So Armstrong skipped that division and challenged the welter champion, who, of all

Louis's seventh defence, June 1939: his sprawling opponent is the Beer Barrel Palooka, Two-Ton Tony Galento, fat, beer-swigging bartender who dropped Joe early on. He paid heavily for it. Arthur Donovan stopped the fight in the fourth

people, was the granite-hard Barney Ross, as tough a fighter as ever came out of New York city and who had previously held the light-weight championship, taken from Tony Canzoneri.

Armstrong swigged gallons of beer in training to gain some weight, but still had to concede well over half a stone, yet gave Ross such a hammering over fifteen rounds the Jewish fighter spent the next three days in bed. Within three months, Armstrong faced Lou Ambers for the lightweight crown, had him down in the fifth and sixth, but got his left eye cut, his lip so badly split it needed twenty-two stitches, and had three rounds taken away for low blows. He still won, and the MC, Harry Balogh, was able to make the unique announcement: 'Armstrong, triple world champion!' It can never be done again. Today a fighter is forced to relinquish one title when he wins another.

Armstrong's later slide into drunkenness and his reformation as a Baptist preacher makes one wish some similar happy outcome awaited Benny Lynch of Scotland, the world flyweight champion (the best since Wilde) who hit the bottle at the time he won the title from Jackie Brown of Manchester in 1935. What might Lynch have achieved but for his fatal weakness? In January 1937, he out-pointed the Filipino challenger, Small Montana, at Wembley in a classic battle of skills. Later the same year he smashed the hitherto unbeaten Peter Kane of Golborne to a thirteenth-round KO at the Shawfield Park dog track in Glasgow, where Lynch had sprung from the Gorbals. W. Barrington Dalby, who counted Kane out, described the fight as the greatest he'd seen. But it was Benny's last good one. The tragic descent began in 1938 when he failed to make 112lbs for a defence against Jackie Jurich of California. Despite refusing food and water for four days Lynch still weighed 118½lbs and had his title stripped from him at the scales. The fight went on, however, and Lynch knocked Jurich out. But his career was dying; he slipped back to the fairground booths where he'd started, until he was too ill for that. He was lifted out of the Glasgow gutter in 1946 and died in hospital, aged thirty-three.

But for the bottle, Lynch could have been a Joe Louis at the other end of the scale. He had skill and timing, the assets of the true champion. What of Louis? His advisers thought Tommy Farr of Wales would be an easy touch for his first defence. British critics thought so. Tommy was never much appreciated in London, despite wins over Ben Foord, Max Baer and Walter Neusel. US writers simply scoffed. One rated his chances 'about as good as Shirley Temple's' (a child movie star of the time). Everyone was wrong. Almost 37,000 people in Yankee Stadium saw Farr from Tonypandy pull out the hard-won skills learned in ten years as a pro to defy Louis over fifteen rounds. The decision was correct, although Welshmen will tell you Tommy-bach was robbed. Ever since the lamentable downfall of Phil Scott against Sharkey, Britain had been laughed at in America as the home of 'horizontal heavyweights'. Farr changed all that in sixty minutes with Louis that won him a lifetime's respect on both sides of the Atlantic.

In June 1938 came Louis's fourth defence: the inevitable return with Schmeling, a fight full of sinister overtones. The inescapable 'revenge' motive attributed to Louis; Schmeling's attack on him in print for the low punches in the first fight; the Nazi creed of Aryan supremacy and the snubbing of negro Jesse Owens by Hitler at the Berlin Olympics. It must be concluded that if the implacable Louis ever hated anyone, which I doubt, he came closest to it in this fight. There was the horrific moment when his right hand sledge-hammered into Schmeling's left side and the German let out a piercing shriek heard well above the roars from 70,000 throats. Schmeling was dropped three times: then the towel came floating in from his corner. Arthur Donovan stopped the fight; 124 seconds . . . that was all it lasted . . . Louis earned his money at the rate of 2832 dollars a second . . . Schmeling never fought another important fight. This could well have been the most concentratedly savage punishment meted out by one man to another with fists in the 200-odd years since James Figg began it all. Louis had the look of the finest fighting machine yet produced.

The next few years were to be gruesome enough as nation tore nation to bits, so let's close the decade lightly with a fleeting glimpse of Two-Ton Tony Galento, the Beer Barrel Palooka, chomping on his cigar, swigging his beer, and muttering of Louis: 'I'll moida da bum.' Well, he did put Joe on the floor, before Joe half-murdered *him*. Schmeling, then Galento, had found a chink in the Louis armour. No man's perfect. But in boxing Louis came as close as anyone.

If you must have a Golden Era, try this one

1940-9

HEAVY: LOUIS, WALCOTT, CHARLES

LIGHT-HEAVY: LESNEVICH, MILLS

MIDDLE: ZALE, GRAZIANO, CERDAN, LA MOTTA

WELTER: ROBINSON

LIGHT: JACK, WILLIAMS

FEATHER: PEP, SADDLER

BANTAM: ORTIZ

FLY: PATERSON

September 1939: *Boxing* magazine: 'So the Big Fight is on, and we are all sworn, as Britishers, to see it through until Right and Justice shall conquer Might and Persecution . . . take what you are forced to take with the heart of a lion, and then retaliate with the ferocity and tenacity of the British Bulldog.'

Chamberlain's government shut down sports meetings 'because if they are hit by a bomb, large numbers of people will be killed', but within two weeks a boxing show was staged at an Army camp, somewhere in southern England, and Crowley, McAvoy, Boon and Berg volunteered exhibitions.

Boxing's last issue before the war carried a reminder that Britain was dragging her feet on the colour problem. 'On what sporting grounds,' it asked, 'can the British Boxing Board justify its ban against coloured British boxers as competitors for British championships?' None whatever. Strangely enough, the same edition drew attention to a rising young middleweight, Dick Turpin, from Leamington. He became Britain's first coloured champion when the ban was lifted – but that was nine years later.

As the embarrassing question was asked, negro Henry Armstrong, the triple champion, met his first defeat in nearly three years, after forty-six consecutive wins. He lost his lightweight title to Lou Ambers in front of 30,000 people, having five rounds taken from him for low blows.

Almost at the same time, negro Ray Robinson won America's Golden Gloves amateur featherweight crown, while Joe Louis was building a reputation that has never dimmed with the passing years. Consider the social implications of Louis's achievements. He was the first negro allowed to fight for the heavyweight title since Jack Johnson almost a quarter of a century earlier. His impeccable dignity, quiet efficiency and an inborn knowledge that his fists could do the most eloquent speaking for him ensured a following in America that no previous black sportsman (and few since) had commanded. Louis and the athlete Jesse Owens, who won four gold medals in the 1936 Berlin Olympics, crashed the racial barrier in sport, clearing the way for men like Jackie Robinson in baseball.

The Bum-of-the-Month Club came into being between December 1940 and June 1941, when Louis put up the title once a month, against Al McCoy, Red Burman, Gus Dorazio, Abe Simon, Tony Musto, Buddy Baer and Billy Conn, the former world light-heavyweight champion. Conn, conceding more than 25lbs, came close to beating Louis with sheer technical efficiency at New York's Polo Grounds, but late in the fight confidence overcame commonsense. Conn threw aside his skill and elected to mix it. A right hand laid him out in the thirteenth. Louis decided on a long rest (three months) before beating Lou Nova next.

Between September 1939 and March 1942, when he enlisted in the US Army, Louis defended his title fourteen times. Money was rolling in, but not being cared for. Golf had become an addiction with him and he was 'suckered' for big bets. He spent unheedingly on a wardrobe which, by 1940, contained twenty suits and thirty-six shirts, while tailors continued to design way-out clothes for him. But basically his problem was income-tax. No one paid it, so that at the very moment of his greatest earning power the seeds of trouble were sown, reaping in time a massive debt amounting to millions of dollars which he could never hope to pay.

By June 1942, daytime restrictions on sports events had been lifted in Britain. One Saturday afternoon 40,000 people streamed into the Tottenham Hotspur soccer ground, with barrage balloons overhead, to see what proved to be Len Harvey's last fight. A pilot officer in the RAF, Len had not fought for almost three years. Facing him was an RAF sergeant, Freddie Mills, ex-milkman and fairground fighter from Bournemouth, a tousle-haired extrovert who liked to wade in throwing punches from all angles. In the second round a right uppercut smashed Harvey out of the ring and on to the Press tables. He could not clamber back in time. (He didn't get the helpful shove someone had given Dempsey against Firpo!)

Harvey was counted out for the first time in twenty-two years and Mills was British cruiserweight champion. In fact, the British Board considered him world champion, a point not resolved until he fought Gus Lesnevich four years later. The end of Harvey and the coming of Mills effectively draws the line between pre- and post-war boxing in Britain.

Peter Kane, the Lancashire man who succeeded tragic Benny Lynch as world flyweight champion, lost the title to Scotland's Jackie Paterson in June 1943, in one of the quickest title fights ever known. Kane, whose little finger on the right hand was amputated after his fight with Jackie Jurich in 1938, had not defended the title in all those years and now he had trouble making the weight (112lbs). Paterson knocked him out in the drenching rain at Hampden Park, Glasgow, in 61 seconds to become, at twenty-two, the first southpaw holder of the flyweight crown.

Paterson was unlucky to box in the shadow of Lynch, who won so much adulation in Scotland there was little left for Paterson, and yet his record at both fly and bantamweight was brilliant. At one time this son of an Ayrshire miner held five titles simultaneously.

America's entry into the war, *via* Pearl Harbor, was about a week away when the world middleweight situation, which had been in confusion since Mickey Walker quit the division ten years earlier, cleared with the advent of Tony Zale, from Gary, Indiana: the Man of Steel, who beat Georgie Abrams in Madison Square Garden on 28 November 1941. At about this time one begins to sense the start of a Golden Era in boxing. Great names appear. In November 1942, Willie Pep wins the world featherweight title against Chalky Wright and will hold it for six years. At twenty, Pep is the youngest world champion at any weight for forty years. In August 1943, Henry Armstrong, on the way down, meets a young man on the way up: Sugar Ray Robinson, still three years away from his first world title.

By now, Joe Louis is touring Army camps giving exhibitions. He did not defend his title between March 1942 and June 1946, by which time the war is over, and we can begin the story of the post-war boom. Note, however, that Louis's first fight in four years was a flop: not financially, for it garnered almost two million dollars at Yankee Stadium, beaten only by the Dempsey-Tunney return fight. But as a spectacle, it certainly was a flop. The man chosen to give Louis his first post-war challenge was Billy Conn, who had come close to beating him five years earlier. Expectations were so great Mike Jacobs was able to charge, for the first time, 100 dollars a

Wartime Saturday afternoon, 1942: and 40,000 people at Tottenham Hotspur soccer ground see a new champion crowned, an old one crash from the ring. Len Harvey, almost 35, is about to topple through the ropes under a hail of blows from fiery young Freddie Mills. Harvey, unable to clamber back, is counted out for the first time in 22 years. Mills becomes British light-heavyweight champion

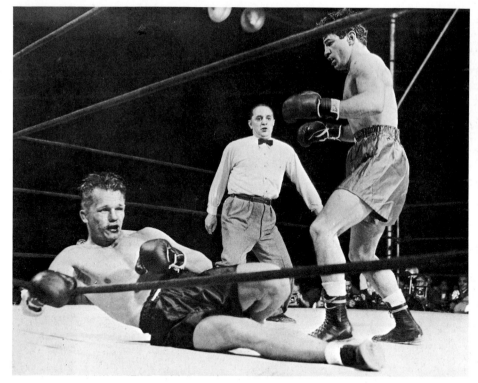

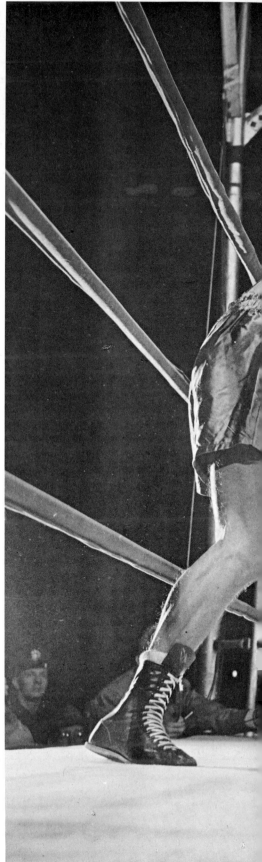

The man on the floor in New York's Yankee Stadium is one of the great middleweight champions: Tony Zale (above), in the first of his three wild fights with Rocky Graziano, reformed army deserter. Zale, from the brink of defeat, wins on a sixth-round KO. Graziano will beat him next time, but Zale regains the crown in their third fight.
In every way, a sad picture (right). Zale is about to lose the title to French-Algerian Marcel Cerdan in Jersey City, 1948. It's Zale's last fight. And a year later, Cerdan dies in an air crash

seat, but only in the first three rows. Conn, however, did not come up to expectations. There was no fire in his belly. He could only retreat, and in so doing proved to the hilt Louis's famous dictum that 'they can run, but they can't hide' by getting knocked out in the eighth.

In Britain, the end of the war coincided almost exactly with the rise to fame of the man on whom Britain's peacetime boom was based. Bruce Woodcock, a Yorkshire railwayman who had won the national amateur light-heavy title in 1939, employed a long jabbing left and a quick right hand to knock out Jack London on the same Spurs ground where Mills sent Harvey flying through the ropes. It was Woodcock's twentieth professional fight and the first major promotion, before 38,000 people, of Jack Solomons, one-time fishmonger, who was laying the foundation of a reign as Britain's Mister Boxing which lasted fifteen years.

As a point of inflationary interest, Woodcock was paid £1000 (Joe Bugner received a reputed £50,000 for fighting Joe Frazier in 1973) and Solomons admitted a profit of £400. Woodcock was promising, but not as good as the public were led to believe, and his hasty promotion to world class led to bitter disillusionment and, for him, severe physical hurt. When you understand how some US champions come to the top, the gap between the States and Britain is obvious. Middleweight Rocky Graziano, from New York city, referred to himself as a 'wild animal of a kid, sworn enemy of the whole human race'. A cop once said: 'Look in his eyes and you see the devil himself. Ten years from now, he'll be in the Death House at Sing Sing.' The cop was wrong. Boxing gave Graziano a route to respectability, but his three amazing title fights with Tony Zale remain among the most bloodcurdling ever recorded. The first in September 1946, was

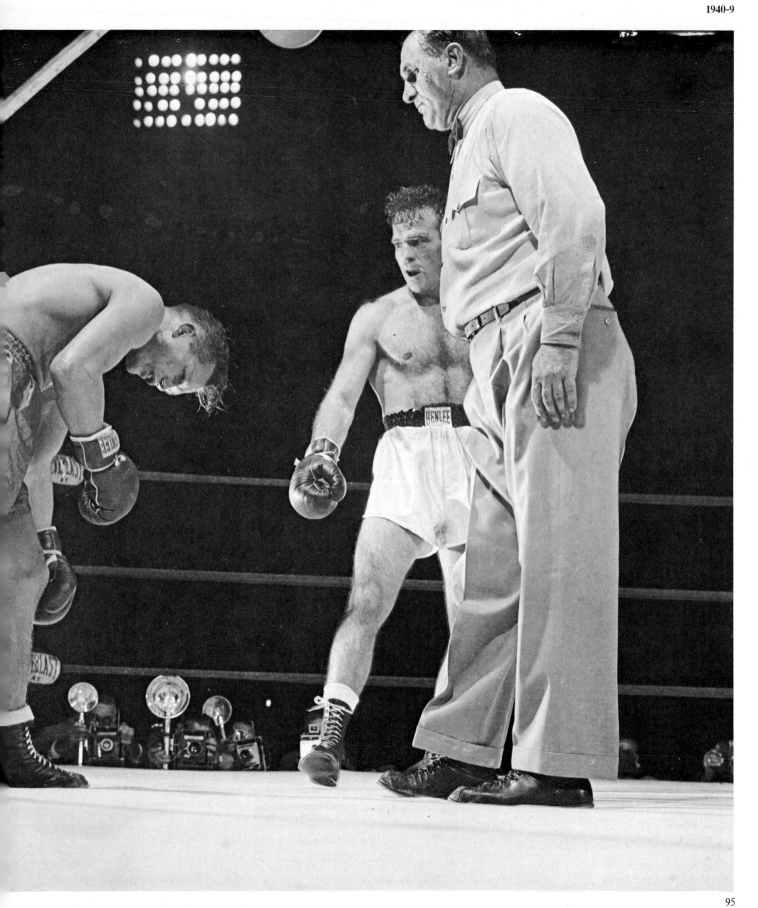

Great moment for Great Britain
(left); Freddie Mills on his
way to outpointing America's
Gus Lesnevich for the world
light-heavyweight title at
London's huge White City
stadium in 1948. Ex-booth
fighter Mills is the first
Britain since Bob Fitzsimmons,
nearly half a century earlier,
to win this crown
Above: tough as he was, Mills
(on the right) never could
successfully give weight to the
big boys. Here he is conceding
20lbs to Bruce Woodcock, heavyweight champion of Britain,
Europe and the Commonwealth,
at the White City in 1949.
Woodcock KO'd him in the 14th
round. It probably helped
soften Freddie for Joey Maxim,
who took the world cruiser
crown from him seven months
later.

When Irish Eyes are Smiling ... that's the song John Joseph
(Rinty) Monaghan is crooning to the Belfast crowd (above).
No wonder. Rinty's just become the first Belfast fighter to
win a world title. That's Jackie Paterson on the floor.
The little Scotsman has lost his flyweight title on a seventh-
round KO in 1948. Paterson found it so hard to make 112 lbs
for this fight he wrapped himself in woollies and sat in front
of a blazing boiler to sweat it off

called 'a throwback to the bareknuckle era of slashing, brutal slugging'. Zale was so badly beaten up in the fifth he should not have survived. Yet, with a broken thumb, he hit Graziano under the heart, then left-hooked him to the temple in the sixth and knocked him out.

Their second fight, in July 1947, killed a suspicion, ridiculous as it may seem now, that Graziano lacked courage in a crisis. With one eye closed and the other cut, he rescued himself in the sixth with a frightening barrage of twenty punches so menacing the referee felt compelled to move in and save Zale.

The final clash in June 1948 (Zale was underdog in all three) produced the most dramatic KO since Louis had cut down Schmeling ten years earlier. A long scything left laid Graziano on his back, out to the world, and Zale became the first to regain the middleweight crown since Ketchel beat Papke in 1908. These three fights grossed over a million dollars and the fact that Zale won two of them places him firmly among the great champions, particularly as Graziano, only 5ft 7ins, was conceded to be the hardest hitter, pound for pound, at the time, other than Louis. He often referred to Zale as the fiercest body-puncher he ever met. No one else, apart from Sugar Ray Robinson, ever stopped him. In later life Graziano became a successful actor, retaining a sharp line in wit. 'Celebrity?' he once said. 'Me? On New York's East side where I come from, they just call me a lucky bum who can punch.'

Zale had one more fight, losing the title to Frenchman Marcel Cerdan, who was later killed in an air crash on his way to fight Jake La Motta, the Bull of the Bronx. La Motta deserves special mention here as the only man to beat Robinson from the time Sugar Ray turned pro in 1940 until he met Randolph Turpin eleven years later!

A month before Louis v. Conn drew 100 dollars a seat in June 1946, Jack Solomons charged twenty guineas ringside for Britain's first post-war world championship: Freddie

Superb ring artist Willie Pep falls to the fists of Sandy Saddler in the first of their four nothing-barred featherweight title fights. Pep's about to lose the title he's held for six years. Saddler KO'd him in the 4th in this one. In fact, he won three of the four fights with Pep

Mills *v.* America's Gus Lesnevich for the undisputed cruiserweight title. Solomons himself called it: 'The most savage fight I've ever seen. Sometimes I'm doubtful about being remembered as the man who promoted it.' Mills, almost unconscious in the second round, recovered to break Lesnevich's nose and close one eye, but in the tenth was hammered to the floor three times, prompting referee Eugene Henderson to end the fight. Henderson was criticized because there were only four seconds of the round remaining, on the grounds that Mills would have had a minute in which to recover. I never understood this. Referees do not carry clocks in their heads. If a man is beaten, he is beaten, if only half a second remains. Timely intervention can save life.

British patriotism was taking a bad beating. Bruce Woodcock, dispatched to New York for a fight with Tami Mauriello, was knocked out in five rounds. It takes some believing now, but three weeks after Mills's savage pasting from Lesnevich and only seventeen days after Woodcock's KO by Mauriello, the two Britons were matched by Solomons in a non-title fight, Woodcock winning on points. Britain's boxing renaissance under Solomons was built upon the broad and willing shoulders of these two, whose courage and resilience were tested to the full, and sometimes beyond. Mills, for example (let's not forget he was only a cruiserweight) was placed against the giant American, Joe Baksi, in November 1946, to be totally obliterated. A few months later Woodcock absorbed the worst beating of his career from Baksi, whose left-hook at the bell shattered the Yorkshireman's jaw, while subsequent blows half-blinded him. The fight was eventually halted in the seventh, but Woodcock has since confessed he remembers nothing after that first bone-splintering punch.

Mills at least reaped world honours when he went in with Lesnevich for the second time in July 1948, on the eve of the London Olympic Games, winning a fifteen-round decision, to stand alongside Fitzsimmons, only other Briton then to have taken the light-heavyweight title. Irrepressible Mills was such a favourite with crowds and had a heart so big he was expected to face impossible odds in other fights. In the summer of 1949 he was matched with Woodcock for the British heavyweight crown, only to be knocked out in the fourteenth, a defeat which may well have made him an easier proposition for America's Joey Maxim in 1950, who ended Mills's reign as world champion by knocking

Back goes the head of once-great Beau Jack (above), as Ike Williams (5ft 9½ins) pushes home the heel of his glove in defence of the world lightweight championship. Jack gets stopped in the sixth round of this 1948 Philadelphia fight. Williams reigned as undisputed lightweight king from 1947-51. Most of his punches were better than this one.

Point at which the supremacy of Joe Louis is first questioned (right). Jersey Joe Walcott (at 33, as old as Louis) drops him in the opening round of their 1947 fight at Madison Square Garden. Louis, champion for 10 years, plods his way to a disputed points win. Six months later, he beats Walcott convincingly, then quits as undefeated champion

With Louis retired, the heavyweight crown is open to all-comers. Right: in Chicago, slightly-built Ezzard Charles (on the left) scores a 15-round points victory over Walcott. But he gets only partial recognition. Louis is already sadly missed

him out in the tenth (and three of his teeth as well). Mills, at thirty, retired to a career in show-business, but took his own life with a gun in 1965.

Sadly, other British fighters who won world titles died violently. Randolph Turpin committed suicide. Jackie Paterson, who lost his world flyweight crown to Rinty Monaghan in 1948, after sitting swathed in woollens in front of a boiler to sweat off excess weight, was stabbed to death in South Africa at the age of

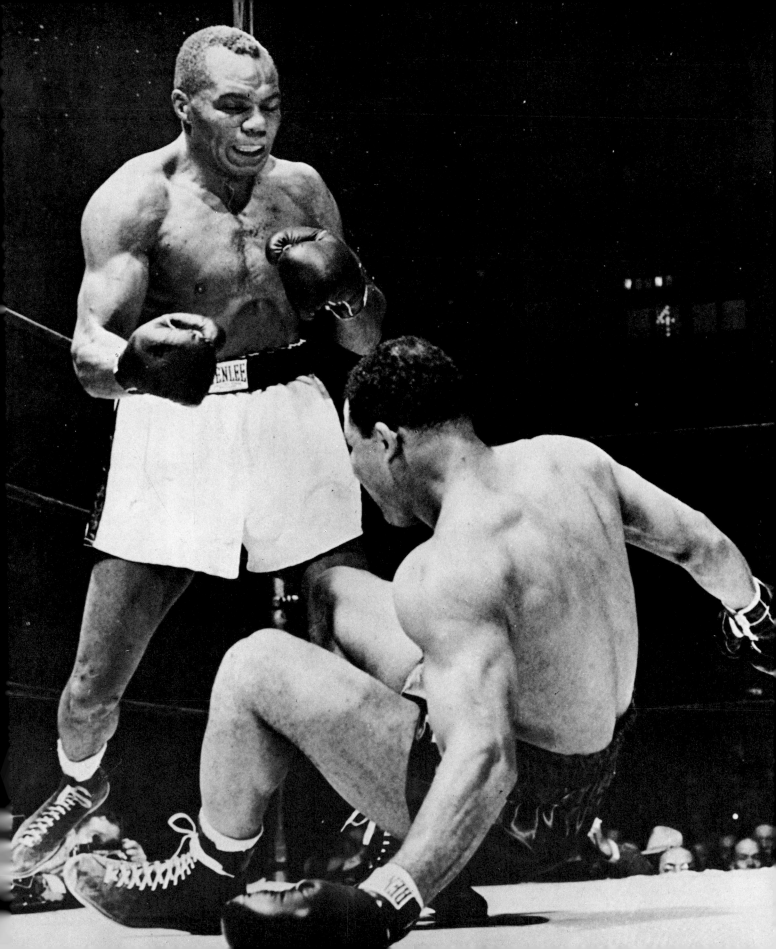

forty-six.

Monaghan, whose nickname Rinty sprang from his boyhood passion for films starring Rin Tin Tin, the Alsatian dog, was the first Belfast boxer to win a world title. Win or lose, he always grabbed the microphone after a fight to warble 'When Irish Eyes are Smiling'.

But back to America, where Willie Pep and Sandy Saddler are having their four famous fights for the featherweight championship. Fights? Brawls, more like it. Saddler won three of them: the first, third and fourth. The last was so dirty the referee wound up on the floor. When Pep failed to come out for the tenth, New York Commissioner Robert Christenberry ordered an inquiry. Wrote one reporter: 'I'm not surprised. It was so rough I wonder they didn't have to order an autopsy.'

The previous fight also ended strangely when Pep failed to come up for the eighth, despite being ahead on all three officials' cards. Pep said his left shoulder was dislocated where Saddler had wrenched him round during the in-fighting. Saddler said, phooey, Pep quit because he couldn't take the body punching. Furthermore, said Sandy, Pep stuck a finger in my eye.

The first fight, in 1948, came not long after Pep had survived an air crash. Rumours of a 'fix' were so strong, New York commissioner Eddie Eagan took them aside at the weigh-in and said: 'I am making you both responsible to uphold the good name of boxing.' Pep was knocked out in the fourth and it later came out that Saddler's manager, Charley Johnston, had guaranteed Willie a purse of nearly £9000, plus a return fight if Saddler won. It was only the second time in 137 fights that Pep had lost.

Saddler was a rough, tough slugger, but Pep was a master boxer, who showed his class in the second fight, which he won on points. It was described by Grantland Rice as 'the greatest exhibition of boxing I have seen in more than 50 years'. John Lardner wrote: 'Pep has the nonchalance and blinding speed to move within half an inch of danger and stay there all night.' And Red Smith said: 'If Willie had chosen a life of crime, he could have been the most accomplished pickpocket since the Artful Dodger. He may be the only man that ever lived who could lift a sucker's wallet while wearing 8-oz. gloves.'

Joe Louis was in decline. In December 1947 came the first of his two fights with Jersey Joe Walcott, who, although nearly thirty-four, was only a few months older than Louis. The fight, not much of an attraction, was relegated to Madison Square Garden in front of 18,000 people and Louis installed as 10–1 on favourite. Walcott had been around seventeen years, but was written off as a 'cutey' who at best would make only a dull fight. However, he dropped Louis in the opening round, again in the fourth, and frequently outboxed the champion. Louis was slow, his timing off, and unable to nail Walcott. After fifteen rounds, referee Ruby Goldstein gave his vote to Walcott, but the two judges scored for Louis. Booing and stamping broke out. Many critics thought Louis lucky to keep his title, the first time in ten years his supremacy had been questioned.

A quick rematch took place in Yankee Stadium. For ten rounds Louis did hardly better than the first time. Still no sign of the short, destructive hand-speed with which he made his name. Walcott then fell into the same trap Billy Conn had dug for himself. He got over-confident, or perhaps did not trust the officials to come up with a points verdict for him. He jettisoned his boxing and went for a kill. Walcott left a gap and Louis slammed three lefts and a right through it. More punches rained on Walcott, who crumpled to the floor and was still there, on all fours, when the count reached ten.

Louis never fought as champion again. Nine months later he announced his retirement, undefeated after twenty-five defences spread across eleven years. If only he could have left it at that. He couldn't. Haunted by mounting tax debt, he had to fight again. But that comes in the next decade.

On 13 November 1949, Sugar Ray Robinson, welterweight champion of the world, turned up in New Orleans to knock out Vern Lester in five rounds. Two nights later, at Harringay, London, Randolph Turpin, rising middleweight and brother of the man who broke Britain's colour bar, smashed America's Pete Mead so hard in the ribs Mead fainted and had to be taken to hospital. At that moment nothing seemed less likely than that Robinson and Turpin would ever face one another in the ring. In fact, they were set on a collision course.

They seldom come back: but Louis, and the world, hoped he might. It's 27 September 1950. Louis hasn't fought for more than two years. Now he challenges NBA champion Ezzard Charles. But Charles, seven years younger, is too quick for him. This left-hook counter from Charles helps him win on points and gain world-wide acclaim as champion

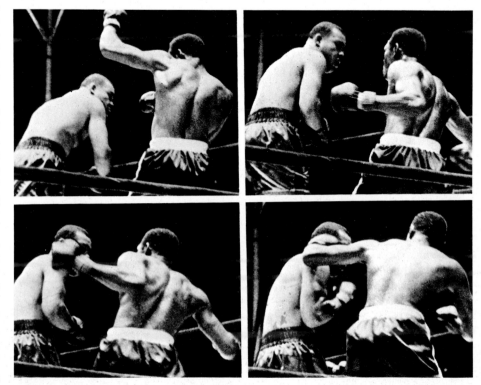

Why did Marciano come along and spoil everything?

1950-9

HEAVY: CHARLES, WALCOTT, MARCIANO, PATTERSON

LIGHT-HEAVY: MOORE

MIDDLE: ROBINSON, TURPIN

WELTER: GAVILAN, BASILIO

LIGHT: BROWN

FEATHER: SADDLER, MOORE

BANTAM: COHEN

FLY: PEREZ

No one who was there will forget the rapture of Randolph Turpin's amazing upset win over Sugar Ray Robinson at Earl's Court in July 1951 (above). Sugar Ray looked jaded, Turpin boxed coolly, and Britain found herself unexpectedly with the world middleweight title

ouis's retirement led to an uncertain groping for a new champion, just as Tunney's had twenty years earlier. Louis suggested that Ezzard Charles and Jersey Joe Walcott meet for the title, which they did. Charles won, but was not universally accepted. In Britain, the Board of Control naïvely endorsed a White City fight between Bruce Woodcock, the battered British champion, and Lee Savold, a thirty-four-year-old American, for the world title. Savold won. The absurdity was laid bare in 1951 when Louis, out of retirement, easily stopped Savold. The British Board was now forced to recognize Louis as champion, when in fact he had failed to regain the title from Ezzard Charles a few months earlier.

Why did Louis come back? He was tied up with the International Boxing Club. Founded in 1949, it was to control all major boxing in the USA from 1950 to 1960. The IBC grip was so strong it took a Supreme Court judgment to break it. Louis's old boss, Mike Jacobs, staged his last show at Madison Square Garden on 20 May 1949. Immediately, James D. Norris, a Chicago grain millionaire who owned racehorses and an ice-hockey team, formed the IBC. He signed a contract to provide seventy live-TV boxing shows a year, sponsored to the tune of £350,000 by Gillette Razor and Pabst Blue Ribbon Beer. IBC power eventually spread to every major fight city in the States. New York columnist Red Smith dubbed it 'Octopus Inc'. By selling big boxing to television, Norris strangled the small arenas, nurseries of the sport. Few would pay to watch second-raters when top stars were free on TV.

Norris persuaded Louis to fight again. The Brown Bomber needed money to pay off his tax and Norris needed a big name to satisfy his sponsors. There was none better than Louis, still fondly regarded as the real champion. But Joe's good days were long gone and although he won eight out of ten comeback fights, he lost the two that mattered: the title fight with Ezzard Charles, and his last fight of all, with Rocky Marciano.

Marciano was one of two Jim Norris trump cards. The other was Sugar Ray Robinson, the welterweight champion, who was about to stir the middleweight division into a frenzy of activity. In 1951 Robinson won a victory as satisfying as any in his career. He was already thirty years old, had been a pro for more than ten years, and in 122 fights had been beaten only once, by Jake La Motta, back in 1943. La Motta, the

Bull of the Bronx, was now middleweight champion, but Robinson beat him for speed, skill and punch. A punch under the heart in the eleventh round set La Motta on the way to a fourteenth-round defeat. For Sugar Ray it was revenge, plus worldwide celebrity.

Muhammad Ali has admitted he used Robinson as a model. Both were masters of publicity. Where Ali relied on his mouth, Robinson, the Black Prince, sleek and worldly, adopted a mock-modest front, but gained notoriety from his extravagant travelling 'circus'. He assessed its cost at £1200 a week. There was the flamingo-pink Cadillac, a retinue of servants, including chauffeur, barber, masseur, golf pro, dwarf jester and three trainers, 100 pieces of luggage, a wife, and the wife's relations. All these came to Europe on barnstorming tours in 1950 and 1951, when Ray surprised the wife of the French President by embracing her at a Paris reception and grandly donating a 10,000-dollar purse to charity.

Jack Solomons, whose grip on boxing in Britain was as firm as the IBC's in America, saw in Robinson an ideal match for muscular young Randolph Turpin of Leamington, who was riding a wave of knockout successes. Turpin, the most exciting post-war fighter in Britain, was clearly dangerous with punches hooked from either flank, but was he ready for Robinson? Solomons said yes, offered Sugar Ray £30,000 and booked Earls Court. The public said no, but bought tickets anyway and packed the place. Turpin had had forty-three fights; Robinson 131. Turpin was raw and strong; Robinson smooth, assured, but aging and weak.

If that seems uncharitable to Turpin, whose great night this was, it must stand as the truth. Perhaps the mad, six-week, six-fight whirl through Europe dulled Robinson's form. No magic ever came. In the seventh, Turpin cut Robinson's left eye, the only incident of note. On stiff, straddled legs, Turpin carried the fight to Robinson. It was enough for a points win, rousing 18,000 delirious fans to sing 'For He's a Jolly Good Fellow'. Robinson, smiling politely, made no excuses, and for sixty-four days Turpin was a national hero.

The contract called for a return within ninety days if Turpin won, and Solomons was not arguing with Norris. On a stifling night in New York's Polo Grounds (61,370 people paid a record non-heavyweight gate of £274,152) Robinson almost lost again. The difference of eight years in age caught up with him in the tenth and once more his eye

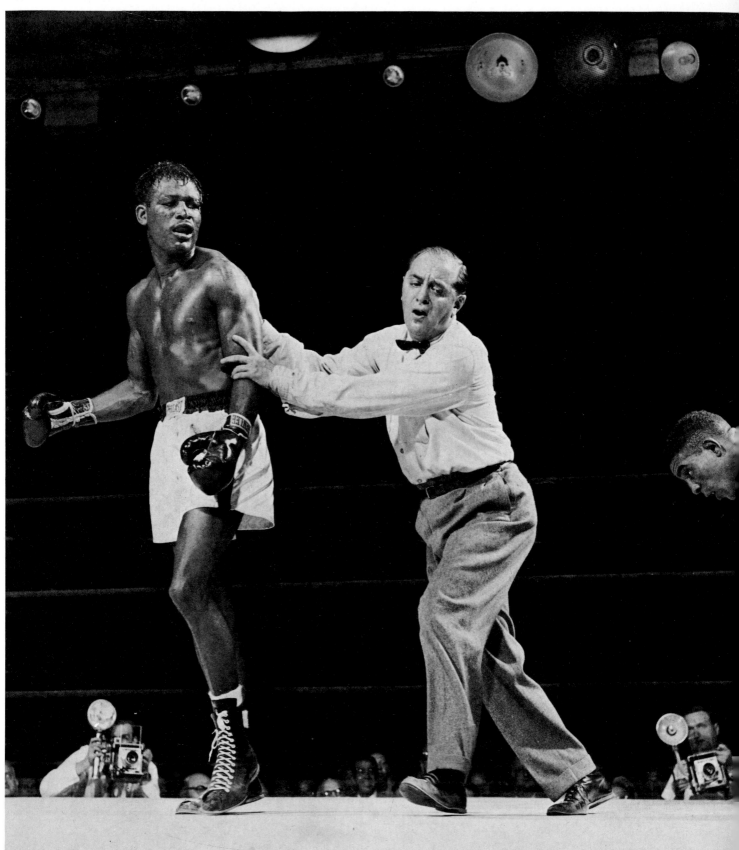

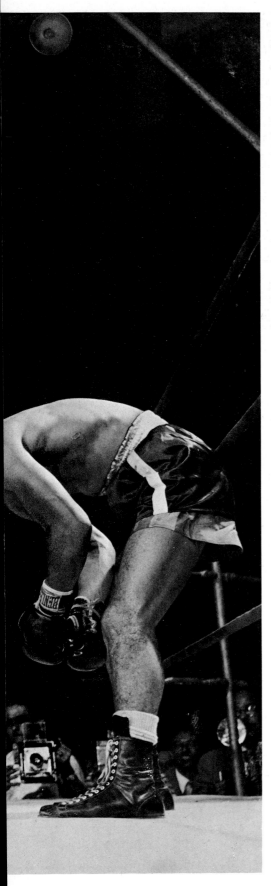

After two hard rights, Freddie Mills is down and out in the 10th round at London's Earl's Court in 1950 (above). Joey Maxim, Italian-American managed by old Doc Kearns, takes over as cruiserweight champion. The rapture lasted just 64 days. Then Turpin took the crown to New York's Polo Grounds (left). In the 10th round, Robinson, left eye split, turned on a barrage of punching which left Turpin swaying unsteadily on the ropes. Ruby Goldstein stops the fight. Robinson has the title back. Turpin never recaptures the magic of 1951

was split. At the ringside, his mother screeched: 'You've got to get him, Ray!' Ray got him. A right cracked on Turpin's brown chin and he fell. When he stood up, Robinson forced him to the ropes and hammered him with blows as Turpin swayed from side to side in the effort to avoid them. A few nights earlier a boxer had died in New York under a similar attack. Now the referee stepped between them and yanked Robinson off. Sugar Ray had his title back. Another eight seconds, and the bell would have saved Turpin. It was a decisive moment in both men's lives. Turpin, declining fast, never fought another great fight. His private life fell apart. He lost everything: fortune, titles, respect, and eventually his life, by his own hand. That night of triumph at Earls Court can be seen now as the top of a slide to oblivion. But for just a few

months Turpin was the most exciting fighter Britain has ever had. Robinson, a marvel of dedication and always a magnetic box-office draw, went on and on, to win the middle-weight crown a record five times.

The downfall of Joe Louis came only six weeks after Turpin's defeat. Norris was now ready to play his other trump, Marciano. An Italian–American from a Boston suburb, he was managed by Al Weill, who when he first set eyes on him in the gym wanted to throw him out. Weill couldn't believe anyone as crude as this could be a prospect, particularly when Marciano explained he always let other guys belt him in the stomach because it tired them out. Little Charley Goldman, Weill's trainer, saw diamond quality in this hunk of granite and said he could 'sculpture' him into something good. He taught Rocky a simple cross-arm defence (other fighters *did* exhaust themselves hitting his arms) and by the time Norris was ready to test him against Louis, who was now thirty-seven, Marciano had won thirty-eight fights in a row. Cynics scoffed. Pushover fights, they said. But when Marciano had Louis in the crucifix position on the ropes and let go the terrible right that laid the old Bomber in a forlorn heap, they conceded he *might* just be good material.

So, farewell to Louis after seventeen magnificent years. Only three defeats in all that time: the first with Schmeling, the come-back fight with Charles, and now Marciano. He had earned nearly five million dollars, with nothing to show other than a massive debt to Internal Revenue. What a condemna-tion of the men who mishandled his affairs.

Boxing now flourished in North and South America, Western Europe, Africa and Asia,

Hogan Bassey of Nigeria won the world featherweight crown in 1957, but this British-based fighter had a long, hard climb. In this 1953 fight in London (above) he had to retire in the fifth with a damaged thumb against ex-French champion, Emile Chemama.

End of the Brown Bomber (right): Louis, 37, is offered as a trial-horse for up-and-coming Rocky Marciano. He's slaughtered in eight rounds in October 1951. The close of 17 magnificent years. Joe never complained when Marciano finished him. He merely said: 'That's OK. I've knocked lots of guys out.'

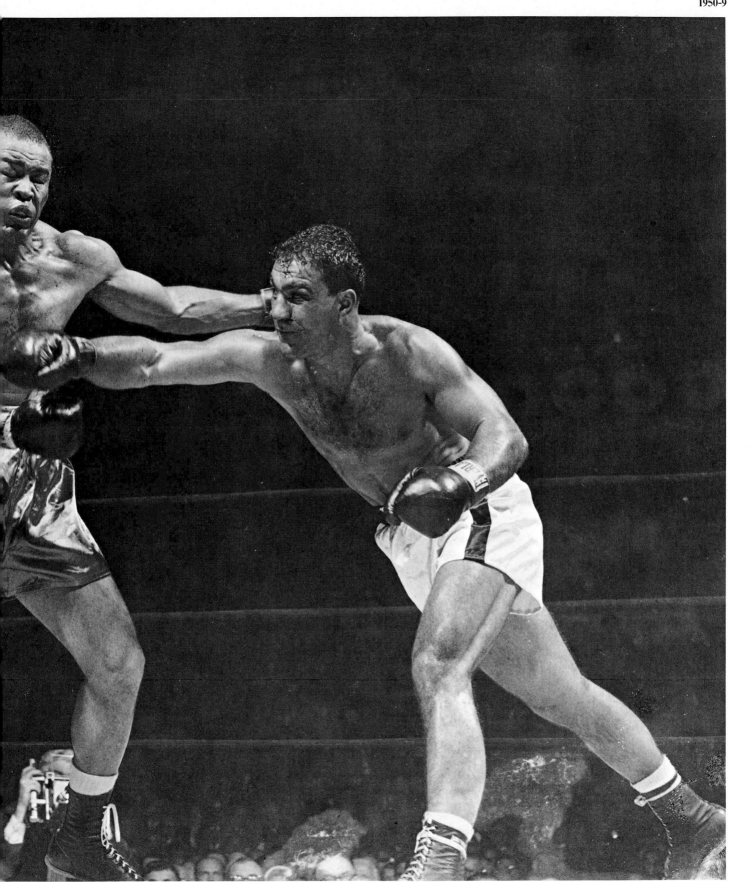

whose little men were about to make successful attacks on the flyweight championship. Britain's traditional hold on the title was maintained for a short time by the Cockney barrow-boy, Terry Allen. But the best flyweight of the decade was Pascual Perez of Argentina, who followed his Olympic triumph of 1948 by winning the professional title in 1954 and reigning for six years. Among his defences was the annihilation of Welshman Dai Dower, a smart mover with no punch, who lasted only 2min 48sec in front of 85,000 people in Buenos Aires.

Europe was producing many good-class men. Ray Famechon of France came close to the world featherweight title. The Spaniards, Luis Romero and Young Martin, were too strong for most of Britain's little men. The remarkable Duilio Loi of Italy, world junior welter champion, lost once only in his first 100 fights. Britain had classy boxers like Ronnie Clayton of Blackpool and Peter Keenan of Glasgow. Both won two Lonsdale Belts. Joe Lucy, a methodical southpaw, had to give way to a better one, Dave Charnley of Dartford, who was unlucky to be seeking the world lightweight crown when it was worn by one of the decade's finest champions, Joe (Old Bones) Brown, of the USA. Aggressive Charnley was Britain's best lightweight since Eric Boon.

Promoter Fred Bamber struck a blow for tolerance by permitting Leo Starosch of Essen to fight middleweight Jonny Sullivan at Preston Public Hall in 1954. Starosch was the first German allowed in a British ring for fourteen years.

Sugar Ray Robinson missed one ambition: that of being a triple world champion like Armstrong and Fitzsimmons. In trying to lift the light-heavyweight title from Joey Maxim, he also found himself fighting the hottest night of the year: 104° in the shade at Yankee Stadium, but more like 150° under the arc lamps. It was so hot the referee, Ruby Goldstein, collapsed and had to be replaced during the fight, while Robinson, ahead on points, fell exhausted at Maxim's feet in the thirteenth round and couldn't get off his stool for the fourteenth. He retired after this, but when his Harlem businesses went bust and his night-club song-and-dance act fizzled out, he had to come back. The 'circus' had soaked up all his money and he went on without it, sometimes champion, sometimes not, but always a great attraction.

Having finished Louis, Marciano was ready to challenge for Joe's old title, now in the hands of thirty-eight-year-old Jersey Joe

End of a triple-crown dream: Ray Robinson (above) flat on his face in Yankee Stadium. Having already won welter and middle titles, he thought he could take the light-heavy crown from Maxim. But a night of relentless, steamy heat beat him. This was the 13th round. He couldn't get off his stool for the 14th. The referee collapsed even earlier and had to be replaced.

For 13 rounds Marciano has taken everything champion Walcott can throw. Now (right), in Jersey Joe's home town of Philadelphia, Rocky throws his Suzy Q – that's what he calls his right hand – and Walcott crumples. The Rock is champion. Just one of 49 fights that Marciano had: he won all of them

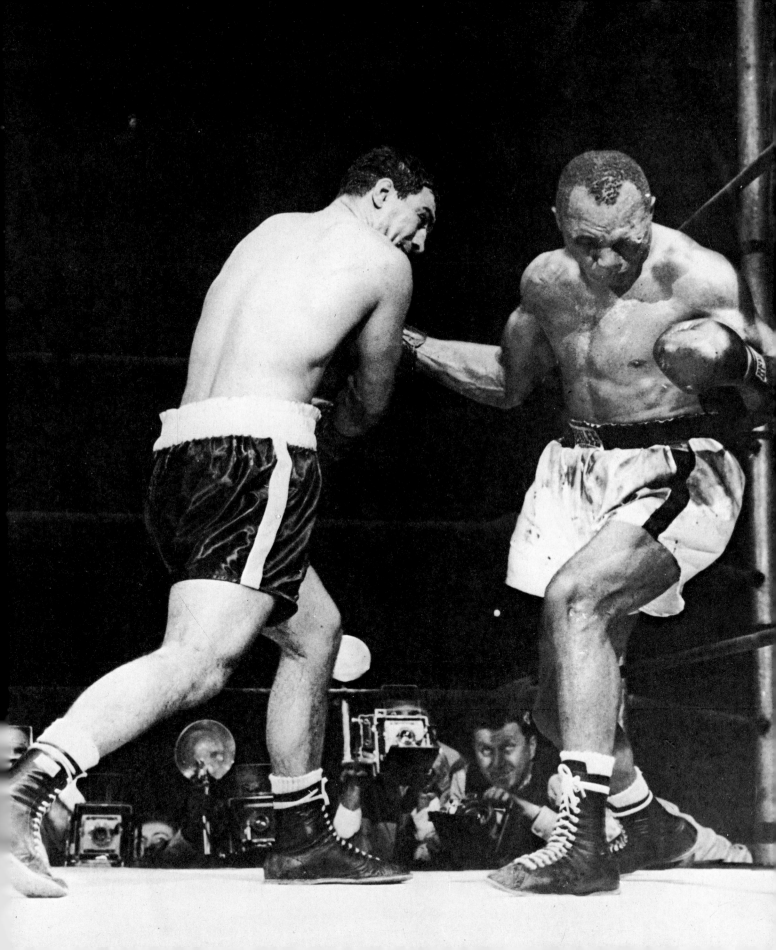

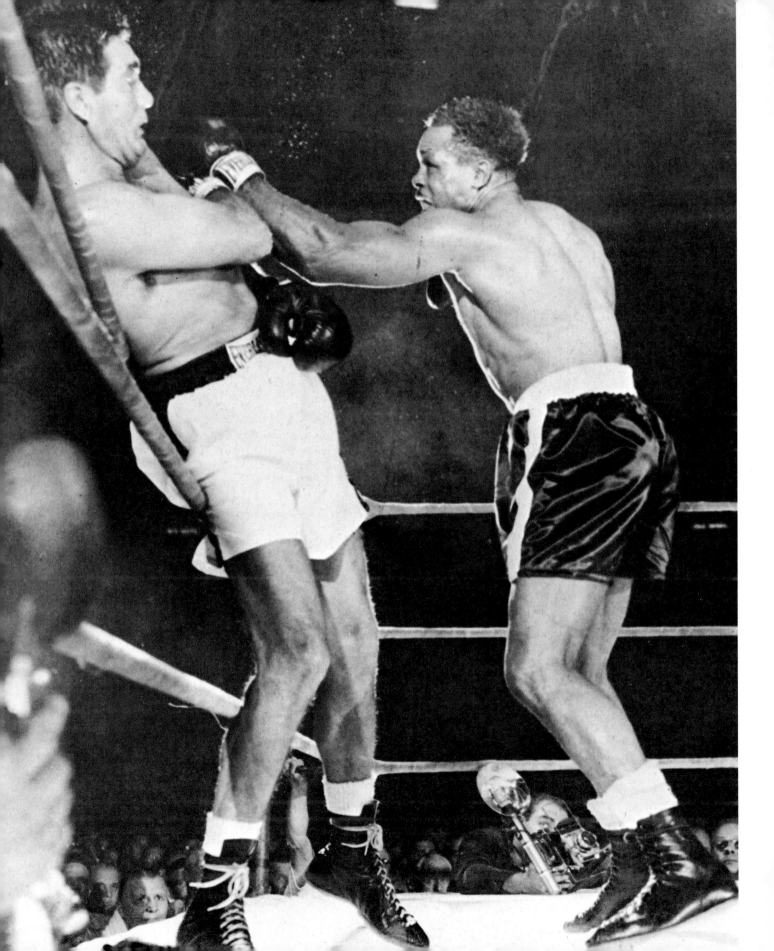

A June night in 1959 which shakes the boxing world: 4-1 underdog Ingemar Johansson of Sweden smashes Floyd Patterson to the floor seven times in the third round at Yankee Stadium (above). Johansson was on top of the world for a year, but never achieved anything as remarkable again.
Archie Moore waited nearly 17 years for a shot at the world cruiser title. But in 1952, Maxim gave him his chance (left). Moore took it with a points victory. Archie was 39 at the time. He held the title until he was 48 !

Walcott, the oldest man ever to win it. The Rock absorbed everything Walcott could throw for thirteen rounds. Left eye shut, right eye gashed, lips swollen, scalp split, Marciano finally smashed home his right – he called it Suzy Q – which sent the old man sprawling. One ringsider described it as the hardest punch he had seen one man land on another. At twenty-eight Marciano was the first

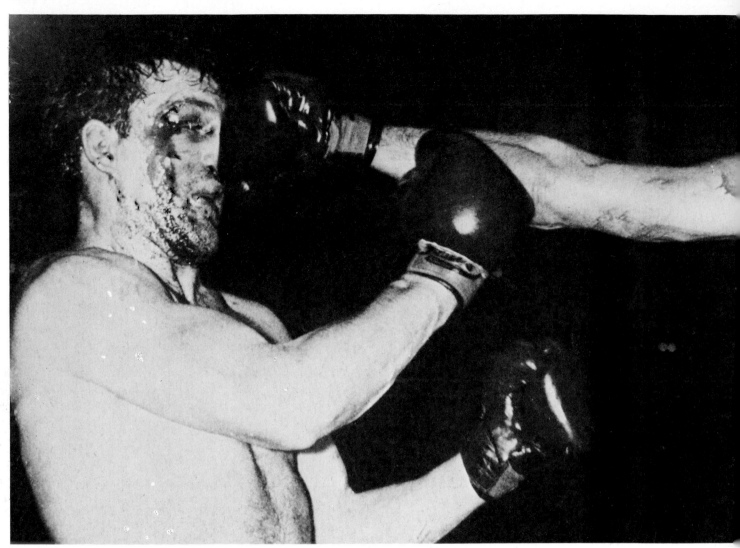

white heavyweight champion since Braddock and for sheer blind ferocity a throwback to Dempsey. Men wondered why 3000 years had been spent learning the arts and crafts of boxing if Marciano could come along and overthrow it all with one savage blow reminiscent of the ancient *caestus*.

Doc Kearns, who had managed Dempsey and had cleaned out Shelby, Montana, in 1923, was still wheeling and dealing in 1952. Archie Moore, arguably the greatest light-heavyweight of them all, had been side-tracked for sixteen years in his pursuit of the world title. Kearns, manager of Joey Maxim, the champion, accepted Moore as a challenger. Moore won, despite being near his fortieth birthday. Who had a piece of Archie from that moment? Doc Kearns. The Doc almost wound up with the heavyweight champion of the world again. Moore tossed a right in 1955 that knocked Rocky Marciano clean off his feet. I swear it could have killed

some men, but Marciano clambered to his feet before the referee had got to 'three'. Probably the best right hand Moore had produced in twenty years of fighting, it still wasn't good enough, and although Archie struggled on for another seven rounds, Marciano got him in the end. Just as he had got Britain's Don Cockell a few months earlier. Cockell, the first Briton to fight for the big title since Tommy Farr, eighteen years earlier, showed tremendous courage, but was later dismissed by Marciano as a 'powderpuff puncher'.

Marciano was a ruthless attacker and a very dirty fighter. He always elbowed and butted. He hit Cockell at least once when Don was down. But he was a charming companion outside the ring and incapable of believing he did any of these things. He was never pulled up for it in America, but had he fought in Britain he might have been disqualified. I never saw him take a backward step. He

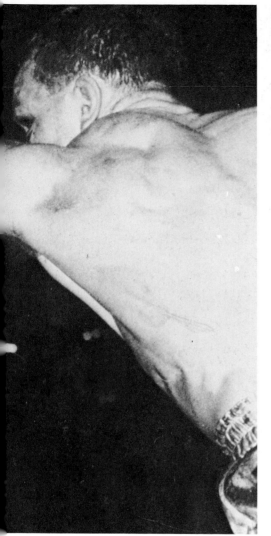

The left that governed Britain's heavyweights for 12 years: Henry Cooper (above) jabs Brian London to defeat at Earl's Court in 1959. It was the beginning of Cooper's long reign as British heavyweight champion which lifted him to the status of national hero. Rocky Marciano (above right): first white heavyweight champion since Braddock, toughest since Dempsey. Game, but unavailing: British champion Don Cockell (right), of Battersea, goes nine rounds with Marciano at San Francisco's Kezar Stadium in 1955. He was Britain's first challenger for the big one since Farr in 1937

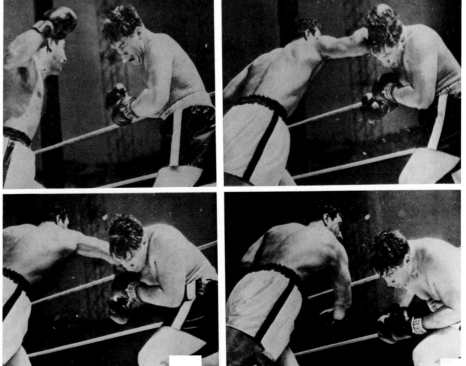

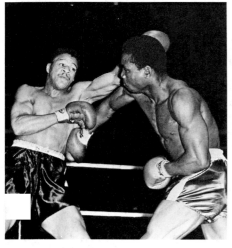

Pascual Perez of Argentina
(top), a brilliant flyweight
champion. Here he flattens
former champion Yoshio Shirai
in Tokyo in the fifth round of
their 1955 fight. Perez won
the title from Shirai the
previous year, defended it
successfully nine times.
Another great Nigerian fighter,
Dick Tiger (above, on the
right), never really made the
grade until he quit Britain for
America. Then he won the world
middle and light-heavy titles.
He lost this 1958 fight in
London to useful US middle
Spider Webb.
Joe 'Old Bones' Brown (right)
made 11 successful defences of
the lightweight championship
from 1956-61

trained nine months in every year to maintain the physical shape his relentless style demanded. Having seen him lay Moore to rest, I would have laid long odds that Ancient Archie would call it a day. In fact, seven months later, Marciano decided to retire, partly because his long confinement in camp put an intolerable strain on his marriage and partly because Moore's right hand had signalled danger. After an explosive reign of just under four years, with six defences, Marciano took with him the perfect record: forty-nine fights, forty-nine wins. No other world champion, at any weight, has come through an entire career in this way.

And Moore? Incredibly, he fought for another eight years, until he was nearly fifty, and was involved in the heavyweight championship again when young Floyd Patterson succeeded Marciano. Cus D'Amato, a crafty manager from Brooklyn, shaped Patterson's style to suit television: peek-a-boo defence with gloves cupped to the head and a kangaroo leap to throw a punch. Nothing of value, mere flashiness to catch the viewer's eye. Moore, nowhere near as dangerous as he had been with Marciano, was easily beaten in five rounds for the vacant title in 1956, and Patterson, at twenty years and ten months, became the youngest man ever to win the crown.

Although he has earned about eight million dollars, Patterson was a vulnerable champion. D'Amato's reluctance to match him with good opponents in his early championship days and Patterson's palpably weak jaw tarnished his reputation. D'Amato devalued the title by allowing an amateur, Pete Rademacher, to challenge for it. Rademacher, Olympic gold medallist of 1956, made his pro début as Patterson's opponent. What's more, he dropped the champion, but was subsequently well beaten, going down seven times.

To his credit, D'Amato refused to allow the powerful IBC to muscle in on Patterson, but undid all the good by creating his own monopoly, spurning good challengers and accepting poor ones, such as Brian London, of Britain. As it happened, the IBC was already under Federal investigation. Evidence showed that between 1949 and 1953 the Club promoted thirty-six of the forty-four world title bouts that had taken place. Jim Norris & Co., found guilty of violating anti-trust laws, were ordered to shut shop and sell their holdings in Madison Square Garden, Frankie Carbo, an underworld figure long suspected of being close to the IBC, was accused of conspiracy and extortion.

In 1957, Henry Cooper almost gave up boxing when he lost three big fights in succession. Joe Bygraves and Ingemar Johansson knocked him out, Joe Erskine outpointed him. Despondent Cooper talked of quitting, but his manager Jim Wicks persuaded him to

Three great black champions of the 1950s: Davey Moore (top), featherweight king, later tragically killed. Kid Gavilan (right), of Cuba, welterweight champion for three years, skilled exponent of the bolo punch. James Carter (left), lightweight champion, made history by twice regaining the title

continue. This must be one of the most valuable pieces of advice ever offered to a boxer. In January 1959, Cooper took the British heavyweight title from Brian London to begin the longest, most popular reign in the history of British boxing. The Swede, Johansson, a moderate fighter from a nation which had only six professional boxers at the time, carried a destructive right hand. It paralysed Cooper, forced Erskine into submission, and knocked out world-ranked American, Eddie Machen, in 2min 16sec. In the summer of 1959, Cus D'Amato brought Johansson to New York to challenge Patterson. At Grossingers, the Catskill Mountain resort where Marciano had once trained, Ingo lounged by the pool, worked lethargically, had his girl-friend Birgit at his side, and told reporters: 'I do not train hard. I conserve power for my fight.' You must be kidding, said the reporters.

A Broadway ticket agency, trying to boost sales, ran a film-loop day and night in its window showing Johansson knocking out Machen over and over again. No one was impressed. Johannson contributed a feature to a magazine describing in words and pictures how he would lure Patterson on to his big right – 'my toonder (thunder) punch.' No one believed him.

On a June night in Yankee Stadium, Johansson carried out his plan to the letter. The right smacked home on Patterson's glass jaw and the champion went down seven times before the fight was stopped amid riotous scenes. Johansson was the first European since Carnera, a quarter of a century earlier, to win the world heavyweight title. Patterson, the protected champion, was humiliated, not for the last time.

These had been ten amazing years, but Johansson's win surpassed all. He would not be champion long, but at least he would not wind up like Louis, who in the mid-1950s was reduced to writhing on the wrestling mat for money to pay the tax man. Two trust funds set up for his children were handed over. By 1957 his tax debt amounted to £430,000. Interest on it was compounding at such a rate he could not have settled if he'd earned a million dollars a year from then on. His third marriage broke up. In 1960, the Government stated: 'We have gotten all we can financially out of Mr Louis' and cancelled the debt. Today Louis scratches a living as best he can selling his name to big-fight promotions and glad-handing visitors to Caesar's Palace in Las Vegas. So much for helping out the IBC.

A gentleman from Louisville has something to say

1960-9

HEAVY: PATTERSON, LISTON, CLAY, FRAZIER

LIGHT-HEAVY: MOORE, TIGER, FOSTER

MIDDLE: TIGER, GRIFFITH

WELTER: NAPOLES

LIGHT: ORTIZ

FEATHER: SALDIVAR, FAMECHON

BANTAM: JOFRE, HARADA, OLIVARES

FLY: HARADA

The 1960s . . . a century under the Queensberry Rules. What is there to show for it? Frankie Carbo, mobster, begins a twenty-five year jail sentence. Good riddance. Power is out of the hands of ringside promoters, and television is taking over. The big new boss is closed-circuit TV: piping of live pictures into cinemas, extending the paying audience a thousandfold. Marciano was unlucky. His career ended before these monster paydays. Patterson, and all his successors, have cashed in.

In Britain, there is another change of power. Jack Solomons, undisputed king since the end of the war, has given way. Harry Levene takes over. Jarvis Astaire, a West End tycoon with a passion for sport, is the first British entrepreneur to sense the satellite-TV boom. Now you can walk into the Odeon, Leicester Square, at 3am and see a big fight taking place on the other side of the Atlantic.

Sugar Ray Robinson, supreme champion of the 1950s, is fading. He fails to win a world middleweight fight against Paul Pender, an ex-fireman from Boston. Johnny Buckley, Pender's manager, mouths a bitter requiem over the close of Robinson's wonderful championship career: 'Promoters and managers will be glad to see the back of him. He wanted every cent for himself and left nothing for anybody else. He squeezed you until the pips squeaked.' Robinson, arrogantly sure of his box-office pull, had indeed called the tune all those years. But he had given value for money.

Pender, a journeyman champion, livened British interest in the middleweights, almost as much as in the days of Turpin and Robinson, by taking on Terry Downes in three fights, one of which Downes won at Wembley in 1961, an unsatisfactory affair. It ended with Pender quitting on his stool. Downes had a short-lived career as world champion. Nose and eye injuries haunted him all his fighting life. But for this he might have done a good deal better.

Born in London, Downes was taken to

Fatal 12th round (right): Cuba's Benny Paret, world welter champion, pinned in a corner at Madison Square Garden by Emile Griffith. Paret mocked Griffith at the weigh-in. Griffith exacted terrible revenge, battering Paret unconscious. The Cuban died in hospital 10 days later

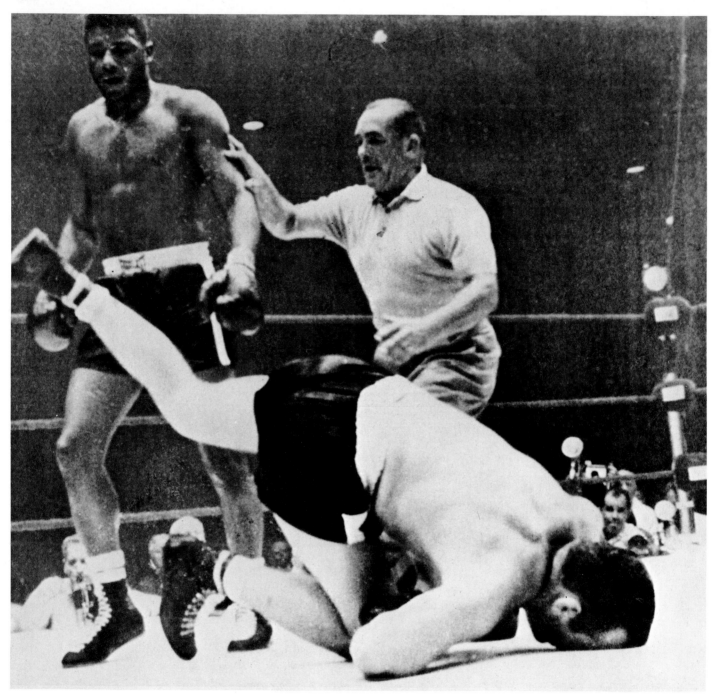

Nose-dive to obscurity taken by Ingemar Johansson (above) in his third fight with Floyd Patterson. The Swede, KO'd in the sixth round, never fought for the heavyweight crown again. Patterson won two of their three fights and was boxing's first man to regain the heavyweight title

America in his early teens, joined the US Marine Corps and won the All-American Services title. He would have been in the US Olympic team of 1956 but for his British background. He came home to fulfil a boast that he would win the British professional crown 'in not more than twenty fights'. As good as his word, he did it in his twentieth fight. A slangy wit went well with his whirlwind style, which was reminiscent of Ted Kid Lewis. I once asked Downes why he had taken a fight with Spider Webb, a good American negro fighter, so early in his career. Webb had beaten him. Downes replied: 'Jack Solomons asked me if I wanted Webb or Sugar Ray Robinson. Blimey, it was like being asked if I wanted to be shot or hanged.'

Later, Downes *did* fight Robinson and beat him. In 1964 he came close to winning the world light-heavyweight title from the brilliant Willie Pastrano of New Orleans. Downes was thumping his way to victory at Belle Vue, Manchester, against a lethargic Pastrano, until manager Angelo Dundee whacked his man on the rump on his way out for the eleventh and said: 'Get going, stupid, unless you want to blow the title.' Unhappily for Downes, Pastrano got the message.

In 1957, Downes had fought Dick Tiger, the great Nigerian boxer. It was Downes's third pro fight, while Tiger was a struggling fighter based in Liverpool, apparently doomed for ever to minor fights for moderate wages. Tiger knocked Terry all over the place at Shoreditch Town Hall, forcing the Cockney to retire after six rounds. The fight cost the matchmaker, Mickey Duff, less than £200. Years later, when Downes had won the middleweight championship and Tiger was in America, where he won both the middle and light-heavyweight championships of the world, Duff reflected that he could not have re-matched them for less than £25,000!

Tiger, like that other good Nigerian, Hogan Kid Bassey, matured late and found qualities under new management that earlier had not been suspected. Until he left for the States in 1959, Tiger's biggest success had been the Empire middleweight crown, but three years later he took the world title from Gene Fullmer, losing it eventually to the flashy Emile Griffith of the Virgin Isles. Then, in his next fight, Tiger won the world cruiser title from Jose Torres, and held it until 1968.

Emile Griffith's fighting style mirrored his personality and his way of dressing. It was bright and showy and, at its best, devastating. Like Tiger, he became a double world

champion, having previously held the welter title. His jaunty manner and his penchant for jewellery and crimson-silk suit linings led some people to the mistaken impression that he was 'cissy'. Benny Paret, who briefly relieved Griffith of the welter title, got this idea and at the weigh in for their third fight, taunted him about it. The outcome was tragic. Griffith gave him such a terrible thrashing in the fight, Paret died from his injuries.

As 1960 opened, Ingemar Johansson was milking his fame as fast as he could, modelling clothes, endorsing cars, signing film and TV contracts – doing everything, in fact, except fight. It was an open secret he would not fight again until the return with Patterson.

Already the youngest man to win the heavyweight crown, Patterson now had his chance to regain it, which no one had ever done. 'They never come back' was boxing's hoariest saying. It has not been heard, however, since 20 June 1960, the night Patterson took his revenge on Johansson. Only once, in the second round, did the Swede's famous right hand threaten destruction. Patterson wobbled but recovered, and in the fifth landed the first of two left-hooks which made history. Johansson crashed on his back, to rise shakily at 'nine'. Patterson went berserk in a wild chase that lasted almost a minute, until the second left-hook found its target. This time Johansson hit his head on the boards as he fell. He lay with one leg quivering ominously and he was counted out. He was unconscious for some time. His seconds

Nino Benvenuti of Italy (above) won an Olympic gold medal in 1960, then went on to outstanding success as a pro. He won his first 65 fights, picked up both junior-middle and middleweight world titles.
Charles (Sonny) Liston (below), ex-convict, for a time regarded as one of history's most fearsome heavyweight champions ... until Cassius Clay twice discredited him

dragged the stool to the centre of the ring and hoisted him on to it. It was the first fight he had ever lost.

This historic win, at twenty-five, was the supreme moment of Patterson's life. Nine months later, he knocked out Johansson again. But already his days as champion were running out. A dark, menacing figure loomed at his shoulder. Sonny Liston, a former jailbird with a history of poverty and violence, had a record of astonishing ferocity both in and out of the ring. He could not be ignored.

Patterson's manager, Cus D'Amato, seeing the destructive path carved by the scowling Liston through the list of contenders, wanted no part of him. Patterson's conscience, however, could not rest with this obvious threat to his credibility as champion. Patterson, not D'Amato, made the decision to fight Liston. It was an honourable move, but I doubt if Patterson enjoyed another truly happy moment in boxing from the moment he made it.

In June 1960, when Patterson became champion again, Cassius Clay was known only to a handful of people who followed amateur boxing. He was eighteen, had enjoyed a comfortable upbringing as the son of a signwriter in Louisville, Kentucky, and was blossoming as a useful light-heavyweight. He won the national AAU title and the Golden Gloves championship. He was picked for the Olympic team to go to Rome, where he won a gold medal. While Patterson revelled in his glory as the man who had come back, Clay pondered his future. On his return from Rome he wandered into a New York amusement arcade (the first time he had set foot in Manhattan) and came away with one of those phoney newspapers which, for 25 cents, carry any headline you care to invent. Clay's headline was: CASSIUS SIGNS FOR PATTERSON FIGHT. He was not even a pro yet. But something in his mind had clicked. He knew where he was going. As soon as he began to fight for money, he told anyone who would listen that he was heading for the world title. He predicted the rounds in which his victims would

Poor Patterson (left): he had two goes with menacing Sonny Liston, and both ended like this, both in just over two minutes. This is how Liston KO'd Patterson in 1963 in Las Vegas, the gambling capital where Liston died in 1970

fall and was invariably right. The bragging and the prophecies quickly attracted national attention. To back them up, there was considerable talent.

He was probably the fastest heavyweight, in both hand and foot, the world had yet seen. Inborn rhythm, natural grace, a genius for showmanship – all were there. But at the time almost nobody could see it. He was nicknamed 'Cass the Gas' and his exploits were good for a laugh. Nobody took him seriously as a threat for the world title.

Charles (Sonny) Liston, however, was as fearsome a challenger as boxing had known. Not so much tall as massively broad, he had impressive measurements. His fists were 15ins in circumference, bigger than any world champion's, from John L. Sullivan to Floyd Patterson. His reach was 84ins, longer than any champion's except Carnera. He was one of twenty-three children born to an Arkansas sharecropper. His life had been one long struggle against authority. He had robbed with violence. Cops had beaten him up; he had beaten them up. He was a marked man in the eyes of the law. Liston came into boxing through a Catholic priest who talked him into it in jail. From 1953 until 1962, when Patterson decided to give him a crack at the title, Liston had lost only one pro fight, a points decision to a man called Marty Marshall, who had broken Liston's jaw early in the fight.

Rumour had it that Liston, in 1962, was much older than the twenty-eight years the record books showed. Rumour also had it (no one would dare say it to his face) that he was a bully who enjoyed beating up weaker men, but whose courage would be called into question when he met his match. Neither allegation seemed remotely true when he met Patterson. The fight, in Chicago's Comiskey Park, where Louis thrashed Braddock, was a farce. At 214lbs Liston was 25lbs heavier, with a reach advantage of 13ins. Patterson, a man of complex and baffling thoughts, saw himself as the avenging angel, the good guy who puts paid to the villain. Disdaining the natural caution of a small man tackling a big one, he tried to slug it out toe-to-toe. In 2min 6sec, Patterson was counted out on his side, face in the dirt, stricken by a huge right hand followed by a left. The humiliation was worse than he had suffered against Johansson and he emphasized it by slinking from the stadium in dark glasses and a false beard, driving far into the night, unable to face anyone. When that story emerged, the obvious question was

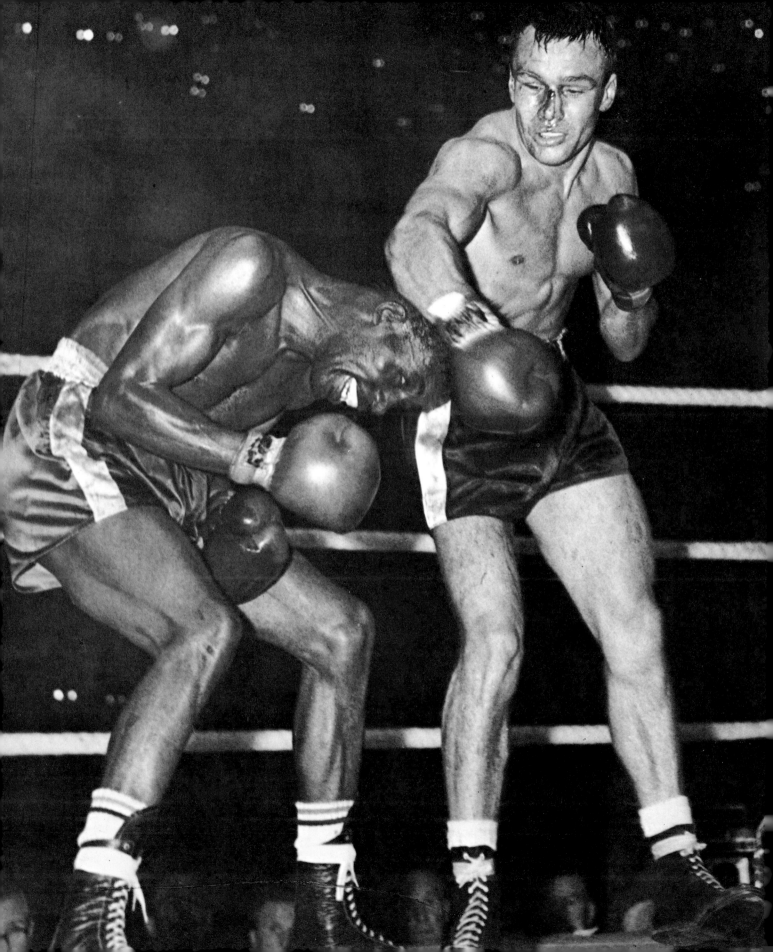

asked: what sort of champion goes to a fight carrying a disguise in his bag?

Liston looked like the best champion since Marciano, in destructive power alone. His left jab was compared favourably with that of Joe Louis and he was apparently impervious to punishment. How could hands-in-gloves hurt a man who'd been worked over by policemen's sticks?

Patterson, living like a recluse, tried to suppress the shame he felt, emerging ten months later for another try at Liston in Las Vegas. He did better . . . but only by four seconds! Liston put him away in 2min 10sec. To suggest at this time that the young Cassius Clay, the Louisville Lip, had the beating of Liston was to invite derision. Clay had already over-reached himself in the forecasting business, failing to beat Doug Jones inside the distance in March 1963. His validity was further questioned that year in London, where he was matched with Henry Cooper, whose only defeat in the previous five years had come from the American, Zora Folley. Cooper came within an ace of beating Clay.

The first appearance of Cassius Clay in England laid the foundation of a popularity with the British that has never waned. His rhyming couplets ('If he wants to jive, he'll fall in five') tickled people's sense of humour. His ever-open mouth, the popping eyes, the incessant boasting intrigued not just boxing fans, but the public at large. He played his part to the full, prophesying a fifth-round defeat for Cooper and brightening a rainy night at Wembley Stadium by walking to the ring with a crown on his head and the legend 'Cassius Clay, The Greatest' flaunted across the back of his red-and-white robe. The rain kept the crowd down. Those who stayed away missed the most famous punch ever thrown in a British ring.

Cooper's vicious left-hook whipped on to Clay's chin in the fourth round when the fleeting figure momentarily paused on the ropes. Clay slumped to the floor amid deafening roars. He was so far gone he did not have the sense to take a long count. Quickly up on tottery legs, he was ripe for the kill, and Cooper surely would have had him had the bell not ended the round at that moment. The entire course of the heavyweight championship could have changed there and then, but for that bell. Clay's eyeballs were still rolling in their sockets as he dropped on to his stool, where Angelo Dundee 'discovered' a rent in Clay's left glove. There was no time to replace it. Clay came out for the

Above: two superb featherweights: Howard Winstone (on the left) had three exciting world title fights with Mexico's Vicente Saldivar. He won none of them, but will be remembered as one of the most skilled Welsh boxers of all time.
Southpaw Dave Charnley (left), one of Britain's best-ever pound-for-pound fighters, failed narrowly in this 1961 fight to grab the world lightweight title from 34-year-old negro Joe Brown, who lost the title to Carlos Ortiz the following year. Charnley beat Brown in 1963 ... too late

fifth wearing the damaged glove. He danced and pranced round the ring, prodding the glove at Cooper's already torn face. It had the desired effect. Cooper's left eye split wider open, blood poured, and referee Tommy Little did the only thing he could: he stopped the fight. Clay's prediction had come true. When the gloves came off, he leant over the ropes and held up one hand to the crowd, showing them the 'five' he had forecast. They booed him lustily for having been right. Cooper was only the second man to drop Clay (Sonny Banks was the first) and Clay was not put down again until he fought Joe Frazier.

With this fight Cooper entered the hearts of the British public, where he has remained. Like his long-reigning predecessor, Bombardier Billy Wells, he was invincible in domestic competition, but had his weaknesses exposed at top level. His eyes cut too easily (they let him down again with Clay in a fight for the world title) and he did not absorb a hard punch well. Floyd Patterson knocked him out in four rounds. Both Wells and Cooper set fine examples of correct behaviour outside the ring. In November 1966, after seven years and ten months as champion, Cooper passed

the Bombardier's record, which had stood for nearly fifty years. A year later he beat Billy Walker to win himself a third Lonsdale Belt, the only man to do this at any weight.

It was a good decade for Britain in world-class terms. From Merthyr in Wales came the brilliant Howard Winstone, a dazzling featherweight despite having lost the tops of three fingers on his right hand in a factory accident. His three fights with world champion Vincente Saldivar of Mexico were classic examples of boxer v. fighter. The Mexican's greater stamina just outweighed Winstone's superior skill in fights in London and Cardiff. The third, in Mexico City, was more decisive. The towel came in from the Welshman's corner at the end of the twelfth, to Saldivar's relief. He at once announced: 'Our three fights have taken too much from both of us. I shall retire as champion.' The title was thus left vacant and Winstone went on to win one version against Mitsunori Seki of Japan, but he was not fully recognized. To the end of his days Winstone will wish he could have beaten Saldivar just once. He held the British title from 1961 to 1966, retiring as undefeated champion.

A world title also eluded bantamweight

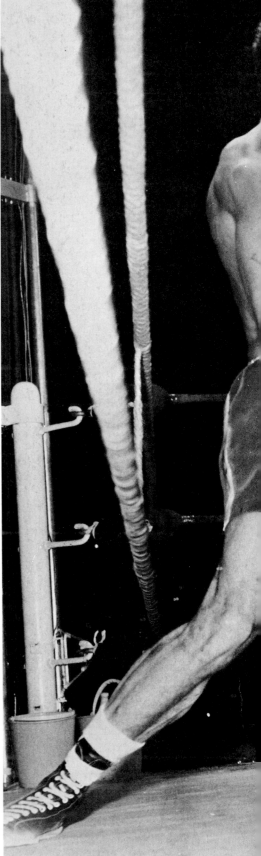

He still remembers this: Muhammad Ali (above) floored`by Henry Cooper's left-hook at Wembley in June, 1963. The bell stopped Cooper following up and he was beaten by cuts in the next round. Eight months later, Ali was world champion.
Muhammad Ali sees victory in sight (right). One look at Henry Cooper's cuts shows that. This was their 1966 world championship in London's Highbury Stadium. All British records for gate receipts were broken, with a take of £210,000 ($504,000) - more than was paid at the World Soccer Cup Final at Wembley the same year

Alan Rudkin of Liverpool, although he tried three times and travelled 60,000 miles in pursuit of it. This compact, aggressive little fighter was unlucky to meet three good champions in a row: Fighting Harada of Japan, Lionel Rose of Australia, and Ruben Olivares of Mexico.

In every decade so far, Britain has found a flyweight good enough to win the world championship and it was true of the 1960s. Walter McGowan, of Scotland, lacked the impressive punching power of a Benny Lynch, but his speed and skill were sufficient to take the title from Salvatore Burruni of Italy in 1966, despite the handicap of a cut eye throughout the second half of the fight. McGowan was the first British world 112lbs champion for sixteen years.

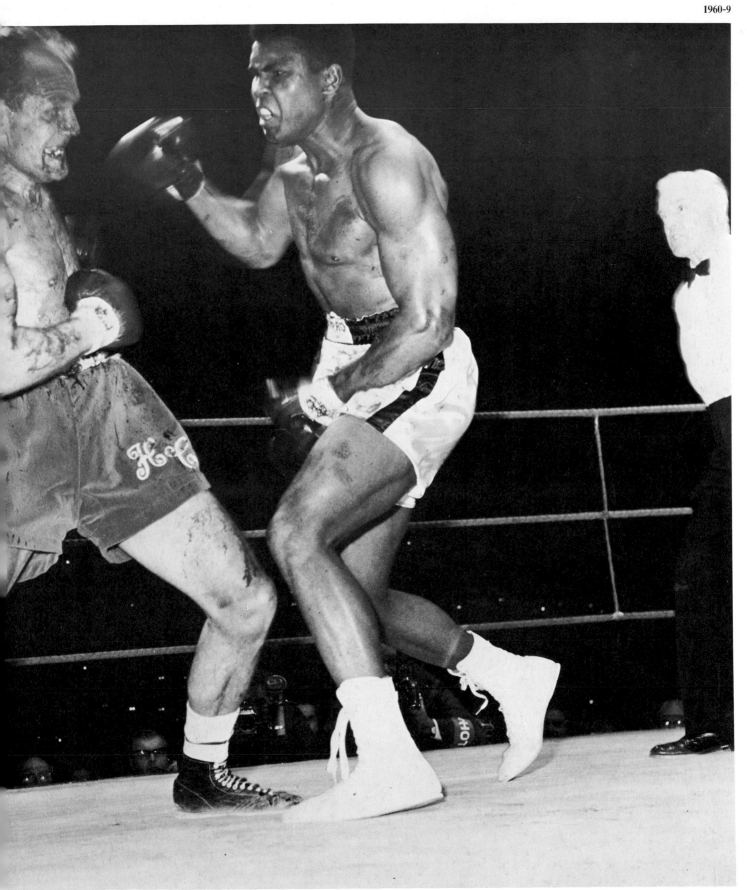

Brilliant little Scot Walter McGowan (right) battles desperately
with a cut eye in his world flyweight championship against
Thailand's Chartchai Chionoi at Wembley in 1967. The fight was
stopped in the seventh.
Ruben Olivares (below right) of Mexico, one of the hardest-
hitting bantams of all time, KO's Lionel Rose, Australian
Aborigine, to win the world title in Los Angeles, 1969.
Talented, Liverpool bantam, Alan Rudkin (left), who flew
50,000 miles in search of the world title, but had to give best
to Fighting Harada in Tokyo, Lionel Rose in Melbourne, and Ruben
Olivares in Los Angeles.
Below: Masahiko 'Fighting' Harada (on the right) from Japan, a
solid fighter who won world fly and bantam titles. This July
1967 fight was in Tokyo and Harada retained his bantam crown
with a clearcut points win over Columbia's Bernado Carabello.
It was his fourth defence

The knockdown of Clay by Cooper confirmed in most people's minds the utter hopelessness of matching Clay against the massive power of Liston. Although he had now come through nineteen fights unbeaten, he was still regarded primarily as a clown who would be ripped apart in short order by the ex-convict. The big jabs would shut the Mouth for good. But Clay, hysterically optimistic as ever, had no doubts: 'I am the Greatest! Bring on the big ugly bear! I'm so pretty! Make it a date, I'll get Sonny in eight!'

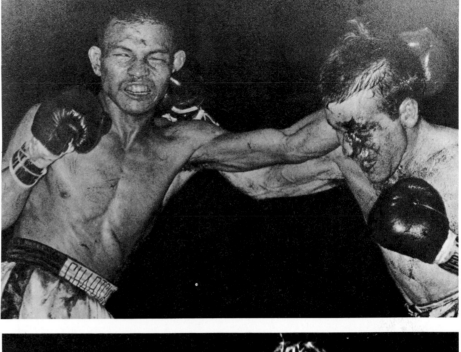

On and on it went, while Liston glowered and mumbled dark threats to 'that crazy kid whistling in the graveyard'. The public waited for the inevitable downfall of Clay. The odds against him in the Liston fight were 7–1. At the weigh-in, on 25 February 1964, Clay strode into Miami Beach Auditorium waving a big stick and screaming insults at Liston, as if he were trying to goad the champion into a fight there and then. Liston looked at him with contempt. Clay kept on yelling. It sounded like pure hysteria. Local boxing officials fined him for misconduct. A doctor took his pulse and announced that he was 'scared to death'. It was suggested he might not even show up for the fight.

He showed up – for a fight which still takes some explaining. Liston was cumbersome and tired quickly. Clay skipped about, but was hesitant in throwing punches. He cut Liston around the face, but by the fourth round was blinking his own eyes and pawing at them with his gloves. At the end of the fifth he went back to his corner and said to Angelo Dundee: 'There's something in my eyes. I can't see properly. I want to quit.' Dundee swore at him, slapped him a few times and shouted: 'Get out there, Daddy-o! This is the big one. Don't louse it up!' So Clay went back to the fight. A round later, Liston flopped on *his* stool and told his handlers he couldn't go on. He had hurt his left shoulder, he said. It was too painful to throw a punch. Let Clay have the title . . .

Clay tore from his corner, threw his arms in the air and began another tirade: 'I told you I was the Greatest. Oh, I am *so* great! You hypocritical reporters, get on your knees and beg forgiveness . . . I *told* you I would beat the Bear! You didn't believe me! . . .' So it went on. The Lip had triumphed over the Scowl.

What happened to Liston? Had the non-stop verbal assault drained him of his will-power? Was there some threat to his life if he won? This theory gained ground when Clay revealed he was now a member of the Black Muslims, a sect based on the Islamic faith, preaching black separatism. Through the uproar, other thoughts returned. What about the allegations against Liston two years earlier? He certainly looked much, much older now, slumped on the stool, tears coursing down the lined black face. Was his courage suspect after all? Doctors probing Liston's injury diagnosed bursitis. A district attorney probed the fight itself, suspecting a fix. Nothing was proved. Clay was champion.

Even that statement was not quite true. Confirming his new allegiance to Allah, Clay said: 'Don't call me Cassius Clay any more. That's my slave name. I am now Muhammad Ali.' (His mother said: 'He's still Cassius to me.') From this moment the extraordinary young man from Louisville became the most publicized sportsman in the world. Everything he said and did was controversial. Less than seventy-two hours before the return fight with Liston in Boston, he collapsed with a hernia and the fight was delayed six months. When it was revealed that Sonny Liston was a major stockholder in the company set up to promote the return (and had been since before the first fight!) boxing commissions looked askance at the rematch. Boston refused to accept it. The World Boxing Association, one of two main governing bodies, stripped Clay of his title. But as far as the public was concerned, he was still champion.

Nonetheless, the return match, in May 1965, was a hole-and-corner affair, tucked away in the derelict mill-town of Lewiston, Maine, on the New England coast, inside a high-school hockey rink where only 2434 people came to see it. It was either the most sensational heavyweight championship of all time, or the most disgraceful affair ever to masquerade in the guise of a title fight. It could be seen either way. It was even more inexplicable than the first fight. In the opening round, Ali threw an innocuous right which grazed Liston's temple. The ex-champion fell to the floor. The referee, Jersey Joe Walcott, looked as amazed as the rest of us, and belatedly started to count. After a few seconds, Liston clambered to his feet and resumed fighting. A great hammering and yelling was heard from little Nat Fleischer, the veteran reporter, sitting next to the timekeeper. He shouted to Walcott: 'Liston was knocked out! The count was ten before he got up!' Walcott was now more confused than before. But under Fleischer's insistent yelling, he stopped the fight and declared

Muhammad Ali the winner by a knockout. The incredible confusion was amplified when the timekeeper announced the knockout time as one minute. My own stopwatch had shown just about two minutes when Walcott stopped the fight. The KO must have come somewhere between 1min 40sec and 1min 50sec.

The cynicism engendered by these two fights prevented Ali's immediate acceptance as a worthy champion. He remained a joke to many people. But in the next two years he gradually won approval. He stopped Floyd Patterson, Henry Cooper, Brian London, Karl Mildenberger, Cleveland Williams and Zora Folley. He outpointed George Chuvalo and Ernie Terrell. The fight with the giant Terrell was notorious for his conversation with an opponent who refused to call him Muhammad Ali. 'What's my name?' he muttered throughout the fight, 'tell me, what's my name?' Terrell would not give in, despite the hammering he took. This protracted torture displayed a vindictive side of Ali's nature.

From the moment he sided with the Black Muslims, Ali became a political liability in US establishment eyes. He repeatedly tried to claim exemption from the military draft. As a Muslim, he said, he was a conscientious objector to the war in Vietnam: 'I ain't got no quarrel with them Vietcongs. They never called me nigger.' The remark split the American nation down the middle. The older generation, many of them ex-servicemen or relatives of men who had been killed in action, turned an implacable hatred on the controversial champion. The younger generation, who were against the Vietnam war anyway, saw in him a folk-hero.

His reiterated pride in being black, his refusal to fight 'the white man's war', resurrected all the bitterness which Jack Johnson had stirred half a century earlier. There was even something curiously similar between Johnson's grinning supremacy in the ring, based on guile and craft, and Ali's mocking domination with speed and skill.

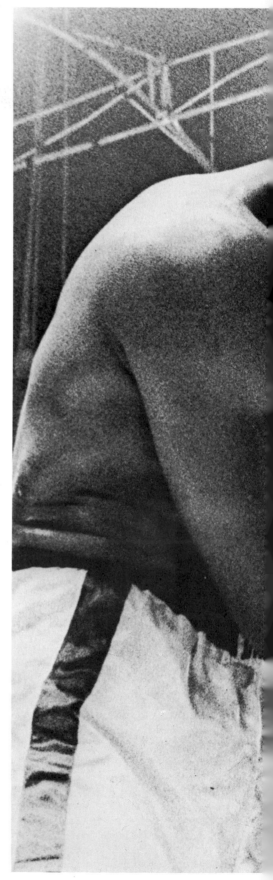

Ali (or Cassius Clay, as he was still known) stuns the world by beating Liston at Miami Beach, 1964 (right). Odds of 7-1 were overturned as the so-called young braggart made good his boasting. Liston, up to now a man of menace, pathetically quit on his stool, pleading a damaged shoulder. He did even worse in their second fight

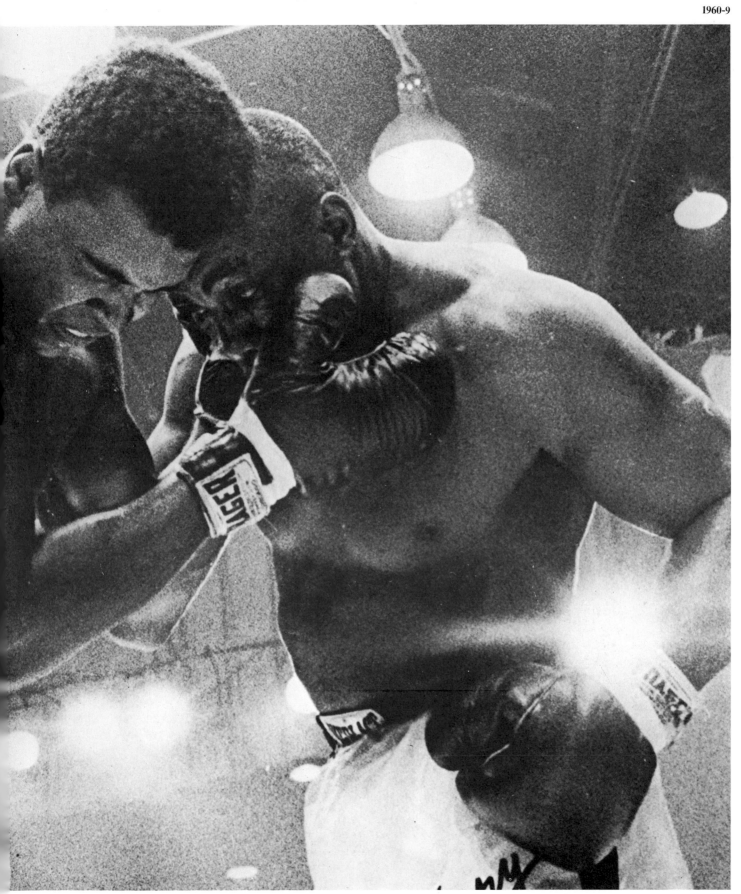

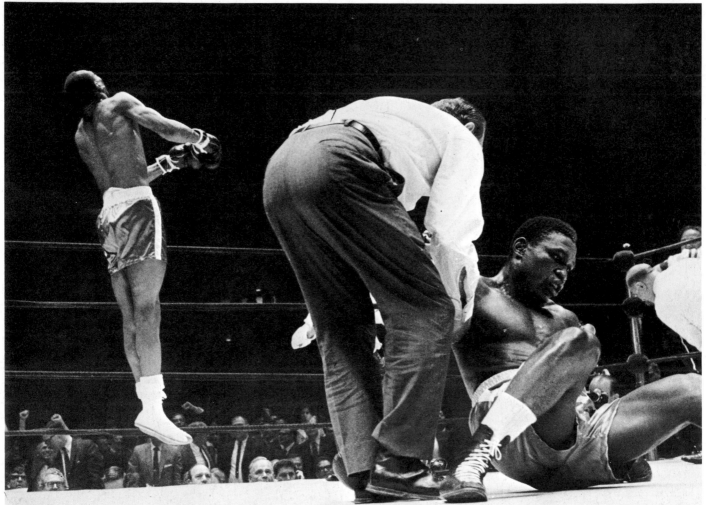

Jump for joy from 6ft 4ins Bob
Foster of Albuquerque (above),
as he wins the world light-
heavyweight championship.
Dick Tiger is KO'd in round
four at Madison Square Garden
in 1968, and Foster starts a
long, brilliant reign: 14
successful defences in six
years

Every appeal he made against the draft was turned down. In 1967 he made his last stand, by refusing to take the oath of allegiance at an induction ceremony in Houston, Texas. He was brought before the courts and sentenced to five years' jail and a 10,000-dollar fine for draft evasion. There began a long legal battle against the sentence. His passport was impounded and he could not leave America.

Every boxing commission in the world stripped him of his heavyweight crown (Britain was the last to do so). Having established himself as the best black champion since Louis, he was no longer permitted to practise his profession. It was impossible not to sympathize with him. There was an appealing candour in his remark, when I asked him if he missed his boxing: 'No,' he said, 'boxing misses me.' He was right.

In 1969, an American company announced a 'computer' fight between Muhammad Ali and Rocky Marciano, the two unbeaten champions. Every available statistic on their styles and records was fed into a computer, which printed out a round-by-round analysis of the fight that could have been expected. The two men agreed to simulate the fight, as told by the computer. Only the ending was kept secret from them. When the film was shown, Marciano was the winner by a knock-out in the thirteenth. Rocky never knew his unbeaten record had been kept intact. He was killed in an air crash before it was shown. For Ali, it was yet another blow. Even the computer was against him. He took it well, with a characteristic comment: 'I always knew I couldn't beat a white guy. The computer was made in Alabama.'

OK, OK—so he IS The Greatest 1970-9

HEAVY: FRAZIER,   FOREMAN,   ALI,   SPINKS

LIGHT-HEAVY: FOSTER,   CONTEH,   SAAD MUHAMMAD

MIDDLE: MONZON,   VALDEZ,   ANTUOFERMO

LIGHT-MIDDLE: MATTIOLI,   HOPE

WELTER: NAPOLES,   STRACEY,   PALOMINO,   BENITEZ,   CUEVAS

LIGHT-WELTER: CERVANTES,   BENITEZ

LIGHT: BUCHANAN,   DURAN,   WATT

JUNIOR-LIGHT: ESCALERA,   SERRANO,   ARGUELLO

FEATHER: LEGRA,   MARCEL,   ARGUELLO

BANTAM: PINDER,   ANAYA,   ZARATE

FLY: SALAVERRIA,   OHBA,   CANTO

LIGHT-FLY: ESTABA,   GUSHIKEN

Midnight struck. 1 January 1970. Boxing now had three men claiming to be world heavyweight champion. There was Jimmy Ellis, of Louisville, Kentucky, an amiable negro from the same city as Muhammad Ali and in the same stable. For years, Ellis had been Ali's principal sparring partner, a talented boxer with a good punch. Now Ellis beat Jerry Quarry, the best white fighter around, to win the World Boxing Association's version of the title they had stripped from Ali.

From Philadelphia came negro Joe Frazier, stumpy, thickset. He was pure aggression. He had won the Olympic heavyweight gold medal in Tokyo 1964. Now, unbeaten as a pro, he was dubbed the 'Black Marciano'. Frazier had the New York State Athletic Commission's blessing as world champion.

The World Boxing Council, yet another 'governing' body, had only lately given up Muhammad Ali as champion. They didn't recognize Ellis or Frazier. The situation was chaotic. In the 200-odd years since Jack Broughton's Rules brought the first sem-blance of order to prizefighting, the professional side of the sport had still not managed to subject itself to the direction of just *one* governing body.

The third claimant, of course, was Muhammad Ali, under sentence for draft evasion but still fighting the conviction in the courts. He had no backing from anyone except the public. Sensing this, he at once coined a new title for himself: the People's Champion. He was shrewd enough to see that the public were not ready to accept Ellis, or Frazier, as champion while he was still around, unbeaten.

Forty-seven days after the chimes heralded a new decade, only two men still claimed the title. Sensibly enough, Ellis and Frazier had been matched with each other in New York. Frazier won decisively, overpowering his man with sheer strength and hitting power. Aged twenty-six, with twenty-five successive wins behind him (all but three inside the distance) Frazier, the former slaughterhouse worker, was now recognized as champion by every boxing commission. Only Muhammad Ali, the People's Champion, stood between him

Final punches of Henry Cooper's long, distinguished career. Joe Bugner outpoints him at Wembley in 1971 (above). The decision raises arguments. Henry takes things calmly and chooses the heated moment to say goodbye to the ring. Scotland's Ken Buchanan (right) in agony at the end of the 13th round of his world lightweight defence against Roberto Duran of Panama. Buchanan claims he's been fouled, but referee Johnny Lobianco, in Madison Square Garden, awards the fight — and the title — to hard-bitten Duran

and full public recognition.

Three years had passed since Ali's refusal to join the US armed forces. In that time public opinion on the Vietnam war had perceptibly shifted – in Ali's direction. His views about not wanting to fight the Vietcong were now widely shared. Young American citizens burned their draft cards and organized protest marches. Slowly, older Americans were coming around to the same views. Amid mounting criticism of US involvement in Vietnam, Ali's stand seemed less controversial. As opinion softened, the first glimmerings of a willingness to let him box again were seen.

New York State was the first to relent. In September 1970, it re-licensed him as a boxer. But his comeback would be made in Atlanta, Georgia, a city where blacks had money and political influence, and where a black Senator pushed so hard on Ali's behalf he overcame the white Governor's objections. In October 1970, Muhammad Ali returned to the ring, his first fight since he knocked out Zora Folley in March 1967.

The return of Ali in Atlanta triggered hysterical black adulation of the resurrected Messiah. In a dilapidated auditorium filled with the black 'beautiful people' of Atlanta – men in ermine cloaks and floppy velvet artists' hats, women in sleek white gowns or daring see-through mini-skirts – he was screamed to victory over white Jerry Quarry, who was stopped in the third round with bad damage to an eye.

Ali was back! The People's Champion! Yes . . . but Frazier was champion. Simple. Match them. And so it was done. The most widely discussed, avidly awaited, comprehensively covered fight of all time. Ali *v.* Frazier, at the superb new Madison Square Garden alongside New York's Penn railroad station, gathered to itself promotional knowhow, electronic aids and the richest financial backing ever given to a sports event. For a guaranteed fee of five million dollars (£1 million each) we had what became known simply as: The Fight.

What else was happening? Henry Cooper, Britain's heavyweight champion, having given up his title in a dispute with the Boxing Board, came back in 1970 to regain it from the clumsy caretaker champion, Jack Bodell. Coming up behind Cooper was the young, blond, Hungarian-born Joe Bugner, who had lived in England since he was six. Criticized incessantly by the Press for lacking natural aggression and a punch, Bugner was matched with the fading Cooper in 1971. The referee's

Lofty Bob Foster, world light-heavy champion, takes 14 rounds to quell the challenge of Britain's courageous Chris Finnegan at Wembley in 1972 (above). Finnegan, completely exhausted, slumps to the floor and is counted out.
Not the end, but very nearly ... British champion Ralph Charles (left) tumbles through the Wembley ropes in his world welter challenge to Cuban-born Jose Napoles. This is the sixth round. In the seventh, smooth, hard hitting Napoles knocks Charles out

decision, in favour of Bugner, roused a storm of protest, but in retrospect it was no bad thing for Cooper, who quit the ring on a wave of popular sympathy. Henceforth, he would be known as the man who never really lost the title. Bugner's fluctuating career dipped badly when he lost the title to Bodell, perked up when he knocked out Germany's Jurgen Blin for the European title, and, in a strangely British way, scaled new heights on the back of two defeats: points decisions lost to both Frazier and Ali.

Overpage: Muhammad Ali, still hopeful of regaining his old title, fills in the time profitably. In European champion Joe Bugner, he finds a white opponent as tall and heavy as himself. Bugner boxes well in Las Vegas and goes the distance

British champion Bunny Sterling down and out in Paris (above).
He tried to take the European middleweight title from Jean-
Claude Bouttier. This is how it ended in the 14th round.
Right: Phil Matthews wasn't upright for long. Champion Bunny
Sterling (on the left) knocked him out in the fifth round of
this British middleweight title fight at Belle Vue, Manchester,
in 1972.
In 1973, Bouttier finds trouble himself (below). At the Roland
Garros stadium in Paris, the Frenchman is floored in each of
the last three rounds by Argentina's world champion, Carlos
Monzon, and loses on points. Monzon must go down in history as
one of the great middleweight champions

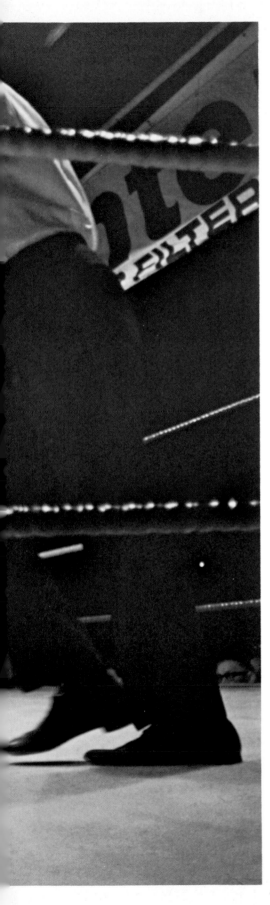

A British lightweight achieved remarkable success, but got precious little credit for it from his own countrymen. Ken Buchanan, of Edinburgh, went to Puerto Rico and beat the reigning world champion, Ismael Laguna. A year later, he took the title to New York and defended it in a return match with Laguna. Despite a seriously damaged eye towards the end of the fight, Buchanan fought with guile and courage, and kept his title.

Not only was he Britain's first world lightweight champion for nearly sixty years (Freddie Welsh was the last), Buchanan was the first Briton to win and defend a world title in America successfully since Ted Kid Lewis. Jubilation? Hardly. His box-office pull in England and Scotland remained mediocre and he won a curious place in British boxing lore: a man whose brilliant left hand was more appreciated in America than it was by his own countrymen.

The 1970s had several good world champions, beside Buchanan. Bob Foster, a spindly negro from Albuquerque, New Mexico, held a long tenure of the world light-heavyweight crown. Despite advancing years, he gave Britain's foxy champion, Chris Finnegan, an ex-Olympic gold medallist, a brutal hammering at Wembley, but was himself punished severely when he stepped out of his weight-class to take on Joe Frazier.

At middleweight, Carlos Monzon, of Argentina, succeeded Nino Benvenuti, of Italy, as world champion, impressing himself upon America and Europe as one of the toughest contemporary champions. At welterweight, an exiled Cuban, Jose Napoles, nicknamed as 'Butterball' because of his sleek, smooth style, exuded the quality known as class. At almost thirty-two, he came to London and knocked out British champion Ralph Charles with the least possible trouble. Charles was thought to be one of Britain's hardest pound-for-pound punchers. Another self-exiled Cuban, Jose Legra, a flashy Muhammad-Ali-in-miniature, dominated European featherweight boxing after he came to live in Spain and even won a version of the world title.

Britain's traditional flyweight supremacy

Bob Foster (on the left) outpoints South African Pierre Fourie in Johannesburg, in defence of his world cruiser crown. This was the first black v. white encounter in a South African ring

seemed to be dying. By 1973, John McCluskey, the British champion from Hamilton, Scotland, was virtually the only 112lbs professional in the land. He had already held the title more than four years without a challenge. Britain had few men at other weights, too. Before the Second World War there had been around 3000 professional boxers; now Britain was down to about 300, and at least 50 per cent of these were immigrants. The Boxing Board brought in a new rule: anyone resident in the United Kingdom for ten years could fight for a British title. Bunny Sterling, born in Jamaica, was the first to take advantage, winning Britain's middleweight title, and later his Jamaican stablemate, Bunny Johnson, became the first black man to hold the British heavyweight crown. British boxing was confined to two spheres: big-fight promotions at Wembley or the Royal Albert Hall, and small dinner-and-boxing club shows up and down the country, which had replaced the local town-hall promotions. Sweden banned professional boxing. West Germany was thinking about it. Spain and Italy were Europe's busiest pro-boxing countries. In South Africa, black man could not fight white.

Whatever the state of professional boxing in each country, The Fight was a talking-point everywhere. Boxing still had this instinctive appeal to people, even if their intellect told them they should not approve. Muhammad Ali had always said his fights were a natural link between the USA and such out-of-favour places as Russia, China and the Arab States. This time he was right.

Before The Fight took place, he had one more comeback appearance, against the white Argentinian, Oscar Bonavena, a bull of a man. With typical Ali panache, he secured a dramatic win in the fifteenth and final round, when a drab points victory seemed certain. He dropped Bonavena three times in the round and, under New York rules, the fight was automatically stopped. He was quick to point out that Frazier, in two fights with Bonavena, had never been able to floor him. On the contrary, Bonavena had knocked Frazier down twice. Nobody needed convincing that Frazier v. Ali was a natural. The Fight was on.

In the build-up period, Ali enjoyed himself, lambasting reporters who doubted if he could win after $3\frac{1}{2}$ years' lay-off: 'You fellas are always picking against me. You never learned your lesson with Liston, did ya? Frazier says he's gonna come out smokin'.

Well, smokin's bad for the lungs, gives you cancer. I'm gonna bring my fire-extinguisher with me. Maybe this will shock and amaze ya – but I'm gonna retire that Joe Frazier!'

Budd Schulberg, in his book, *Loser and Still Champion*, stabbed a finger knowingly at the way public opinion assessed The Fight: 'Almost 75 per cent of America was now agreeing with Ali that we had no moral justification for fighting in Vietnam. Only here was a young man whose protest march was a walkout on million-dollar purses, a walkout on the championship that is every boxer's dream, a walkout on the big Christmas tree of material goodies . . . to walk away from all that, stay out of jail, and finally make the world you had defied pay 2½ million dollars to watch you come back on your own terms – there was something outrageously American about the saga that attracted not only hippies and blacks, but millions of middle-class citizens . . . who respond to boldness and originality, backed up by ability.'

Experts were split in their prediction of the outcome. Of the two unbeaten men, Frazier had greater support. He was younger, still making progress, and could well be strong enough to take Ali's best shots and come back from them. As it turned out, this was about right.

Ali's backers were forced to ignore the long lay-off, put their trust in his speed (which in the fights with Quarry and Bonavena had not been at its old level) and hope that his pre-fight verbal campaign might have 'got at' Frazier, as it apparently had at Liston (but that was seven years ago).

The Fight, when it came, was a curious mixture of the deft, the daft and the dramatic. The audience in Madison Square Garden was celebrity-studded in a way not seen at most big fights since the heyday of Joe Louis. Among those present were John Lindsay, the mayor of New York, Frank Sinatra, Burt Bacharach, Bernadette Devlin, Edward Kennedy and astronaut Alan Shepard. Ringside seats cost 150 dollars (£60), but on the night fetched five times that. Closed-circuit TV carried The Fight to 350 outlets in the USA and Canada, thirty-three more in the UK. More than thirty countries took the

Joe Frazier has the look of a winner in this March 1971 battle (right). So he was. It was the first time Muhammad Ali had lost a title fight

fight by TV satellite. Ali's 2½ million dollars would make him the richest fighter in history, passing Floyd Patterson's 7¼ million dollars. As a last-minute TV gimmick, Ali opened an envelope in his dressing-room, revealing his prediction: six rounds. Frazier had said before The Fight: 'When the bell rings, it's just the two of us.'

As expected, Ali at first moved fast in his German-made shuffle shoes, with bobbing tassles on the laces. He skipped and danced, poking lefts into the lumbering Frazier's face. Frazier moved to cut him off and get in close. When he did, he thumped him hard in the body, to draw the strength and speed. Frazier was giving away height, weight and reach. He could hardly afford to concede much else.

Once Ali's speed went, The Fight entered a psychological phase. Ali had to convince Frazier he was still there with a chance. Frazier had to convince *himself* it wasn't so. As the fight progressed, so Ali's rests on the ropes became longer. He let Frazier hit him, shaking his head from side to side as if to say: 'No, you're just not hurting me.' But any punch Frazier catches you with hurts. The sixth round came and went . . . so did the prediction.

Now Ali was tapping silly pat-a-cake punches at Frazier's head, light taps that meant nothing, yet Frazier, oddly enough, started doing it back. This was daft. Why were so many of Ali's fights strange? By the tenth, Ali had done most of his best work, but Frazier was still there, stomping forward on those thick legs, his face raised in welts where the jabs had bitten. Frazier was forcing himself ahead on points. The going was harder and harder for Ali. Reaching down into his reserves, he staged a good fourteenth. But the fifteenth brought the moment that irrevocably separated them, It was the moment Ali became a beaten man for the first time.

A left-hook reduced Ali to the ranks of the mortals. US Governments, US courts he could defy. These he could beat. But Frazier's left-hook (and what a man *he* was this night to produce such a punch at this stage of The Fight) could not be beaten. It whanged home on Ali's jaw and he sprawled on the seat of his pants, just as he had done eight years earlier with Cooper. He got up. Yes, but he could no longer win. He was brave enough to survive the closing moments, but his right cheek bulged where Frazier had belted him, for all the world as if he had a giant toothache. All three officials scored Frazier the winner. And so he was, without a doubt.

Ali swings into action against Frazier at Madison Square Garden (left). But he couldn't produce enough of this to subdue the champion.
Ali, looking for a way back to the world title, doesn't find it (above). He's dropped by Joe Frazier's left-hook in the 15th round of 'The Fight' at Madison Square Garden in March 1971. He gets up, to lose on points. Frazier remains world champion and, suddenly, Ali looks like a has-been

Overpage: George Foreman walks away from Joe Frazier, towards the heavyweight title. Frazier was down six times in a round and a half of this Kingston, Jamaica, fight

Both men had to go to hospital, Ali for only a short time, until it was verified his jaw had not been broken. Frazier was in hospital much, much longer, while rumours spread that he had kidney trouble. One report, after The Fight, even had him shot dead. It was the beginning of a realization that, although Frazier had won The Fight, he would come out of it a loser in all but hard financial terms. The ultimate irony was that although Ali had been proved not to be The Greatest any longer, it made no difference to the way people thought of him.

He helped things along with incessant chatter, playing up Frazier's lengthy stay in hospital as an indication that he had been badly hurt that night. Eventually, he managed to convince people the decision had not been fair; that he, Ali, had really won more rounds than Frazier. Frazier, true to style,

John Conteh (above), of
Liverpool, lifts British
boxing high in 1974. He beats
Jorge Ahumada of Argentina to
win the WBC cruiser title.
Conteh is Britain's first world
champion at this weight since
the late Freddie Mills.
Left: looks as if John Conteh
(on the left) and Jorge Ahumada
are engaged in secret
conversation at Wembley, 1974.
Maybe Conteh was telling the
Argentinian: 'This light-
heavyweight crown is mine.'

Overpage: Boxing's unbelievable
moment: Ali's right hand
catches Foreman in Kinshasa,
just before dawn. Within a few
seconds, Ali will be world
champion

said little, fought a couple of nobodies in defence of his title, and did little to capitalize on the win. Meanwhile, Ali had his conviction for draft evasion quashed by the US Supreme Court.

For a time, it seemed unarguable: The Fight had drained from them as much as either could give, or would ever give again. The evidence was piling up. In 1973, Frazier staked his title against the giant George Foreman, who had never been beaten, but had never met class. Frazier, smashed to the canvas six times in a round and a half, lost the championship. That same year, Ali took a hard-hitting Californian negro, Ken Norton, too lightly, had his jaw broken (really broken this time) and lost again.

The age-old truth of boxing, that you are only as good as your last fight, had been confirmed. Within two years, Ali and Frazier, heroes of The Fight, bore all the marks of has-beens. And yet, in that curious, cussed way boxing has of making any prediction precarious, the time was just ahead when all such thoughts would be reversed. That is not quite strong enough. Things would happen which were almost unbelievable.

Nowhere in boxing history can a parallel be found for the extraordinary events of 1974. First, Muhammad Ali erased the memory of his defeat by Frazier with a copy-book twelve rounds in which he dug back into his past to find the skills and speed we suspected had been lost. In Madison Square Garden, that January night, I was convinced Ali had produced the best fight of his life to outpoint Frazier.

I was wrong. Something much more start-ling would be fashioned by Ali in the Central African state of Zaïre (once known as the Belgian Congo), where a fight twice as expensive and ten times more bizarre than any before had been conjured in a crazy combination of financial and political juggling between President Mobutu Sese Seko of Zaïre (his country was in it up to the neck – about nine-million-dollars' worth) and a handful of British and US closed-circuit TV whiz-kids.

· The outcome was this: George Foreman, conqueror of Frazier in less than five minutes, winner of all his forty professional fights, ex-Olympic heavyweight champion, a big, brooding and apparently indestructible champion, would fight Muhammad Ali, and they would share, equally, a mammoth purse of ten million US dollars (over £4,000,000), every cent of which had to be deposited in a Paris bank before either would sign the contract.

There was only one sensible way to look at it. For five million dollars, Ali was being tempted to suffer the humiliating blows from Foreman which would blast him out of boxing for ever at the age of thirty-two. Win or lose, he said, this would be his last fight. Ali had never thought of anything but win-ning before. He picked up a line or two of the local dialect, got the crowd to chant: 'Ali – boom-aye-yay!' ('Ali will kill him!') and we awaited the inevitable.

Shortly before dawn on Wednesday, 30 October (the fight was scheduled to start at 4am in Zaïre, to satisfy US demands: New York is six hours behind) some 70,000 Africans and a world-wide representation of Pressmen gathered in Kinshasa's vast soccer stadium to witness the going-down of the bright star that had been Muhammad Ali.

Laid before them was a performance which eclipsed anything Ali had achieved before and must rank as the most remarkable single effort under pressure from any heavyweight boxer who has ever been faced with the simple choice: conquer, or quit. Ali did not just beat Foreman. He swallowed him, savouring every morsel. He dissected him. He broke him apart, mentally and physically. He deliberately turned his own chosen philo-sophy of boxing inside-out, so as to cope with the awesome power· of Foreman. He was unpredictable in· every phase.

Foreman expected him to run away, and Ali stood his ground. No, by God, he did better than that. He *attacked* from the first bell. He actually ran at Foreman and dared the big man to fight it out. Foreman expected him to dance in the ring and use every inch of it to hide. So Ali went to the ropes, laid back on them, and invited Foreman to hit him. This is not quite as suicidal as it sounds. Ali *allowed* Foreman to hit him where he was prepared to be hit: in the body, which was braced against the blows.

Whatever Ali did appeared to be un-orthodox. And yet, in the light of morning, when it was over, the unorthodoxy could be seen as an amalgam of commonsense, expertly welded to suit the occasion and the opponent. What happened was that the lumbering unco-ordinated Foreman thrashed his arms about in the hot and humid African night until he was wrecked, trem-bling with frustration, exhausted, feeble to the point of incompetence, and ripe for extinc-tion. One final piece of impertinence was saved for last. Ali sagged on the ropes in the eighth round, shoulders dropped, arms hang-

Foreman spreadeagled (above): just as he had discredited Liston all those years ago, so Ali reduces the towering Foreman to size. It's the eighth round. Foreman can't beat the count. Ali follows Floyd Patterson into the record books by regaining the heavyweight crown. As he always said he would

ing, to all appearances as weak as Foreman himself. From such apparent helplessness, he launched himself off the ropes, moved Foreman out to where he could hit him, and looped a long right to the champion's head. Foreman crashed like an axed tree. He lay on his back, just the head and shoulders coming up like a drowning man trying to avoid the dark waters engulfing him. He was groping about on the floor when he was counted out.

So Ali was champion again, ten years after he had first won the title. Gone now was the talk of retiring. It was all incomparably better than when Patterson had regained the title from Johansson. As Schulberg had so prophetically written, without ever knowing what would come, Ali made the world watch him come back on his own terms and once more it would respond 'to boldness and originality, backed up by ability'.

How many years had I been hearing Ali say: 'I am the Greatest?' Always I had listened, laughed, enjoyed, and yet kept a doubt aflame in my mind. The Greatest? With Johnson, Dempsey, Louis, Marciano there before him?

As the sun came up in Zaïre and I sat below that seething ring full of screeching men trampling Ali underfoot (he fell beneath the mass of humanity trying to embrace him) I reflected on what I had just seen and admitted to myself: yes, very likely he is The Greatest.

That month, October '74, launched Britain on wave after wave of success. John Conteh began it. A lithe, light-heavyweight half-caste, a mixture of West African and Lancashire blood, John had the golden touch. His hands were small-boned, the fingers long and elegant, like a violinist's. They looked fragile and were later proved to be. He used them fast and hard. Conteh had a racy wit, the Liverpudlian's quick banter, and a consuming desire for fame. Within three years of leaving the amateurs, Conteh pounded the experienced Argentine, Jorge Ahumada, at Wembley to become world champion. Only Freddie Mills in 1948 and Bob Fitzsimmons in 1903 had done as much for Britain at the weight.

John H. Stracey, from Bethnal Green, crossed the Atlantic and won a world title. Ted Kid Lewis, back in World War I, had done something similar. Stracey won Ted's old title, the welterweight championship, from Jose Napoles in six rounds in a Mexico City bullring, smashing Napoles into permanent retirement. Although he reigned a mere six months (America's Carlos Palomino cut him down in

June, 1976) Britain revelled in her new role as a power in the boxing world.

An astute manager played a large part in it all. Terry Lawless, from his gym over a pub in London's dockland, churned out British, European and World champions. A former shipping clerk, Lawless entered boxing in the 1950's, lugging a fighter-friend's bag, and stayed on to become the most gifted and successful manager Britain has known. Working closely with Mickey Duff, hyper-salesman on both sides of the Atlantic, Lawless produced three world champions in little more than three years.

Stracey was the first. Then, in the spring of '79, Lawless had Maurice Hope and Jim Watt winning world titles within 44 days. Hope, born in Antigua, had lived in London since he was nine. Immigrant boxers now played a vital

British role (Cornelius Boza-Edwards, a refugee from Idi Amin's rule in Uganda, would win the WBC junior-lightweight title in the 80's: he was one who somehow escaped the Lawless net).

Hope was a quiet, dignified man of sober talents. His sole concession to the lurid was the slogan stitched in glittering silver across the back of his robe: "Let's Go, Mo!" Mo went quietly to Italy and in a San Remo circus-tent quietly slung a southpaw left-hook to drop Rocky Mattioli in the first 15-seconds, gave him a beating for eight rounds, and quietly came home with the WBC light-middleweight title. Unfortunately, Hope never quite caught the public imagination. He suspected it was because he hadn't been born in Britain. But the Scot, Ken Buchanan, had the same problem.

The Lawless master-stroke was with Jim

Historic fight: Muhammad Ali, on the ropes, beating Leon Spinks in the New Orleans Superdome, 1978, to become the first man to win the heavyweight crown three times. Yet Ali was already on the slide. His last great fight was in 1975.

Watt, a capable southpaw Scottish lightweight who'd been around a long time with only moderate success, partly because he lived in Buchanan's shadow. In 1976, after eight lean years, Watt turned to Lawless. Twelve fights later, he won the WBC lightweight championship, stopping Alfredo Pitalua (Colombia) in 12 rounds in Glasgow. This fair-skinned Scot, not far off 30, was transformed from cautious counter-punching to all-round proficiency. He captured Scottish hearts in a way Buchanan had never done. His title defences in Glasgow were huge fiestas of skirling bagpipes and swirling kilts, of fierce Scots' pride fuelled by the best malt whisky. Watt's name could now be mentioned in the same peaty breath as Benny Lynch's.

Where was Conteh, who'd begun this run of British victories? In 1979 he tried, unsuccessfully, to win back his world title, now in the hands of Matthew Saad Muhammad. He should never have let it go the way he did. He had too many "friends" telling him what to do. In 1977, when he should have gone to Monte Carlo to defend against Argentina's Miguel Angel Cuello, Conteh refused. His case was argued in court. He didn't want to go to Monte Carlo. His share of the purse, £117,000 (340,000 dollars), wasn't enough. He objected to the wording of the TV contract. The court listened. But they had no power over the World Boxing Council, who stripped Conteh of his title. In three attempts, he never got it back. In 1982, the London *Daily Star* summed it up: "Rampages of drink and drugs outside the ring left him a battered wreck needing psychiatric treatment . . . he is still the most talented fighter Britain has produced in the last 20 years."

And Muhammad Ali? That man was still fighting in 1975, despite the assertion before Foreman that "win or lose, this is my last fight". In the nine months after Zaire, Ali knocked off Chuck Wepner and Ron Lyle inside the distance and trudged through a bloodless, well-paid encounter in Malaysia with Joe Bugner. At which point, Super Fight Three was fanfared. Ali would have a third go with Frazier. You had to be some sort of zombie not to feel the pulse quicken.

Ali, 33, two years older than Frazier, was still hauling some 50 "beautiful people" round the world. Yes, here they were again, occupying good suites at the Manila Hilton, headquarters of Super Fight Three, Ali as usual footing the bill. "I need my friends around me when I fight," he explained. Friends? Well, it was his money and he was getting 4½ million dollars for this one, Frazier 2 million.

Even by his standards, Ali's entourage was unusual. Late in the day his wife Belinda turned up. Who should she find already installed but 19-year-old Veronica Porche, soon to become Mrs. Ali No. 3. Belinda, mother of Ali's four children, had flown 10,000 miles to the Philippines. She took Ali into a room. Voices, I'm told, could be heard from the corridor. Then Belinda swept out and caught the next plane, heading for home in Chicago.

Imperturbably, Ali shrugged it off: "She's got two Rolls-Royces, four beautiful children and two million dollars in the bank. She knows I love her." We all calmed down and they got on with the fight. Ali and Frazier, that is. I had been out to Deer Lake, Pennsylvania, Ali's private camp, to watch him prepare. Part of his daily routine was a punch-up with a stuffed gorilla, i.e. Frazier. When I put it to him that equating his old rival with a gorilla was harsh stuff, he said: "Yeah, but I had to find something to rhyme with Manila, so I thought of gorilla. Then I said it would be a thriller, a chiller and a killer when I got that gorilla in Manila."

His predictions were always uncanny. It *was* a thriller, and a chiller. Damn nigh a killer. In a tatty arena in Quezon City, a suburb of Manila, they staged conceivably the hardest encounter of all time in the professional ring. Ali had long since lost the sleek trim of the young athlete. He weighed 224 lb. The flab sagged over the top of his trunks. He genuinely believed the head punches would take Frazier out early on. Wrong. Joe thought he could destroy the man with blows to the ageing ribs. Wrong. They flogged each other unmercifully until the rounds dissolved into some private nightmare. Bundini yelled at Ali: "Force yourself, champ! Go down to the well once more!" And that's just what Ali did, dredging up right hands that changed the shape of Frazier's face.

After the 14th, Eddie Futch told Joe he was pulling him out. Frazier wanted no part of that. Quit? He'd never quit in his life. But Futch was right. It wasn't quitting, just protection. He couldn't let his man take any more. I climbed into the ring for the ritual interview and saw Ali slump to the floor in his corner. Everyone denies it now. But I saw him fall. He collapsed once he knew Frazier was gone. It was the greatest fight I've seen, but it took too much from both of them. Neither man was ever the same again. Ali, of course, found words to match the fight: "Man, I hit him with punches that would bring down the walls of a city . . . it was like death . . . closest thing to dying I know of." And a few days later came the line that foretold the close of Ali's amazing career: "I'm tired of being the whole game!" He was right.

Jim Watt's face tells the story: his two-year reign as WBC lightweight champion is ending under the accurate fire of superb champion Alexis Arguello, of Nicaragua.

He'd carried boxing for too long.

Had he retired at this point, respect and adulation would have been his for the rest of his life. He succumbed to that inane belief, the prop of lesser men, that something better is just around the corner. Oh, he won more fights. True enough. But there were no more great deeds. In 1978 came the pathetic loss to the undisciplined professional novice, Leon Spinks of the gap-toothed grin. In only his eighth pro fight, Spinks hammered an ungainly points win out of the tired old man who'd given it all in Manila. The saving grace was the tempered manner in which Ali received defeat, praising Spinks, making no excuse for himself. He allowed himself one flash of the familiar flamboyant impudence. In the sadness of his deserted room in Las Vegas (where were the 50 hangers-on?) Ali clenched his fist at the camera, stuck his face in the lens and roared: "I shall return!"

Exactly seven months later he kept his word. The immature Spinks, already a discredited champion whose private life had fallen apart under pressure, was outpointed, so badly you wondered how he'd ever come to beat Ali in the first place. Records tumbled. The massive New Orleans Superdome housed 63,350 people, the biggest indoor boxing crowd of all time. They forked out nearly 5 million dollars, by far the biggest indoor gate in boxing history. The seven-month reign was the shortest of any world heavyweight champion's. And Ali was the first man to win boxing's greatest prize three times – the Third Coming, as it was blasphemously dubbed.

Yet none of it was comparable with the magnificent fights against Foreman and Frazier. In any case, Ali's title was now recognised only by the WBA. Larry Holmes, for years the unpublicised straight man in hundreds of sparring sessions with Ali, had taken over the WBC title.

In 1979 Ali came up with the decision he should have made years earlier. He was giving up boxing, almost 20 years after he'd won Olympic gold in Rome. The 80's would have to make do without him.

If only it had been true.

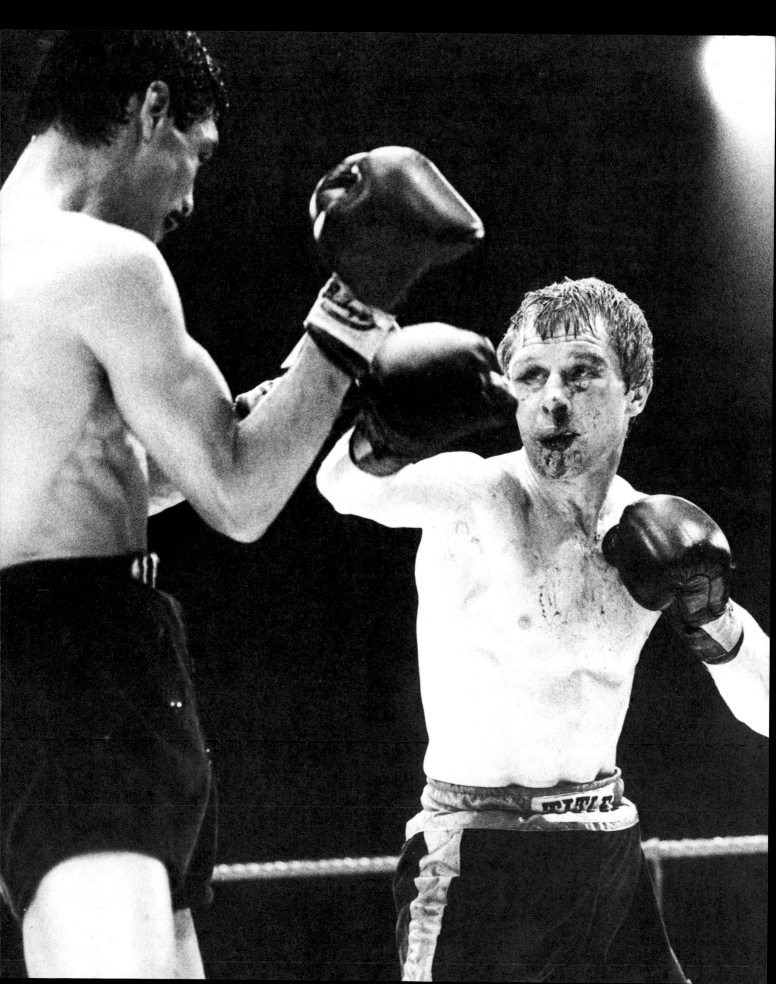

Call yourself Sugar Ray? You'd better be good 1980-?

HEAVY: HOLMES, COONEY

CRUISER: DE LEON

LIGHT-HEAVY: BRAXTON, SPINKS

MIDDLE: MINTER, HAGLER

LIGHT-MIDDLE: BENITEZ, LEONARD

WELTER: HEARNS, LEONARD

LIGHT-WELTER: PRYOR, MAMBY

LIGHT: ARGUELLO

JUNIOR-LIGHT: BOZA-EDWARDS, NAVARETTE

FEATHER: PEDROZA, SANCHEZ

LIGHT-FEATHER: PALMA, GOMEZ

BANTAM: OWEN, PINTOR

FLY: AVELAR

LIGHT-FLY: ZAPATA

NOT FORGETTING LIGHT-BANTAM, OR IS IT SUPER-FLY?

Britain's Tony Sibson, short for a middleweight, but formidable. In the early 1980's Sibson was looking towards Marvin Hagler's world title. Since World War II, Randolph Turpin, Terry Downes and Alan Minter have all won the middleweight crown for Britain.

Allow me, if you will, a flashback to July 31, 1976. U.S. patrons, paying a mere 24-dollars ringside, are getting good value in the Montreal Forum. The night of the Olympic finals has produced among others three champions: Leo Randolph (USA, fly); Howard Davis Jnr (USA, light); Sugar Ray Leonard (USA, light-welter); Mike Spinks (USA, middle); and Leon Spinks (USA, light-heavy). Quite a bunch. They all impressed us a pros.

Randolph became world junior-feather-weight champion. Davis went on to fight Jim Watt for the world lightweight title. Leon Spinks beat Ali. Brother Mike, in 1981, became WBA light-heavyweight champion. The Spinks Bros., unique in winning Olympic gold medals side by side in Canada, became the first brothers to win officially-recognised world professional titles. But from that list of Montreal winners, one name would eventually stand out, just as Cassius Clay's did from the 1960 Olympic rollcall.

A temptation in boxing, if you happen to be named Ray, is to add the prefix Sugar, in the hope that some of the glamour of the original Sugar Ray will rub off. Ray Leonard, only 20 in Montreal, was pushing his luck, I thought, to promote himself this way. Yet looking at my notes of the time, I see I fell for his cheek. I wrote: "Sugar is making sweet progress through the field." He'd won on points over five opponents and the sixth was Aldama of Cuba, who went the same way. (Oddly, in the previous Munich Olympics, the same weight had been won by . . . Sugar Ray Seales!)

Leonard created a record in his first pro fight, collecting 38,000-dollars. The man hired to guide him was Angelo Dundee, who'd been through it all with Ali. Yet if you looked for Leonard on any of the big Ali occasions, you were disappointed. Leonard never fought "under" anyone. He was a star from the start. He topped all his bills, even as a novice pro. He was never drawn into the Ali camp. By the time he reached his 20th pro fight, this one-time choirboy from Maryland, with baby-soft features, was picking up a regular 200,000-dollars a fight. In fight No. 26, in the dying days of '79, he stopped the brilliant Puerto Rican, Wilfredo Benitez, with just six seconds to go to

Welshman Johnny Owen lies stricken on the ring floor in Los Angeles' Olympic Auditorium after a violent blow from Mexico's Lupe Pintor. Owen's family, from Merthyr Tydfil, kept vigil at his bedside for six weeks. The wait was in vain.

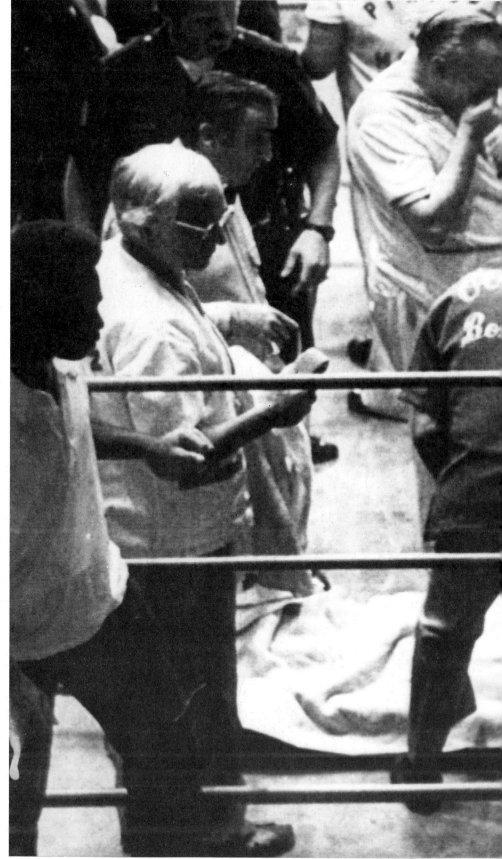

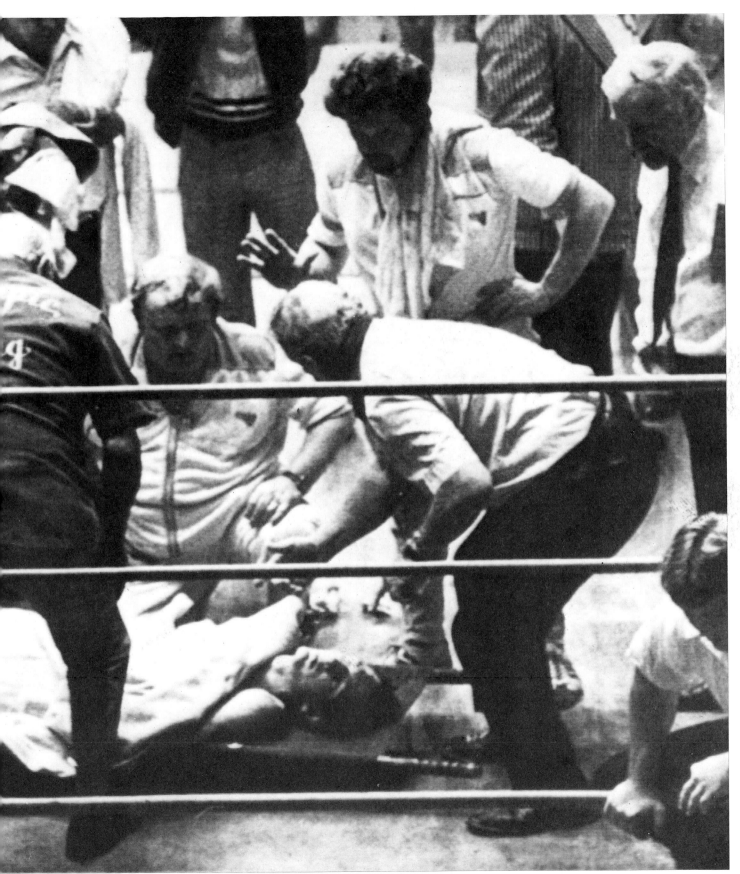

win the WBC welterweight championship. The super-star of the 80's had been found.

Unfortunately, the former super-star couldn't stay away. One year after retirement, Ali was back. It was eerie and unpleasant. He was too jaded to revive the familiar act. When he did speak, his tongue got in the way. The dread words "slurred speech" appeared in reports. His doctor, Ferdie Pacheco, constantly warned him to stay retired. But Larry Holmes had Ali's old title. And Ali could not forget that Holmes was once his sparring partner. Besides, he needed more money... more, after 60-million dollars in purses! Three wives, 50 hangers-on, innumerable Muslim charities had swallowed most of it. Now suppose, just suppose, he beat Larry Holmes ...the *Fourth* Coming!

The Holmes-Ali encounter was depressingly sad. Ali couldn't fight any more. Holmes kept hitting him, but didn't really want to. When the time came to drag Ali out to safety, Bundini was still screaming for a miracle. But the miracles were part of the 60's and 70's. They could not be summoned up in the 80's. Ali was through and had forfeited most of the world-wide admiration acquired in the good years. Public memory is short. Ali was a joke gone sour. He shuffled off the world stage in silent despair. The Mouth that made the world chuckle, the hands and feet that dazzled all, were now weirdly unco-ordinated.

October, 1980, was a bad month. As Ali destroyed himself, a young Briton lay close to death in a Los Angeles hospital. Johnny Owen, 24, from Wales, had been carried out of the Olympic Auditorium on a stretcher. A frail, beguiling matchstick-man, Owen's ability and courage carried him through 12 rounds of a world bantam fight with the hard Mexican, Lupe Pintor, until one violent right swept him to the floor, where he lay unconscious. Forty-six days later, he died, to remind the world how brutal boxing can be, to raise again those doubts civilised man must always have about the sport.

His death was a tragic blow amid continued British success. Alan Minter, a highly competent middleweight who'd been side-tracked for years, journeyed to Las Vegas, tied the crude Vito Antuofermo in knots for 15 rounds and won the undisputed world title. Minter was the first fighter from Britain to lift a world title in the United States since Ted Kid Lewis in 1917. When Antuofermo came to London for the return, Minter hacked him to bits in eight rounds.

Minter, a national celebrity now, caught the attention of a tatty minority of white racists.

When they heard Minter was defending his title in London against Marvin Hagler, a black slugger from Brockton, Massachusetts (Marciano's home town) they threw their unsolicited weight on Minter's side. Things were not helped by an incautious remark from Minter himself days before the fight: "I don't intend losing my title to a black guy."

When Minter and Hagler met at Wembley, the flag-waving and singing disguised something menacing, an undeniable feeling that Minter MUST win. Instead, he suffered his worst beating in eight years as a pro.

Shaven-headed Hagler, a thickset muscle-man, came to fight and Minter made the mistake of taking him on, when he should have boxed clever. Old wounds were ripped apart on Minter's face and in three rounds it was over. Wembley, deprived of celebration, resorted to fury. Plastic bottles, filled with liquid, were slung at Hagler, who dived for cover behind a posse of police. No-one blamed Hagler, 18 months later, when he said he would not be returning to Britain, thank you, to defend his title against the new British star, Tony Sibson.

Maurice Hope carried on as WBC light-middle champion into the 80's with quiet courage. Following a laser-beam operation to heal the torn retina of his right eye. Hope made two more successful defences until he was caught in Las Vegas by one of the most vicious rights I have seen one man land on another. It was thrown by Wilfredo Benitez, the man Sugar Ray Leonard had beaten in '79, and it won Benitez his third world title.

Less than a month later, Jim Watt, now 32, lost his lightweight title to Alexis Arguello of Nicaragua, who joined Benitez, Armstrong and Fitzsimmons as a super-champion capable of winning world titles at three different weights. Yes, of course it is easier to win a world title when it's split in two: WBA and WBC. But Benitez and Arguello would have been great champions at any time in history.

The new super-star had his bright light briefly dimmed. Sugar Ray Leonard ("svelte, charming, handsome, marketable piece of manhood" was the gushing tribute from one girl reporter) put up his WBC welter title against the long-serving Roberto Duran in front of 46,000 people in Montreal's Big O, the outdoor Olympic stadium, for a mammoth, record-breaking fee of £3-million (nearly six-million dollars).

Duran – was it really 1972 when he beat Buchanan? – hammered his way to a points win, Leonard's first defeat since an amateur setback in 1974. It was Duran's proudest moment, yet five months later, in New Orleans,

he uncharacteristically turned his back in the 8th and walked away from Leonard, provoking sneers of "chicken" from the very people who previously had called him hero.

Leonard's fame and fortune grew. When he wasn't fighting he worked as a TV commentator and paid the biggest taxes of anyone in Maryland, a smaller, nimbler, less lippy successor to Muhammad Ali. There were no Black Power rantings from Leonard to upset American whites. He trod a conventional path through black-and-white politics, thus upsetting some American blacks. In 1981 he stepped out of his weight to thrash the previously unbeaten, formidable Ugandan, Ayub Kalule, and take the WBA light-middleweight title, which he later returned.

There followed boxing's first major confrontation of the decade. Thomas Hearns, a beanstalk fighter from Detroit, held the WBA welter title and therefore cast doubt on Leonard's supremacy. Hearns, known as the Detroit Hit-Man or Motown Cobra, stood 6ft.2in. and had a reach of 78-inches, longer than that of Louis, Charles or Walcott! And he'd never lost a fight.

Hearns and Leonard came together in the wide open spaces at the back of Caesar's Palace, Las Vegas, where one month later they built a Grand Prix track to stage the climax of the 1981 Formula One world drivers' championships. A crowd of 24,000 and millions more around the world watching closed-circuit TV saw these two men earn their massive guarantees: Leonard 8-million dollars, Hearns 5-million.

Artist v Hit Man . . . Superstar v Freak . . . oh, here was a promotion to match the craziest Ali days. Wonder of wonders, they conjured a fight to live up to it all, Hearns, behind that freakish reach, outboxed the superstar. The 13th, and Leonard was losing! Only one course left. The Hit Man must be hit. So Leonard hit him and when the bell came Hearns was sitting dazed on the ropes. But he was still ahead on all the judges' cards. The 14th: Hearns *only* had to stay the course to win. *Only*.

Leonard bolted off his stool and smashed the wobbling Hit Man with everything he could muster. Pinned in a corner, trying to cover up,

The ill-starred encounter at Wembley, London, between Alan Minter and the black muscleman Marvin Hagler (USA). When Hagler was declared winner and middleweight champion of the world, bottles started flying.

Right: Superstar of the 80's: Sugar Ray Leonard, former Olympic champion. His immense talent and good PR will make him the richest boxer of all time.

Once Muhammad Ali's regular sparring partner, Larry Holmes found it hard to win public acclaim when he took Ali's place as heavyweight champion. Like Ali, he beat off rival after rival. He just didn't have the words to go with it.

Multi-million dollar white hope: Gerry Cooney, giant Irish-American, son of a pro fighter, unbeaten challenger for Larry Holmes' heavyweight title.

Hearns looked beaten. So the referee stopped it. Leonard undisputed welterweight champion of the world! Superstar of the 80's! In the end he banked close on 10-million dollars from this one fight. His earnings were already at the 50-million mark. He was set to pass the entire lifetime earnings of Ali: and not a hanger-on in sight.

Joe Louis died in 1981, aged 66. Peter Wilson, undisputed champion of British scribes, soon to pass on himself, wrote the final tribute: "Every negro heavyweight should go down on his knees every night to salute the memory of Joe Louis."

Larry Holmes kept winning, but the public still wasn't ready to enjoy heavyweight boxing after the long affair with Ali. They needed a new face. What about a white face? There hadn't been a white heavyweight champion since Ingemar Johansson, and only two in close on 50 years.

In 1981 Gerry Cooney, a white giant, Irish-American, 6ft. 5in., 224-lb., knocked Ken Norton over in 54-seconds, his 25th consecutive win. The moneymen rubbed hands and promised Holmes and Cooney 10-million dollars apiece for a showdown.

In Gleason's gym, New York, I watched Cooney train. I asked an American standing by me: "What do you think?" He scowled: "Cooney? Beat Holmes? Nah, the guy's just a lucky bum with a punch." Right. That's what they said about Marciano, just before he beat Walcott.

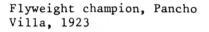

Results
of World   Championships

Light-flyweight (inaugurated 1975)

1975 4 Apl	Franco Udella dis 12 Valentin Martinez, Milan	
1975 23 Aug	Jaime Rios pts 15 Rigoberto Marcano, Panama City (WBA)	
1975 13 Sep	Luis Estaba ko 4 Rafael Lovera, Caracas (WBC)	
1975 17 Dec	Luis Estaba rsf 10 Takenobu Shimabukuro, Okinawa (WBC)	
1976 14 Feb	Luis Estaba pts 15 Leo Palacios, Caracas (WBC)	
1976 1 May	Luis Estaba pts 15 Juan Alvarez, Caracas (WBC)	
1976 8 July	Juan Guzman pts 15 Jaime Rios, Santo Domingo (WBA)	
1976 19 July	Luis Estaba ko 3 Franco Udella, Caracas (WBC)	
1976 26 Sep	Luis Estaba ret 10 Rodolfo Rodriguez, Caracas (WBC)	
1976 10 Oct	Yoko Gushiken ko 7 Juan Guzman, Kofu (WBA)	
1976 21 Nov	Luis Estaba rsf 9 Valentin Martinez, Caracas (WBC)	
1977 30 Jan	Yoko Gushiken pts 15 Jaime Rios, Tokio (WBA)	
1977 15 May	Luis Estaba pts 15 Rafael Pedroza, Caracas (WBC)	
1977 22 May	Yoko Gushiken pts 15 Rigoberto Marcano, Sapporo (WBA)	
1977 17 July	Luis Estaba pts 15 Ricardo Estupinan, Puerta La Cruz (WBC)	
1977 28 Aug	Luis Estaba ko 10 Juan Alvarez, Puerto La Cruz (WBC)	
1977 18 Sep	Luis Estaba ko 15 Orlando Hernandez, Caracas (WBC)	
1977 9 Oct	Yoko Gushiken rsf 4 Montsayarm Mahachai, Beppu (WBA)	
1977 29 Oct	Luis Estaba pts 15 Netrnoi Vorasingh, Caracas (WBC)	
1978 29 Jan	Yoko Gushiken rsf 14 Anecito Vargas, Nagoya (WBA)	
1978 19 Feb	Freddy Castillo rsf 14 Luis Estaba, Caracas (WBC)	
1978 6 May	Netrnoi Vorasingh pts 15 Freddy Castillo, Bangkok (WBC)	
1978 7 May	Yoko Gushiken rsf 13 Jaime Rios, Hiroshima (WBA)	
1978 29 July	Netrnoi Vorasingh ret 5 Luis Estaba, Caracas (WBC)	
1978 30 Sep	Kim Sung-Jun ko 3 Netrnoi Vorasingh, Seoul (WBC)	
1978 15 Oct	Yoko Gushiken ko 5 Chung Sang-Il, Tokio (WBA)	
1979 7 Jan	Yoko Gushiken ko 7 Rigoberto Marcano, Kawasaki (WBA)	
1979 31 Mar	Kim Sung-Jun dr 15 Hector Ray Melendez, Seoul (WBC)	
1979 8 Apl	Yoko Gushiken ko 7 Alfonso Lopez, Tokio (WBA)	
1979 28 July	Yoko Gushiken pts 15 Rafael Pedroza, Kitakyushu (WBA)	
1979 28 July	Kim Sung-Jun pts 15 Siony Carupo, Seoul (WBC)	
1979 21 Oct	Kim Sung-Jun pts 15 Hector Melendez, Seoul (WBC)	
1979 28 Oct	Yoko Gushiken rsf 7 Tito Abella, Tokio (WBA)	
1980 3 Jan	Shigeo Nakajima pts 15 Kim Sung-Jun, Tokio (WBC)	
1980 27 Jan	Yoko Gushiken pts 15 Kim Yung-Hyun, Osaka (WBA)	
1980 23 Mar	Hilario Zapata pts 15 Shigeo Nakajima, Tokio (WBC)	
1980 1 June	Yoko Gushiken rsf 8 Martin Vargas, Koichi (WBA)	
1980 7 June	Hilario Zapata pts 15 Kim Choi Bok, Seoul (WBC)	
1980 16 Aug	Hilario Zapata pts 15 Hector Melendez, Caracas (WBC)	
1980 17 Sep	Hilario Zapata rsf 11 Shigeo Nakajima, Tokio (WBC)	
1980 12 Oct	Yoko Gushiken pts 15 Pedro Flores, Kanazawa (WBA)	
1980 1 Dec	Hilario Zapata pts 15 Reynaldo Becerra, Caracas (WBC)	
1981 8 Feb	Hilario Zapata ret 13 Joey Olivo, Panama City (WBC)	
1981 8 Mar	Pedro Flores ret 12 Yoko Gushiken, Naha (WBA)	
1981 24 Apl	Hilario Zapata pts 15 Rudy Crawford, San Francisco (WBC)	
1981 19 July	Kim Hwan Jen rsf 13 Pedro Flores, Seoul (WBA)	
1981 15 Aug	Hilario Zapata pts 15 German Torres, Panama City (WBC)	
1981 11 Oct	Kim Hwan Jen pts 15 Alfonso Lopez, Seoul (WBA)	
1981 6 Nov	Hilario Zapata rsf 10 Netrnoi Vorasingh, Kortat (WBC)	
1981 16 Dec	Katsuo Takashiki pts 15 Kim Hwan Jen, Sendai (WBA)	
1982 Mar	Amado Ursua (Mex) rsf 2 Hilario Zapata (Pan) (WBC)	
1982 4 Apl	Katsuo Takashiki pts 15 Lupe Madera, Sendai (WBA)	

Flyweight

1916 18 Dec	Jimmy Wilde ko 11 Young Zulu Kid, London, Eng.	
1923 18 June	Pancho Villa ko 7 Jimmy Wilde, New York	
1923 13 Oct	Pancho Villa pts 15 Benny Schwartz, Baltimore	
1924 30 May	Pancho Villa pts 15 Frankie Ash, Brooklyn	
1925 22 Aug	Fidel La Barba pts 10 Frankie Genaro, Los Angeles (US only)	
1927 21 Jan	Fidel La Barba pts 12 Elky Clark, New York	
1927 16 Dec	Izzy Schwartz pts 15 Newsboy Brown, New York (NY only)	
1928 6 Feb	Frankie Genaro pts 10 Frenchy Belanger, Toronto (NBA only)	
1929 2 Mar	Emile Pladner ko 1 Frankie Genaro, Paris (Eur only)	
1929 18 Apl	Frankie Genaro dis 5 Emile Pladner, Paris	
1930 21 Mar	Midget Wolgast pts 15 Black Bill, New York (NY only)	
1930 26 Dec	Frankie Genaro dr 15 Midget Wolgast, New York	
1931 25 Mar	Frankie Genaro dr 15 Victor Ferrand, Madrid	
1931 30 July	Frankie Genaro ko 6 Jackie Harmon, Waterbury, Conn.	
1931 3 Oct	Frankie Genaro pts 15 Valentin Angelmann, Paris	
1931 27 Oct	Young Perez ko 2 Frankie Genaro, Paris	
1932 31 Oct	Jackie Brown ret 13 Young Perez, Manchester, Eng.	
1933 12 June	Jackie Brown pts 15 Valentin Angelmann, London, Eng.	
1933 11 Sep	Jackie Brown pts 15 Valentin Angelmann, Manchester, Eng.	
1933 11 Dec	Jackie Brown pts 15 Ginger Foran, Manchester, Eng.	
1934 18 June	Jackie Brown dr 15 Valentin Angelmann, Manchester, Eng.	
1935 9 Sep	Benny Lynch ret 2 Jackie Brown, Manchester, Eng.	
1936 16 Sep	Benny Lynch ko 8 Pat Palmer, Glasgow	
1937 19 Jan	Benny Lynch pts 15 Small Montana, London, Eng.	
1937 13 Oct	Benny Lynch ko 13 Peter Kane, Glasgow	
1938 22 Sep	Peter Kane pts 15 Jackie Jurich, Liverpool	
1943 19 June	Jackie Paterson ko 1 Peter Kane, Glasgow	
1946 10 July	Jackie Paterson pts 15 Joe Curran, Glasgow	
1948 23 Mar	Rinty Monaghan ko 7 Jackie Paterson, Belfast	
1949 5 Apl	Rinty Monaghan pts 15 Maurice Sandeyron, Belfast	
1949 30 Sep	Rinty Monaghan dr 15 Terry Allen, Belfast	
1950 25 Apl	Terry Allen pts 15 Honore Pratesi, London, Eng.	
1950 1 Aug	Dado Marino pts 15 Terry Allen, Honolulu	
1951 1 Nov	Dado Marino pts 15 Terry Allen, Honolulu	
1952 19 May	Yoshio Shirai pts 15 Dado Marino, Tokyo	
1952 15 Nov	Yoshio Shirai pts 15 Dado Marino, Tokyo	
1953 18 May	Yoshio Shirai pts 15 Tanny Campo, Tokyo	
1953 27 Oct	Yoshio Shirai pts 15 Terry Allen, Tokyo	
1954 23 May	Yoshio Shirai pts 15 Leo Espinosa, Tokyo	
1954 26 Nov	Pascual Perez pts 15 Yoshio Shirai, Tokyo	
1955 30 May	Pascual Perez ko 5 Yoshio Shirai, Tokyo	
1956 11 Jan	Pascual Perez pts 15 Leo Espinosa, Buenos Aires	
1956 30 June	Pascual Perez ret 11 Oscar Suarez, Montevideo	
1957 30 Mar	Pascual Perez ko 1 Dai Dower, Buenos Aires	
1957 7 Dec	Pascual Perez ko 3 Young Martin, Buenos Aires	
1958 19 Apl	Pascual Perez pts 15 Ramon Arias, Caracas	
1958 15 Dec	Pascual Perez pts 15 Dommy Ursua, Manila	
1959 10 Aug	Pascual Perez pts 15 Kenji Yonekura, Tokyo	
1959 5 Nov	Pascual Perez ko 13 Sadao Yaoita, Osaka	
1960 16 Apl	Pone Kingpetch pts 15 Pascual Perez, Bangkok	
1960 22 Sep	Pone Kingpetch rsf 8 Pascual Perez, Los Angeles	
1961 27 June	Pone Kingpetch pts 15 Mitsunori Seki, Tokyo	
1962 30 May	Pone Kingpetch pts 15 Kyo Noguchi, Tokyo	
1962 10 Oct	Fighting Harada ko 11 Pone Kingpetch, Tokyo	
1963 12 Jan	Pone Kingpetch pts 15 Fighting Harada, Bangkok	
1963 18 Sep	Hiroyuki Ebihara ko 1 Pone Kingpetch, Tokyo	
1964 23 Jan	Pone Kingpetch pts 15 Hiroyuki Ebihara, Bangkok	
1965 23 Apl	Salvatore Burruni pts 15 Pone Kingpetch, Rome	
1965 2 Dec	Salvatore Burruni ko 13 Rocky Gattellari, Sydney	
1966 14 June	Walter McGowan pts 15 Salvatore Burruni, London, Eng.	
1966 30 Dec	Chartchai Chionoi rsf 9 Walter McGowan, Bangkok	
1967 26 July	Chartchai Chionoi ko 3 Puntip Keosuriya, Bangkok	
1967 19 Sep	Chartchai Chionoi rsf 7 Walter McGowan, London, Eng.	
1968 28 Jan	Chartchai Chionoi rsf 13 Efren Torres, Mexico City	
1968 10 Nov	Chartchai Chionoi pts 15 Bernabe Villacampo, Bangkok	
1969 23 Feb	Efren Torres rsf 8 Chartchai Chionoi, Mexico City	
1969 28 Nov	Efren Torres pts 15 Susumu Hanagata, Guadalajara	
1970 20 Mar	Chartchai Chionoi pts 15 Efren Torres, Bangkok	
1970 7 Dec	Erbito Salavarria rsf 2 Chartchai Chionoi, Bangkok	
1971 30 Apl	Erbito Salavarria pts 15 Susumu Hanagata, Manila	
1971 20 Nov	Betulio Gonzales dis Erbito Salavarria, Maracaibo (WBC only)	
1972 4 Mar	Masao Ohba pts 15 Susumu Hanagata, Tokyo (WBA only)	
1972 29 Sep	Venice Borkorsaw ret 10 Betulio Gonzales, Bangkok (WBC only)	
1973 17 May	Chartchai Chionoi rsf 4 Fritz Chervet, Bangkok (WBA only)	
1973 4 Aug	Betulio Gonzales pts 15 Miguel Canto, Maracaibo (WBC only)	
1973 27 Oct	Chartchai Chionoi pts 15 Susumu Hanagata, Bangkok (WBA only)	

1973 17 Nov	Betulio Gonzales rsf 11 Alberto Morales, Caracas (WBC only)
1974 27 Apl	Chartchai Chionoi pts 15 Fritz Chervet, Zurich (WBA only)
1974 20 July	Betulio Gonzales rsf 10 Franco Udella, Lignano Sabbiadoro (WBC only)
1974 1 Oct	Shoji Oguma pts 15 Betulio Gonzales, Tokyo (WBC only)
1974 18 Oct	Susumu Hanagata rsf 6 Chartchai Chionoi, Yokahama (WBA only)
1975 8 Jan	Miguel Canto pts 15 Shoji Oguma, Sendai, (WBC only)
1975 1 Apl	Erbito Salavarria pts 15 Susumu Hanagata, Toyama (WBA only)
1975 24 May	Miguel Canto pts 15 Betulio Gonzalez, Monterrey (WBC)
1975 23 Aug	Miguel Canto rsf 11 Jiro Takada, Merida (WBC)
1975 7 Oct	Erbito Salavarria pts 15 Susumu Hanagata, Yokohama (WBA)
1975 13 Dec	Miguel Canto pts 15 Ignacio Espinal, Merida (WBC)
1976 27 Feb	Alfonso Lopez rsf 15 Erbito Salavarria, Manila (WBA)
1976 21 Apl	Alfonso Lopez pts 15 Shoji Oguma, Tokio (WBA)
1976 15 May	Miguel Canto pts 15 Susumu Hanagata, Merida (WBC)
1976 2 Oct	Guty Espadas rsf 13 Alfonso Lopez, Los Angeles (WBA)
1976 3 Oct	Miguel Canto pts 15 Betulio Gonzalez, Caracas (WBC)
1976 19 Nov	Miguel Canto pts 15 Orlando Javierto, Los Angeles (WBC)
1977 1 Jan	Guty Espadas ret 7 Jiro Takada, Tokio (WBA)
1977 25 Apl	Miguel Canto pts 15 Reyes Arnal, Caracas (WBC)
1977 30 Apl	Guty Espadas ko 13 Alfonso Lopez, Mexico City (WBA)
1977 15 June	Miguel Canto pts 15 Kimio Furesawa, Tokio (WBC)
1977 17 Sep	Miguel Canto pts 15 Martin Vargas, Merida (WBC)
1977 19 Nov	Guty Espadas ko 8 Alex Santana, Los Angeles (WBA)
1977 30 Nov	Miguel Canto pts 15 Martin Vargas, Santiago (WBC)
1978 2 Jan	Guty Espadas rsf 7 Kimio Furesawa, Tokio (WBA)
1978 4 Jan	Miguel Canto pts 15 Shoji Oguma, Koriyama (WBC)
1978 18 Apl	Miguel Canto pts 15 Shoji Oguma, Tokio (WBC)
1978 13 Aug	Betulio Gonzalez pts 15 Guty Espadas, Maracay (WBA)
1978 4 Nov	Betulio Gonzalez rsf 12 Martin Vargas, Maracay (WBA)
1978 20 Nov	Miguel Canto pts 15 Tacomron Viboonchai, Houston (WBC)
1979 29 Jan	Betulio Gonzalez dr 15 Shoji Oguma, Hamatsu (WBA)
1979 10 Feb	Miguel Canto pts 15 Antonio Avelar, Merida (WBC)
1979 18 Mar	Park Chan-Hee pts 15 Miguel Canto, Seoul (WBC)
1979 19 May	Park Chan-Hee pts 15 Tsutomo Igarashi, Seoul (WBC)
1979 13 July	Betulio Gonzalez ko 12 Shoji Oguma, Utsonomiya (WBA)
1979 6 Sep	Park Chan-Hee dr 15 Miguel Canto, Seoul (WBC)
1979 16 Nov	Luis Ibarra pts 15 Betulio Gonzalez, Maracay (WBA)
1979 16 Dec	Park Chan-Hee ko 2 Guty Espadas, Pusan (WBC)
1980 9 Feb	Park Chan Hee pts 15 Arnel Arrozal, Seoul (WBC)
1980 17 Feb	Kim Tae-Shik ko 2 Luis Ibarra, Seoul (WBA)
1980 18 May	Shoji Oguma ko 9 Park Chan-Hee, Seoul (WBC)
1980 26 July	Shoji Oguma pts 15 Kim Sung-Jun, Tokio (WBC)
1980 18 Oct	Shoji Oguma pts 15 Park Chan-Hee, Tokio (WBC)
1980 13 Dec	Peter Mathebula pts 15 Kim Tae-Shik, Los Angeles (WBA)
1981 3 Feb	Shoji Oguma pts 15 Park Chan-Hee, Tokio (WBC)
1981 28 Mar	Santos Laciar rsf 7 Peter Mathebula, Soweto (WBA)
1981 12 May	Antonio Avelar ko 7 Shoji Oguma, Mito (WBC)
1981 6 June	Luis Ibarra pts 15 Santos Laciar, Buenos Aires (WBA)
1981 30 Aug	Antonio Avelar ko 2 Kim Tae-Shik, Seoul (WBC)
1981 26 Sep	Juan Herrera ko 11 Luis Ibarra, Merida (WBA)
1981 26 Dec	Juan Herrera rsf 7 Betulio Gonzalez, Merida (WBA)
1982 20 Mar	Prudencio Cardona ko 1 Antonio Avelar, Tampico (WBC)

Super-Flyweight (inaugurated 1980)

1980 2 Feb	Rafael Orono pts 15 Deun Hoon Lee, Caracas (WBC)
1980 12 Apl	Rafael Orono pts 15 Ramon Soria, Caracas (WBC)
1980 28 July	Rafael Orono dr 15 Willie Jensen, Caracas (WBC)
1980 15 Sep	Rafael Orono rsf 3 Jovito Rengifo, Barquisimeto (WBC)
1981 24 Jan	Choul Ho Kim ko 9 Rafael Orono, San Cristobal (WBC)
1981 24 Apl	Choul Ho Kim pts 15 Jiro Watanabe, Seoul (WBC)
1981 29 July	Choul Ho Kim ko 13 Willie Jensen, Pusan (WBC)
1981 12 Sep	Gustavo Ballas rsf 8 Suk Chul Bae, Buenos Aires (WBA)
1981 18 Nov	Choul Ho Kim rsf 9 Ryotsu Maruyama, Pusan (WBC)
1981 5 Dec	Rafael Pedroza pts 15 Gustavo Ballas, Panama City (WBA)

| 1982 10 Feb | Choul Ho Kim ko 8 Koki Ishii, Taegu (WBC) |

Bantamweight

1888 10 May	George Dixon dr 9 Tommy Kelly, Boston
1890 27 June	George Dixon rsf 18 Nunc Wallace, London, Eng.
1890 23 Oct	George Dixon pts 40 Johnny Murphy, Providence, RI
1892 9 May	Billy Plimmer pts 10 Tommy Kelly, Coney Island, NY
1894 15 Sep	Jimmy Barry ko 28 Casper Leon, Lamont, Ill. (US only)
1897 6 Dec	Jimmy Barry ko 20 Walter Croot, London, Eng.
1898 30 May	Jimmy Barry dr 20 Casper Leon, New York
1898 29 Dec	Jimmy Barry dr 20 Casper Leon, Davenport, Iowa
1899 12 Sep	Terry McGovern ko 1 Pedlar Palmer, Tuckahoe, NY
1901 18 Mar	Harry Harris pts 15 Pedlar Palmer, London, Eng.
1903 27 Feb	Harry Forbes pts 10 Andy Tokell, Detroit
1903 13 Aug	Frankie Neil rsf 2 Harry Forbes, San Francisco
1903 4 Sep	Frankie Neil ko 15 Billy de Coursey, Los Angeles
1903 16 Oct	Frankie Neil dr 20 Johnny Reagan, Los Angeles
1904 17 June	Frankie Neil ko 3 Harry Forbes, Chicago
1904 17 Oct	Joe Bowker pts 20 Frankie Neil, London, Eng.
1905 20 Oct	Jimmy Walsh pts 15 Digger Stanley, Chelsea, Mass.
1010 6 Mar	Johnny Coulon ko 19 Jim Kendrick, New Orleans
1910 19 Dec	Johnny Coulon pts 5 Earl Denning, Memphis
1911 26 Feb	Johnny Coulon pts 20 Frankie Conley, New Orleans
1912 3 Feb	Johnny Coulon pts 20 Frankie Conley, Vernon, Cal.
1912 18 Feb	Johnny Coulon pts 20 Frankie Burns, New Orleans
1912 18 Oct	Johnny Coulon no-dec. 10 Kid Williams, New York
1914 9 June	Kid Williams ko 3 Johnny Coulon, Vernon
1915 6 Dec	Kid Williams dr 20 Frankie Burns, New Orleans
1916 7 Feb	Kid Williams dr 20 Pete Herman, New Orleans
1917 9 Jan	Pete Herman pts 20 Kid Williams, New Orleans
1917 5 Nov	Pete Herman pts 20 Frankie Burns, New Orleans
1920 22 Dec	Joe Lynch pts 15 Pete Herman, New York
1921 25 July	Pete Herman pts 15 Joe Lynch, Brooklyn
1921 23 Sep	Johnny Buff pts 15 Pete Herman, New York
1921 10 Nov	Johnny Buff pts 15 Jack Sharkey, New York
1922 10 July	Joe Lynch ko 14 Johnny Buff, New York
1922 22 Dec	Joe Lynch pts 15 Midget Smith, New York
1924 21 Mar	Abe Goldstein pts 15 Joe Lynch, New York
1924 16 July	Abe Goldstein pts 15 Charles Ledoux, New York
1924 8 Sep	Abe Goldstein pts 15 Tommy Ryan, Long Island City
1924 19 Dec	Eddie Cannonball Martin pts 15 Abe Goldstein, New York
1925 20 Mar	Charlie Phil Rosenberg pts 15 Eddie Martin, New York
1925 23 July	Charlie Phil Rosenberg ko 4 Eddie Shea, New York
1926 2 Mar	Charlie Phil Rosenberg pts 10 George Butch, St Louis
1927 24 June	Charles Bud Taylor pts 10 Tony Canzoneri, Chicago (NBA only)
1929 18 June	Panama Al Brown pts 15 Vidal Gregorio, New York
1929 28 Aug	Panama Al Brown pts 10 Knud Larsen, Copenhagen
1930 4 Oct	Panama Al Brown pts 15 Eugene Huat, Paris
1931 11 Feb	Panama Al Brown pts 10 Nick Bensa, Paris
1931 25 Aug	Panama Al Brown pts 15 Pete Sanstol, Montreal
1931 27 Oct	Panama Al Brown pts 15 Eugene Huat, Montreal
1932 10 July	Panama Al Brown pts 15 Kid Francis, Marseilles
1932 19 Sep	Panama Al Brown ko 1 Emile Pladner, Toronto
1933 18 Mar	Panama Al Brown pts 12 Dom Bernasconi, Milan
1933 3 July	Panama Al Brown pts 15 Johnny King, Manchester, Eng.
1934 19 Feb	Panama Al Brown pts 15 Young Perez, Paris
1935 1 June	Baltazar Sangchilli pts 15 Panama Al Brown, Valencia
1936 29 June	Tony Marino ko 14 Baltazar Sangchilli, New York
1936 31 Aug	Sixto Escobar ko 13 Tony Marino, New York
1936 13 Oct	Sixto Escobar ko 1 Indian Quintana, New York
1937 21 Feb	Sixto Escobar pts 15 Lou Salica, San Juan, PR
1937 23 Sep	Harry Jeffra pts 15 Sixto Escobar, New York
1938 20 Feb	Sixto Escobar pts 15 Harry Jeffra, San Juan
1939 2 Apl	Sixto Escobar pts 15 Kayo Morgan, San Juan
1940 24 Sep	Lou Salica pts 15 Georgie Pace, New York
1941 13 Jan	Lou Salica pts 15 Tommy Forte, Philadelphia
1941 25 Apl	Lou Salica pts 15 Lou Transparenti, Baltimore

1941 16 June	Lou Salica pts 15 Tommy Forte, Philadelphia	
1942 7 Aug	Manuel Ortiz pts 12 Lou Salica, Hollywood	
1943 1 Jan	Manuel Ortiz pts 10 Kenny Lindsay, Portland, Ore.	
1943 27 Jan	Manuel Ortiz ko 10 Georgie Frietas, Oakland, Cal.	
1943 10 Mar	Manuel Ortiz ko 11 Lou Salica, Oakland	
1943 28 Apl	Manuel Ortiz ko 6 Lupe Cardoza, Ft. Worth, Tex.	
1943 26 May	Manuel Ortiz pts 15 Joe Robleto, Long Beach, Cal.	
1943 12 July	Manuel Ortiz ko 7 Joe Robleto, Seattle	
1943 1 Oct	Manuel Ortiz ko 4 Leonardo Lopez, Hollywood	
1943 23 Nov	Manuel Ortiz pts 15 Benny Goldberg, Los Angeles	
1944 14 Mar	Manuel Ortiz pts 15 Ernesto Aguilar, Los Angeles	
1944 4 Apl	Manuel Ortiz pts 15 Tony Olivera, Los Angeles	
1944 12 Sep	Manuel Ortiz ko 4 Luis Castillo, Los Angeles	
1944 14 Nov	Manuel Ortiz ko 9 Luis Castillo, Los Angeles	
1946 25 Feb	Manuel Ortiz ko 13 Luis Castillo, San Francisco	
1946 26 May	Manuel Ortiz ko 5 Kenny Lindsay, Hollywood	
1946 10 June	Manuel Ortiz ko 11 Jackie Jurich, San Francisco	
1947 6 Jan	Harold Dade pts 15 Manuel Ortiz, San Francisco	
1947 11 Mar	Manuel Ortiz pts 15 Harold Dade, Los Angeles	
1947 30 May	Manuel Ortiz pts 15 David Kui Kong Young, Honolulu	
1947 20 Dec	Manuel Ortiz pts 15 Tirso del Rosario, Manila	
1948 4 July	Manuel Ortiz ko 8 Memo Valero, Mexicali	
1949 1 Mar	Manuel Ortiz pts 15 Dado Marino, Honolulu	
1950 31 May	Vic Toweel pts 15 Manuel Ortiz, Johannesburg	
1950 2 Dec	Vic Toweel ret 10 Danny O'Sullivan, Johannesburg	
1951 17 Nov	Vic Toweel pts 15 Luis Romero, Johannesburg	
1952 26 Jan	Vic Toweel pts 15 Peter Keenan, Johannesburg	
1952 15 Nov	Jimmy Carruthers ko 1 Vic Toweel, Johannesburg	
1953 21 Mar	Jimmy Carruthers ko 10 Vic Toweel, Johannesburg	
1953 13 Nov	Jimmy Carruthers pts 15 Henry Pappy Gault, Sydney	
1954 2 May	Jimmy Carruthers pts 12 Chamrern Songkitrat, Bangkok	
1954 19 Sep	Robert Cohen pts 15 Chamrern Songkitrat, Bangkok	
1955 3 Sep	Robert Cohen dr 15 Willie Toweel, Johannesburg	
1956 29 June	Mario D'Agata ret 6 Robert Cohen, Rome	
1957 1 Apl	Alphonse Halimi pts 15 Mario D'Agata, Paris	
1957 6 Nov	Alphonse Halimi pts 15 Raton Macias, Los Angeles	
1959 8 July	Joe Becerra ko 8 Alphonse Halimi, Los Angeles	
1960 4 Feb	Joe Becerra ko 9 Alphonse Halimi, Los Angeles	
1960 23 May	Joe Becerra pts 15 Kenji Yonakura, Tokyo	
1960 25 Oct	Alphonse Halimi pts 15 Freddie Gilroy, London, Eng. (EBU only)	
1960 18 Nov	Eder Jofre ko 6 Eloy Sanchez (NBA only)	
1961 30 May	Johnny Caldwell pts 15 Alphonse Halimi, London, Eng. (EBU only)	
1962 18 Jan	Eder Jofre rsf 10 Johnny Caldwell, Sao Paulo	
1962 4 May	Eder Jofre rsf 10 Herman Marques, San Francisco	
1962 11 Sep	Eder Jofre ko 6 Joe Medel, Sao Paulo	
1963 4 Apl	Eder Jofre ko 3 Katsutoshi Aoki, Tokyo	
1963 18 May	Eder Jofre ret 11 Johnny Jamito, Manila	
1964 27 Nov	Eder Jofre ko 7 Bernardo Caraballo, Bogota	
1965 17 May	Fighting Harada pts 15 Eder Jofre, Nagoya	
1965 30 Nov	Fighting Harada pts 15 Alan Rudkin, Tokyo	
1966 1 June	Fighting Harada pts 15 Eder Jofre, Tokyo	
1967 3 Jan	Fighting Harada pts 15 Joe Medel, Nagoya	
1967 4 July	Fighting Harada pts 15 Bernardo Caraballo, Tokyo	
1968 27 Feb	Lionel Rose pts 15 Fighting Harada, Tokyo	
1968 2 July	Lionel Rose pts 15 Takao Sakurai, Tokyo	
1968 6 Dec	Lionel Rose pts 15 Jesus Castillo, Los Angeles	
1969 8 Mar	Lionel Rose pts 15 Alan Rudkin, Melbourne	
1969 22 Aug	Ruben Olivares ko 5 Lionel Rose, Los Angeles	
1969 12 Dec	Ruben Olivares rsf 2 Alan Rudkin, Los Angeles	
1970 18 Apl	Ruben Olivares pts 15 Jesus Castillo, Los Angeles	
1970 16 Oct	Jesus Castillo rsf 14 Ruben Olivares, Los Angeles	
1971 3 Apl	Ruben Olivares pts 15 Jesus Castillo, Los Angeles	
1971 25 Oct	Ruben Olivares rsf 14 Kazuyoshi Kanazawa, Nagoya	
1972 19 Mar	Rafael Herrera ko 8 Ruben Olivares, Mexico City	

1972 29 July	Enrique Pinder pts 15 Rafael Herrera, Panama City	
1973 20 Jan	Romeo Anaya ko 3 Enrique Pinder, Panama City (WBA only)	
1973 14 Apl	Rafael Herrera rsf 12 Rodolfo Martinez, Monterrey (WBC only)	
1973 13 Oct	Rafael Herrera pts 15 Venice Borkorsaw, Los Angeles (WBC only)	
1973 3 Nov	Arnold Taylor ko 14 Romeo Anaya, Johannesburg (WBA only)	
1974 26 May	Rafael Herrera ko 6 Romeo Anaya, Mexico City (WBC only)	
1974 3 July	Soo Hwan Hong pts 15 Arnold Taylor, Durban (WBA only)	
1974 7 Dec	Rodolfo Martinez rsf 4 Rafael Herrera, Merida (WBC only)	
1974 28 Dec	Soo Hwan Hong pts 15 Fernando Cabanela, Seoul (WBA only)	
1975 14 Mar	Alfonso Zamora ko 4 Soo Hwan Hong, Los Angeles (WBA only)	
1975 31 May	Rodolfo Martinez rsf 7 Nestor Jiminez, Bogota (WBC)	
1975 30 Aug	Alfonso Zamora ko 4 Thanomjit Sukothai, Anaheim (WBA)	
1975 8 Oct	Rodolfo Martinez pts 15 Hisami Numata, Sendai (WBC)	
1975 6 Dec	Alfonso Zamora ko 2 Socrates Batoto, Mexico City (WBA)	
1976 30 Jan	Rodolfo Martinez pts 15 Venice Borkorsaw, Bangkok (WBC)	
1976 3 Apl	Alfonso Zamora ko 2 Eusebio Pedroza, Mexicali (WBA)	
1976 8 May	Carlos Zarate ko 9 Rodolfo Martinez, Los Angeles (WBC)	
1976 10 July	Alfonso Zamora ko 3 Gilberto Illueca, Juarez (WBA)	
1976 10 July	Alfonso Zamora ko 3 Gilberto Illueca, Juarez (WBA)	
1976 28 Aug	Carlos Zarata rsf 12 Paul Ferreri, Los Angeles (WBC)	
1976 16 Oct	Alfonso Zamora rsf 12 Soo Hwan Hong, Inchon (WBA)	
1976 13 Nov	Carlos Zarate ko 4 Waruinge Nakayama, Culiacan (WBC)	
1977 5 Feb	Carlos Zarate rsf 3 Fernando Cabanella, Mexico City (WBC)	
1977 29 Oct	Carlos Zarate rsf 6 Danilo Batista, Los Angeles (WBC)	
1977 19 Nov	Jorge Lujan ko 10 Alfonso Zamora, Los Angeles (WBA)	
1977 2 Dec	Carlos Zarate rsf 5 Juan Francisco Rodriguez, Madrid (WBC)	
1978 25 Feb	Carlos Zarate rsf 8 Alberto Davila, Los Angeles (WBC)	
1978 18 Mar	Jorge Lujan rsf 11 Roberto Rubaldino, San Antonio (WBA)	
1978 22 Apl	Carlos Zarate rsf 13 Andres Hernandez, San Juan (WBC)	
1978 9 June	Carlos Zarate ko 4 Emilio Hernandez, Las Vegas (WBC)	
1978 15 Sep	Jorge Lujan pts 15 Alberto Davila, New Orleans (WBA)	
1979 10 Mar	Carlos Zarata ko 3 Mensah Kpalogo, Los Angeles (WBC)	
1979 8 Apl	Jorge Lujan rsf 15 Cleo Garcia, Los Angeles (WBA)	
1979 3 June	Lupe Pintor pts 15 Carlos Zarate, Las Vegas (WBC)	
1979 6 Oct	Jorge Lujan ko 11 Roberto Rubaldino, McAllen, Tex. (WBA)	
1980 9 Feb	Lupe Pintor rsf 12 Alberto Sandoval, Los Angeles (WBC)	
1980 2 Apl	Jorge Lujan rsf 9 Shuichi Isogami, Tokio (WBA)	
1980 11 June	Lupe Pintor dr 15 Eijiro Murata, Tokio (WBC)	
1980 29 Aug	Julian Solis pts 15 Jorge Lujan, Miami (WBA)	
1980 19 Sep	Lupe Pintor rsf 12 Johnny Owen, Los Angeles (WBC)	
1980 14 Nov	Jeff Chandler rsf 14 Julian Solis, Miami Beach (WBA)	
1980 19 Dec	Lupe Pintor pts 15 Alberto Davila, Las Vegas (WBC)	
1981 31 Jan	Jeff Chandler pts 15 Jorge Lujan, Philadelphia (WBA)	
1981 22 Feb	Lupe Pintor pts 15 Jose Uziga, Houston (WBC)	
1981 4 Apl	Jeff Chandler dr 15 Eijiro Murata, Tokio (WBA)	
1981 25 July	Jeff Chandler ko 7 Julian Solis, Atlantic City (WBA)	
1981 26 July	Lupe Pintor rsf 8 Jovito Rengifo, Las Vegas (WBC)	
1981 22 Sep	Lupe Pintor ko 15 Hurricane Teru, Nagoya (WBC)	
1981 10 Dec	Jeff Chandler rsf 13 Eijiro Murata, Atlantic City (WBA)	
1982 27 Mar	Jeff Chandler rsf 6 Johnny Carter, Philadephia (WBA)	

Junior-featherweight (inaugurated 1976)

1976 3 Apl	Rigoberto Riasco ret 8 Waruinge Nakayama, Panama City (WBC)	
1976 12 June	Rigoberto Riasco rsf 10 Livio Nolasco, Panama City (WBC)	
1976 1 Aug	Rigoberto Riasco pts 15 Dong-Kyun Yum, Seoul (WBC)	
1976 9 Oct	Royal Kobayashi rsf 8 Rigoberto Riasco, Tokio (WBC)	
1976 24 Nov	Dong-Kyun Yum pts 15 Royal Kobayashi, Seoul (WBC)	
1977 13 Feb	Dong-Kyun Yum pts 15 Jose Cervantes, Seoul (WBC)	
1977 21 May	Wilfredo Gomez rsf 12 Dong-Kyun Yum, San Juan (WBC)	
1977 12 July	Wilfredo Gomez ko 5 Raul Tirado, San Juan (WBC)	
1977 26 Nov	Soo Hwan-Hong ko 3 Hector Carrasquilla, Panama City (WBA)	
1978 19 Jan	Wilfredo Gomez ko 3 Royal Kobayashi, Kitakyushu (WBC)	

1978	1 Feb	Soo Hwan-Hong pts 15 Mararu Kasahara, Tokio (WBA)
1978	8 Apl	Wilfredo Gomez rsf 7 Juan Antonio Lopez, Bayamon (WBC)
1978	7 May	Ricardo Cardona rsf 12 Soo Hwan-Hong, Seoul (WBA)
1978	2 June	Wilfredo Gomez rsf 3 Sakad Porntavee, Kortat (WBC)
1978	2 Sep	Ricardo Cardona pts 15 Ruben Valdes, Cartegena (WBA)
1978	9 Sep	Wilfredo Gomez rsf 13 Leo Cruz, San Juan (WBC)
1978	28 Oct	Wilfredo Gomez rsf 5 Carlos Zarate, San Juan (WBC)
1978	12 Nov	Ricardo Cardona pts 15 Soon-Hyun Chung, Seoul (WBA)
1979	9 Mar	Wilfredo Gomez ret 5 Nestor Jiminez, New York (WBC)
1979	16 June	Wilfredo Gomez ko 5 Julio Hernandez, San Juan (WBC)
1979	23 June	Ricardo Cardona pts 15 Soon-Hyun Chung, Seoul (WBA)
1979	6 Sep	Ricardo Cardona pts 15 Yukio Segawa, Hachinohe (WBA)
1979	28 Sep	Wilfredo Gomez rsf 10 Carlos Mendoza, Las Vegas (WBC)
1979	15 Dec	Ricardo Cardona pts 15 Sergio Palma, Barranquilla (WBA)
1980	3 Feb	Wilfredo Gomez ret 6 Ruben Valdes, Las Vegas WBC)
1980	4 May	Leo Randolph rsf 15 Ricardo Cardona, Seattle (WBA)
1980	9 Aug	Sergio Palma ko 6 Leo Randolph, Spokane (WBA)
1980	22 Aug	Wilfredo Gomez rsf 5 Derrick Holmes, Las Vegas (WBC)
1980	8 Nov	Sergio Palma ko 9 Ulises Morales, Buenos Aires (WBA)
1980	13 Dec	Wilfredo Gomez ko 3 Jose Cervantes, Miama Beach (WBC)
1981	4 Apl	Sergio Palma pts 14 Leonardo Cruz, Buenos Aires (WBA)
1981	15 Aug	Sergio Palma rsf 12 Ricardo Cardona, Buenos Aires (WBA)
1981	3 Oct	Sergio Palma pts 15 Wilchit Muangroi-Et, Buenos Aires (WBA)
1982	27 Mar	Wilfredo Gomez rsf 6 Juan Kid Meza, Atlantic City (WBC)

Featherweight

1889	31 Mar	Ike O'Neil Weir dr 80 Frank Murphy, Kouts, Indiana
1890	13 Jan	Billy Murphy ko 14 Ike O'Neil Weir, San Francisco
1891	31 Mar	George Dixon rsf 22 Cal McCarthy, Troy, NY (US only)
1891	28 July	George Dixon rsf 5 Abe Willis, San Francisco
1892	27 June	George Dixon ko 14 Fred Johnson, Coney Island, NY
1892	6 Sep	George Dixon ko 8 Jack Skelly, New Orleans
1893	Aug	George Dixon ko 3 Eddie Pierce, Coney Island
1893	25 Sep	George Dixon ko 7 Solly Smith, Coney Island
1894	29 June	George Dixon dr 10 Young Griffo, Boston
1895	27 Aug	George Dixon pts 15 Johnny Griffin, Boston
1897	4 Oct	Solly Smith pts 20 George Dixon, San Francisco
1898	26 Sep	Dave Sullivan ret 5 Solly Smith, Coney Island
1898	11 Nov	George Dixon dis 10 Dave Sullivan, New York
1898	29 Nov	George Dixon pts 25 Oscar Gardner, New York
1899	17 Jan	George Dixon ko 10 Young Pluto, New York
1899	15 May	George Dixon pts 20 Kid Broad, Buffalo, NY
1899	2 June	George Dixon pts 25 Joe Bernstein, New York
1899	1 July	George Dixon pts 20 Tommy White, Denver
1899	11 Aug	George Dixon dr 20 Eddie Santry, New York
1899	2 Nov	George Dixon pts 25 Will Curley, New York
1899	21 Nov	George Dixon pts 25 Eddie Lenny, New York
1900	9 Jan	Terry McGovern rsf 8 George Dixon, New York
1900	1 Feb	Terry McGovern ko 5 Eddie Santry, Chicago
1900	9 Mar	Terry McGovern ko 3 Oscar Gardner, New York
1900	12 June	Terry McGovern ko 3 Tommy White, Coney Island
1900	2 Nov	Terry McGovern ko 7 Joe Bernstein, Louisville, Ky.
1901	30 Apl	Terry McGovern ko 4 Oscar Gardner, San Francisco
1901	29 May	Terry McGovern ko 5 Auerio Herrera, San Francisco
1901	28 Nov	Young Corbett ko 2 Terry McGovern, Hartford, Conn.
1901	20 Oct	Abe Attell dr 20 George Dixon, Cripple Creek
1901	28 Oct	Abe Attell pts 15 George Dixon, St Louis
1904	1 Feb	Abe Attell rsf 5 Harry Forbes, St Louis
1905	22 Feb	Abe Attell dr 15 Kid Goodman, Boston
1906	4 July	Abe Attell pts 20 Frankie Neil, Los Angeles
1906	30 Oct	Abe Attell pts 20 Harry Baker, Los Angeles
1906	7 Dec	Abe Attell ko 8 Jimmy Walsh, Los Angeles
1907	18 Jan	Abe Attell ko 8 Harry Baker, Los Angeles
1907	24 May	Abe Attell ko 20 Kid Solomon, Los Angeles
1907	29 Oct	Abe Attell ko 4 Freddie Weeks, Los Angeles
1908	1 Jan	Abe Attell dr 25 Owen Moran, San Francisco
1908	7 Sep	Abe Attell dr 23 Owen Moran, San Francisco

1909	26 Mar	Abe Attell ko 8 Frankie White, Dayton, Ohio
1910	28 Feb	Abe Attell ko 7 Harry Forbes, New York
1912	22 Feb	Johnny Kilbane pts 20 Abe Attell, Vernon, Cal.
1912	21 May	Johnny Kilbane dr 12 Jimmy Walsh, Boston
1913	29 Apl	Johnny Kilbane dr 20 Johnny Dundee, Vernon
1916	4 Sep	Johnny Kilbane ko 3 George Chaney, Cedar Point
1920	21 Apl	Johnny Kilbane ko 7 Alvie Miller, Lorain, Ohio
1921	17 Sep	Johnny Kilbane ko 7 Danny Frush, Cleveland
1923	2 June	Eugene Criqui ko 6 Johnny Kilbane, New York
1923	26 July	Johnny Dundee pts 15 Eugene Criqui, New York
1925	2 Jan	Louis Kid Kaplan ko 9 Danny Kramer, New York
1925	27 Aug	Louis Kid Kaplan dr 15 Babe Herman, Waterbury, Conn.
1925	13 Dec	Louis Kid Kaplan pts 15 Babe Herman, New York
1927	19 Sep	Benny Bass pts 10 Red Chapman, Philadelphia
1928	10 Feb	Tony Canzoneri pts 15 Benny Bass, New York
1928	28 Sep	Andre Routis pts 15 Tony Canzoneri, New York
1929	27 May	Andre Routis ko 3 Buster Brown, Baltimore
1929	23 Sep	Battling Battalino pts 15 Andre Routis, Hartford, Conn.
1930	12 Dec	Battling Battalino pts 15 Kid Chocolate, New York
1931	22 May	Battling Battalino pts 15 Fidel La Barba, New York
1931	1 July	Battling Battalino pts 10 Irish Bobby Brady, Jersey City
1931	23 July	Battling Battalino pts 10 Freddie Miller, Cincinnati
1931	4 Nov	Battling Battalino pts 10 Earl Mastro, Chicago
1932	26 May	Tommy Paul pts 15 Johnny Pena, Detroit (NBA only)
1933	13 Jan	Freddie Miller pts 10 Tommy Paul, Chicago (NBA only)
1934	21 Sep	Freddie Miller pts 15 Nel Tarleton, Liverpool, Eng.
1935	17 Feb	Freddie Miller ko 1 Jose Girones, Barcelona
1935	12 June	Freddie Miller pts 15 Nel Tarleton, Liverpool, Eng.
1935	22 Oct	Freddie Miller pts 15 Vernon Cormier, Boston
1936	18 Feb	Freddie Miller pts 12 Johnny Pena, Seattle
1936	2 Mar	Freddie Miller pts 15 Petey Sarron, Coral Gables
1936	11 May	Petey Sarron pts 15 Freddie Miller, Washington, DC
1936	22 July	Petey Sarron pts 15 Baby Manuel, Dallas
1937	4 Sep	Petey Sarron pts 12 Freddie Miller, Johannesburg
1937	29 Oct	Henry Armstrong ko 6 Petey Sarron, New York
1938	17 Oct	Joey Archibald pts 15 Mike Belloise, New York (NY only)
1938	29 Dec	Leo Rodak pts 10 Leone Efrati, Chicago (NBA only)
1939	18 Apl	Joey Archibald pts 15 Leo Rodak, Providence, RI
1939	28 Sep	Joey Archibald pts 15 Harry Jeffra, Washington, DC
1940	20 May	Harry Jeffra pts 15 Joey Archibald, Baltimore
1940	29 July	Harry Jeffra pts 15 Spider Armstrong, Baltimore
1941	12 May	Joey Archibald pts 15 Harry Jeffra, Washington, DC
1941	11 Sep	Chalky Wright ko 11 Joey Archibald, Washington, DC
1942	19 June	Chalky Wright ko 10 Harry Jeffra, Baltimore
1942	25 Sep	Chalky Wright pts 15 Lulu Constantine, New York
1942	20 Nov	Willie Pep pts 15 Chalky Wright, New York
1943	8 June	Willie Pep pts 15 Sal Bartolo, Boston
1944	29 Sep	Willie Pep Pts 15 Chalky Wright, New York
1945	19 Feb	Willie Pep pts 15 Phil Terranova, New York
1946	7 June	Willie Pep ko 12 Sal Bartolo, New York
1947	22 Aug	Willie Pep ko 12 Jock Leslie, Flint
1948	24 Feb	Willie Pep ko 10 Humberto Sierra, Miami
1948	29 Oct	Sandy Saddler ko 4 Willie Pep, New York
1949	11 Feb	Willie Pep pts 15 Sandy Saddler, New York
1949	20 Sep	Willie Pep ko 7 Eddie Compo, Waterbury, Conn.
1950	16 Jan	Willie Pep ko 5 Charley Riley, St Louis
1950	17 Mar	Willie Pep pts 15 Ray Famechon, New York
1950	8 Sep	Sandy Saddler ret 8 Willie Pep, New York
1951	26 Sep	Sandy Saddler ret 9 Willie Pep, New york
1955	25 Feb	Sandy Saddler pts 15 Teddy Davis, New York
1956	18 Jan	Sandy Saddler rsf 13 Flash Elorde, San Francisco
1957	24 June	Hogan Kid Bassey rsf 10 Charif Hamia, Paris
1958	1 Apl	Hogan Kid Bassey ko 3 Ricardo Moreno, Los Angeles
1959	18 Mar	Davey Moore ret 13 Hogan Kid Bassey, Los Angeles
1959	19 Aug	Davey Moore ret 10 Hogan Kid Bassey, Los Angeles
1960	29 Aug	Davey Moore pts 15 Kazuo Takayama, Tokyo

Featherweight champion, Sandy
Saddler, 1954

1961	8 Apl	Davey Moore ko 1 Danny Valdez, Los Angeles
1961	13 Nov	Davey Moore pts 15 Kazuo Takayama, Tokyo
1962	17 Aug	Davey Moore rsf 2 Olli Maki, Helsinki
1963	21 Mar	Sugar Ramos ret 10 Davey Moore, Los Angeles
1963	13 July	Sugar Ramos pts 15 Joe Rafiu King, Mexico City
1964	28 Feb	Sugar Ramos ret 6 Mitsunori Saki, Tokyo
1964	9 May	Sugar Ramos pts 15 Floyd Robertson, Accra, Gha.
1964	26 Sep	Vicente Saldivar rsf 11 Sugar Ramos, Mexico City
1964	6 Dec	Vicente Saldivar rsf 11 Delfino Rosales, Leon, Mex.
1965	7 May	Vicente Saldivar ko 15 Raul Rojas, Los Angeles
1965	7 Sep	Vicente Saldivar pts 15 Howard Winstone, London, Eng.
1966	12 Feb	Vicente Saldivar ko 2 Floyd Robertson, Mexico City
1966	7 Aug	Vicente Saldivar pts 15 Mitsunori Seki, Mexico City
1967	29 Jan	Vicente Saldivar rsf 7 Mitsunori Seki, Mexico City
1967	15 June	Vicente Saldivar pts 15 Howard Winstone, Mexico City
1967	14 Oct	Vicente Saldivar ret 12 Howard Winstone, Mexico City
1968	23 Jan	Howard Winstone rsf 9 Mitsunori Seki, London, Eng. (not WBA)
1968	24 July	Jose Legra rsf 5 Howard Winstone, Porthcawl, Wales (not WBA)
1969	21 Jan	Johnny Famechon pts 15 Jose Legra, London, Eng.
1969	28 July	Johnny Famechon pts 15 Fighting Harada, Sydney
1970	6 Jan	Johnny Famechon ko 14 Fighting Harada, Tokyo
1970	9 May	Vicente Saldivar pts 15 Johnny Famechon, Rome
1970	11 Dec	Kuniaki Shibata rsf 12 Vicente Saldivar, Tijuana
1971	3 June	Kuniaki Shibata ko 1 Raul Cruz, Tokyo (WBC only)
1971	10 Nov	Kuniaki Shibata dr 15 Ernesto Marcel, Matsuyama (WBC only)
1972	5 Feb	Antonio Gomez ko 7 Raul Martinez, Maracay (WBA only)
1972	19 May	Clemente Sanchez ko 3 Kuniaki Shibata, Tokyo (WBC only)
1972	19 Aug	Ernesto Marcel pts 15 Antonio Gomez, Maracay, Ven. (WBA)
1972	2 Dec	Ernesto Marcel rsf 6 Enrique Garcia, Panama City (WBA only)
1972	16 Dec	Jose Legra rsf 10 Clemente Sanchez, Monterrey (WBC only)
1973	5 May	Eder Jofre pts 15 Jose Legra, Brasilia (WBC)
1973	14 July	Ernesto Marcel ret 11 Antonio Gomez, Panama City (WBA only)
1973	8 Sep	Ernesto Marcel ko 9 Shigemitsu Nemoto, Panama City (WBA only)
1973	21 Oct	Eder Jofre ko 4 Vicente Saldivar, Salvador (WBC only)
1974	16 Feb	Ernesto Marcel pts 15 Alexis Arguello, Panama City (WBA only)
1974	9 July	Ruben Olivares rsf 7 Zensuke Utagawa, Los Angeles (WBA only)
1974	7 Sep	Bobby Chacon rsf 9 Alfredo Marcano, Los Angeles (WBC only)
1974	23 Nov	Alexis Arguello ko 13 Ruben Olivares, Los Angeles (WBA only)
1975	1 Mar	Bobby Chacon ko 2 Jesus Estrada, Los Angeles (WBC only)
1975	15 Mar	Alexis Arguello rsf 8 Leonel Hernandez, Caracas (WBA only)
1975	31 May	Alexis Arguello rsf 2 Rigoberto Riasco, Granada (WBA)
1975	20 June	Ruben Olivares rsf 2 Bobby Chacon, Los Angeles (WBC)
1975	20 Sep	David Kotey pts 15 Ruben Olivares, Los Angeles (WBC)
1975	12 Oct	Alexis Arguello ko 5 Royal Kobayashi, Tokio (WBA)
1976	6 Mar	David Kotey rsf 12 Flipper Uehara, Accra (WBC)
1976	19 June	Alexis Arguello ko 3 Salvador Torres, Los Angeles (WBA)
1976	16 July	David Kotey rsf 3 Shig Fukuyama, Tokio (WBC)
1976	6 Nov	Danny Lopez pts 15 David Kotey, Accra (WBC)
1977	15 Jan	Rafael Ortega pts 15 Francisco Coronado, Panama City (WBA)
1977	29 May	Rafael Ortega pts 15 Flipper Uehara, Okinawa (WBA)
1977	13 Sep	Danny Lopez rsf 7 Jose Torres, Los Angeles (WBC)
1977	17 Dec	Cecilio Lastra pts 15 Rafael Ortega, Torrelavega (WBA)
1978	15 Feb	Danny Lopez rsf 6 David Kotey, Las Vegas (WBC)
1978	16 Apl	Eusebio Pedroza rsf 13 Cecilio Lastra, Panama City (WBA)
1978	23 Apl	Danny Lopez rsf 6 Jose de Paula, Los Angeles (WBC)
1978	2 July	Eusebio Pedroza rsf 12 Ernesto Herrera, Panama City (WBA)
1978	15 Sep	Danny Lopez ko 2 Juan Malvarez, New Orleans (WBC)
1978	21 Oct	Danny Lopez dis 4 Fel Clemente, Pessaro (WBC)

1978	27 Nov	Eusebio Pedroza pts 15 Enrique Solis, San Juan (WBA)
1979	9 Jan	Eusebio Pedroza ret 13 Royal Kobayashi, Tokio (WBA)
1979	10 Mar	Danny Lopez ko 2 Roberto Castanon, Salt Lake City (WBC)
1979	8 Apl	Eusebio Pedroza rsf 11 Hector Carrasquilla, Panama City (WBA)
1979	17 June	Danny Lopez ko 15 Mike Ayala, San Antonio (WBC)
1979	21 July	Eusebio Pedroza ret 12 Ruben Olivares, Houston (WBA)
1979	25 Sep	Danny Lopez rsf 3 Jose Caba, Los Angeles (WBC)
1979	17 Nov	Eusebio Pedroza rsf 11 John Aba, Port Moresby (WBA)
1980	22 Jan	Eusebio Pedroza pts 15 Shig Nemoto, Tokio (WBA)
1980	2 Feb	Salvador Sanchez rsf 13 Danny Lopez, Pheonix (WBC)
1980	29 Mar	Eusebio Pedroza rsf 9 Juan Malvarez, Panama City (WBA)
1980	12 Apl	Salvador Sanchez pts 15 Ruben Castillo, Tucson (WBC)
1980	21 June	Salvador Sanchez rsf 14 Danny Lopez, Las Vegas (WBC)
1980	20 July	Eusebio Pedroza ko 9 Kim Sa Wang, Seoul (WBA)
1980	13 Sep	Salvador Sanchez pts 15 Patrick Ford, San Antonio (WBC)
1980	4 Oct	Eusebio Pedroza pts 15 Rocky Lockridge, Great Gorge (WBA)
1980	13 Dec	Salvador Sanchez pts 15 Juan Laporte, El Paso (WBC)
1981	14 Feb	Eusebio Pedroza ko 13 Patrick Ford, Panama City (WBA)
1981	22 Mar	Salvador Sanchez rsf 10 Roberto Castanon, Las Vegas (WBC)
1981	1 Aug	Eusebio Pedroza ko 7 Carlos Pinango, Caracas (WBA)
1981	21 Aug	Salvador Sanchez rsf 8 Wilfredo Gomez, Las Vegas (WBC)
1981	5 Dec	Eusebio Pedroza ko 5 Bashew Sibaca, Panama City (WBA)
1981	12 Dec	Salvador Sanchez pts 15 Pat Cowdell, Houston (WBC)
1982	24 Jan	Eusebio Pedroza pts 15 Juan Laporte, Atlantic City (WBA)

Junior-lightweight

1921	18 Nov	Johnny Dundee pts 15 Jack Sharkey, New York
1922	8 July	Johnny Dundee dis 5 George Chaney, New York
1923	2 Feb	Johnny Dundee pts 15 Elino Flores, New York
1923	30 May	Jack Bernstein pts 15 Johnny Dundee, New York
1923	17 Dec	Johnny Dundee pts 15 Jack Bernstein, New York
1924	20 June	Kid Sullivan pts 10 Johnny Dundee, Brooklyn
1924	15 Oct	Kid Sullivan ko 5 Mike Ballerino, New York
1925	1 Apl	Mike Ballerino pts 10 Kid Sullivan, Philadelphia
1925	2 Dec	Tod Morgan ko 10 Mike Ballerino, Los Angeles
1926	19 Nov	Tod Morgan pts 15 Carl Duana, New York
1928	24 May	Tod Morgan pts 15 Eddie Cannonball Martin, New York
1928	18 July	Tod Morgan pts 15 Eddie Cannonball Martin, New York
1929	5 Apl	Tod Morgan pts 10 Santiago Zorrilla, Los Angeles
1929	20 May	Tod Morgan pts 10 Baby Sal Sorio, Los Angeles
1929	19 Dec	Benny Bass ko 2 Tod Morgan, New York
1931	15 July	Kid Chocolate rsf 7 Benny Bass, Philadelphia
1933	26 Dec	Frankie Klick ko 7 Kid Chocolate, Philadelphia
1959	20 July	Harold Gomes pts 15 Paul Jorgensen, Providence, R.I. (NBA only)
1960	16 Mar	Flash Elorde rsf 7 Harold Gomes, Manila
1960	17 Aug	Flash Elorde ko 1 Harold Gomes, San Francisco
1961	19 Mar	Flash Elorde pts 15 Joey Lopes, Manila
1961	16 Dec	Flash Elorde ko 1 Sergio Caprari, Manila
1962	23 June	Flash Elorde pts 15 Auburn Copeland, Manila
1963	16 Feb	Flash Elorde pts 15 Johnny Bizzarro, Manila
1963	16 Nov	Flash Elorde dis 11 Love Allotey, Manila
1964	27 July	Flash Elorde rsf 12 Teruo Kosaka, Tokyo
1965	5 June	Flash Elorde ko 15 Taruo Kosaka, Manila
1965	4 Dec	Flash Elorde pts 15 Suh Kang II, Manila
1966	22 Oct	Flash Elorde pts 15 Vicente Derado, Manila
1967	15 June	Yoshio Numata pts 15 Flash Elorde, Tokyo
1967	14 Dec	Hiroshi Kobayashi ko 12 Yoshio Numata, Tokyo
1968	30 Mar	Hiroshi Kobayashi dr 15 Rena Barrientos, Tokyo
1968	6 Oct	Hiroshi Kobayashi pts 15 Jaime Valladares, Tokyo
1969	6 Apl	Hiroshi Kobayashi pts 15 Antonio Amaya, Tokyo
1969	9 Nov	Hiroshi Kobayashi pts 15 Carlos Canete, Tokyo

World lightweight championship,
26 June 1972: Ken Buchanan of
Scotland loses to Roberto
Duran of Panama

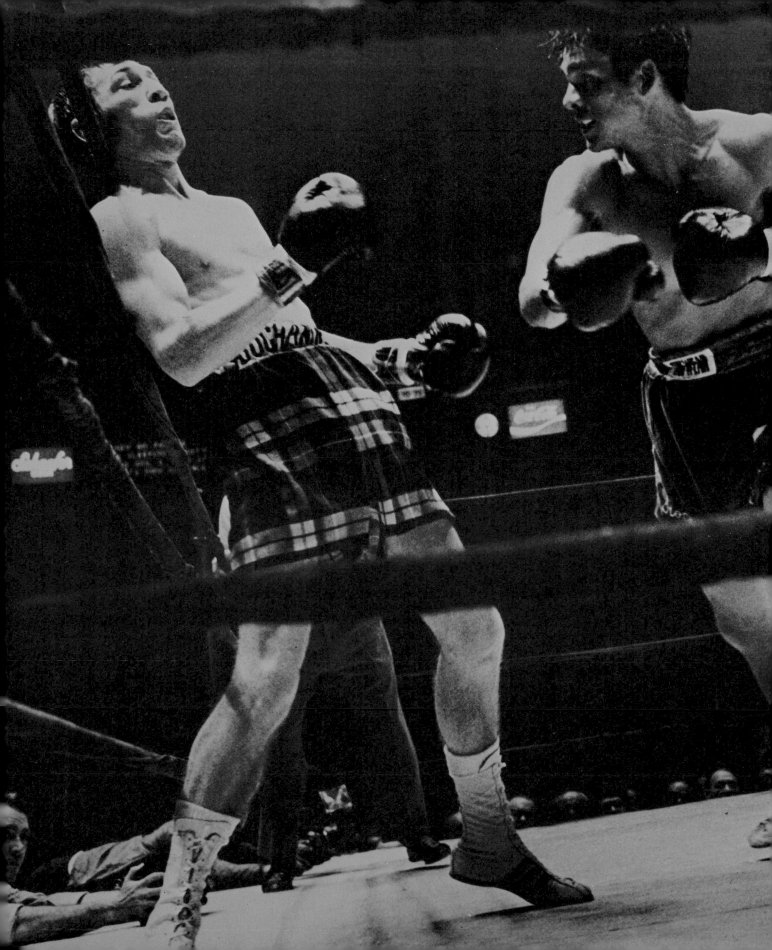

1970 24 Aug	Hiroshi Kobayashi pts 15 Antonio Amaya, Tokyo	
1971 4 Mar	Hiroshi Kobayashi pts 15 Ricardo Arredondo, Tokyo	
1971 29 July	Alfredo Marcano rst Hiroshi Kobayashi, Aomori	
1971 7 Nov	Alfredo Marcano rsf 4 Kenji Iwata, Caracas	
1972 29 Jan	Ricardo Arredondo pts 15 Jose Isaac Marin, Costa Rica (WBC only)	
1972 22 Apl	Ricardo Arredondo ko 5 William Martinez, Mexico City (WBC only)	
1972 25 Apl	Ben Villaflor pts 15 Alfredo Marcano, Honolulu (WBA only)	
1972 5 Sep	Ben Villaflor dr 15 Victor Echegarry, Honolulu (WBA only)	
1972 15 Sep	Ricardo Arredondo ko 12 Susumu Okabe, Tokyo (WBC only)	
1973 6 Mar	Ricardo Arredondo pts 15 Apollo Yoshio, Fukuoka (WBC only)	
1973 12 Mar	Kuniaki Shibata pts 15 Ben Villaflor, Honolulu (WBA only)	
1973 19 June	Kuniaki Shibata pts 15 Victor Echegarry, Tokyo (WBA only)	
1973 1 Sep	Ricardo Arredondo rsf 6 Morito Kashiwaba, Tokyo (WBC only)	
1973 17 Oct	Ben Villaflor ko 1 Kuniaki Shibata, Honolulu (WBA only)	
1974 28 Feb	Kuniaki Shibata pts 15 Ricardo Arredondo, Tokyo (WBC only)	
1974 14 Mar	Ben Villaflor dr 15 Apollo Yoshio, Toyama (WBA only)	
1974 27 June	Kuniaki Shibata pts 15 Antonio Amaya, Tokyo (WBC only)	
1974 24 Aug	Ben Villaflor rsf 2 Yasu Uehara, Honolulu (WBA only)	
1974 3 Oct	Kuniaki Shibata rsf 15 Ramiro Bolanos, Tokyo (WBC only)	
1975 14 Mar	Ben Villaflor pts 15 Hyun Chi Kim, Manila (WBA only)	
1975 5 July	Alfredo Escalera ko 2 Kuniaki Shibata, Nakamachi (WBC)	
1975 20 Sep	Alfredo Escalera dr 15 Leonel Hernandez, Caracas (WBC)	
1975 12 Dec	Alfredo Escalera rsf 9 Sven-Erik Paulsen, Oslo (WBC)	
1976 12 Jan	Ben Villaflor rsf 13 Morito Kashiwaba, Tokio (WBA)	
1976 20 Feb	Alfredo Escalera rsf 13 Jose Fernandez, San Juan (WBC)	
1976 1 Apl	Alfredo Escalera no-dec 6 Buzzsaw Yamabe, Nara (WBC)	
1976 13 Apl	Ben Villaflor dr 15 Sam Serrano, Honolulu (WBA)	
1976 1 July	Alfredo Escalera pts 15 Buzzsaw Yamabe, Ashihara (WBC)	
1976 18 Sep	Alfredo Escalera ret 12 Ray Lunny, San Juan (WBC)	
1976 16 Oct	Sam Serrano pts 15 Ben Villaflor, San Juan (WBA)	
1976 30 Nov	Alfredo Escalera pts 15 Tyrone Everett, Philadelphia (WBC)	
1977 15 Jan	Sam Serrano ko 11 Alberto Herrera, Guayaquil (WBA)	
1977 17 Mar	Alfredo Escalera rsf 6 Ronnie McGarvey, San Juan (WBC)	
1977 16 May	Alfredo Escalera ko 8 Carlos Becceril, Landover (WBC)	
1977 26 June	Sam Serrano pts 15 Leonel Hernandez, Puerto de la Cruz (WBA)	
1977 27 Aug	Sam Serrano pts 15 Apollo Yoshio, San Juan (WBA)	
1977 10 Sep	Alfredo Escalera pts 15 Sigfrido Rodriguez, San Juan (WBC)	
1977 19 Nov	Sam Serrano rsf 10 Tae Ho Kim, San Juan (WBA)	
1978 28 Jan	Alexis Arguello rsf 13 Alfredo Escalera, San Juan (WBC)	
1978 18 Feb	Sam Serrano pts 15 Mario Martinez, San Juan (WBA)	
1978 29 Apl	Alexis Arguello rsf 5 Rey Tam, Los Angeles (WBC)	
1978 3 June	Alexis Arguello ko 1 Diego Alcala, San Juan (WBC)	
1978 8 July	Sam Serrano rsf 9 Young Ho Oh, San Juan (WBA)	
1978 10 Nov	Alexis Arguello pts 15 Arturo Leon, Las Vegas (WBC)	
1978 29 Nov	Sam Serrano pts 15 Takeo Maruki, Nagoya (WBA)	
1979 3 Feb	Alexis Arguello ko 13 Alfredo Escalera, Rimini (WBC)	
1979 18 Feb	Sam Serrano pts 15 Julio Valdez, San Juan (WBA)	
1979 15 Apl	Sam Serrano rsf 8 Ngosana Mgxaji, Cape Town (WBA)	
1979 8 July	Alexis Arguello rsf 11 Rafael Limon, New York (WBC)	
1979 16 Nov	Alexis Arguello ret 7 Bobby Chacon, Los Angeles (WBC)	
1980 20 Jan	Alexis Arguello rsf 11 Ruben Castillo, Tucson (WBC)	
1980 3 Apl	Sam Serrano rsf 13 Kiyoshi Kazama, Nara (WBA)	
1980 27 Apl	Alexis Arguello rsf 4 Rolanda Navarette, San Juan (WBC)	
1980 2 Aug	Flipper Uehara ko 6 Sam Serrano, Detroit (WBA)	
1980 20 Nov	Flipper Uehara pts 15 Leonel Hernandez, Tokio (WBA)	
1980 11 Dec	Rafael Limon rsf 15 Idelfonso Bethelmi, Los Angeles (WBC)	
1981 8 Mar	Cornelius Boza-Edwards pts 15 Rafael Limon, Stockton (WBC)	
1981 9 Apl	Sam Serrano pts 15 Flipper Uehara, Wakayama (WBA)	
1981 30 May	Cornelius Boza-Edwards ret 15 Bobby Chacon, Las Vegas (WBC)	
1981 29 Aug	Rolando Navarette ko 5 Cornelius Boza-Edwards, Viareggio (WBC)	
1981 10 Dec	Sam Serrano rsf 12 Hikaru Tomonari, San Juan (WBA)	
1982 16 Jan	Rolando Navarette ko 11 Choi Chung-Il, Manila (WBC)	

Lightweight

1887 16 Nov	Jack McAuliffe dr 74 Jem Carney, Revere, Mass.	
1896 1 June	George Kid Lavigne ko 17 Dick Burge, London, Eng.	
1896 27 Oct	George Kid Lavigne ko 24 Jack Everhardt, New York	
1897 8 Feb	George Kid Lavigne pts 25 Kid McPartland, New York	
1897 28 Apl	George Kid Lavigne ko 11 Eddie Connolly, New York	
1897 29 Oct	George Kid Lavigne pts 12 Joe Walcott, San Francisco	
1898 17 Mar	George Kid Lavigne dr 20 Jack Daly, Cleveland	
1898 28 Sep	George Kid Lavigne dr 20 Frank Erne, Coney Island, NY	
1898 25 Nov	George Kid Lavigne pts 20 Tom Tracey, San Francisco	
1899 3 July	Frank Erne pts 20 George Kid Lavigne, Buffalo, NY	
1899 4 Dec	Frank Erne dr 25 Jack O'Brien, Coney Island	
1900 23 Mar	Frank Erne ret 12 Joe Gans, New York	
1902 12 May	Joe Gans ko 1 Frank Erne, Fort Erie	
1902 17 Sep	Joe Gans ko 5 Gus Gardner, Baltimore	
1903 11 Mar	Joe Gans ko 11 Steve Crosby, Hot Springs	
1904 28 Mar	Joe Gans pts 10 Gus Gardner, Saginaw, Mich.	
1904 31 Oct	Joe Gans dis 5 Jimmy Britt, San Francisco	
1906 3 Sep	Joe Gans dis 42 Battling Nelson, Goldfield, Nev.	
1907 9 Sep	Joe Gans ko 6 Jimmy Britt, San Francisco	
1907 27 Sep	Joe Gans pts 20 George Memsie, Los Angeles	
1908 14 May	Joe Gans ko 11 Rudy Unholz, San Francisco	
1908 4 July	Battling Nelson ko 17 Joe Gans, San Francisco	
1908 9 Sep	Battling Nelson ko 21 Joe Gans, Colma, Cal.	
1909 29 May	Battling Nelson ko 23 Dick Hyland, Colma	
1909 22 June	Battling Nelson ko 5 Jack Clifford, Oklahoma City	
1910 22 Feb	Ad Wolgast ko 40 Battling Nelson, Port Richmond	
1912 4 July	Ad Wolgast ko 13 Joe Rivers, Vernon, Cal.	
1912 28 Nov	Willie Ritchie dis 16 Ad Wolgast, Daly City, Cal.	
1913 4 July	Willie Ritchie ko 11 Joe Rivers, San Francisco	
1914 17 Apl	Willie Ritchie pts 20 Tommy Murphy, San Francisco	
1914 7 July	Freddie Welsh pts 20 Willie Ritchie, London, Eng.	
1916 4 Sep	Freddie Welsh pts 20 Charley White, Colorado Springs	
1917 28 May	Benny Leonard ko 9 Freddie Welsh, New York	
1917 25 July	Benny Leonard ko 3 Johnny Kilbane, Philadelphia	
1920 5 July	Benny Leonard ko 9 Charley White, Benton Harbour, Mich.	
1920 26 Nov	Benny Leonard ko 14 Joe Welling, New York	
1921 14 Jan	Benny Leonard ko 6 Richie Mitchell, New York	
1922 10 Feb	Benny Leonard pts 15 Rocky Kansas, New York	
1922 4 July	Benny Leonard rsf 8 Rocky Kansas, Michigan City	
1923 24 July	Benny Leonard pts 15 Lew Tendler, New York	
1925 13 July	Jimmy Goodrich ko 2 Stanislaus Loayza, Long Island City	
1925 7 Dec	Rocky Kansas pts 15 Jimmy Goodrich, Buffalo, NY	
1926 3 July	Sammy Mandell pts 10 Rocky Kansas, Chicago	
1928 21 May	Sammy Mandell pts 15 Jimmy McLarnin, New York	
1929 2 Aug	Sammy Mandell pts 10 Tony Canzoneri, Chicago	
1930 17 July	Al Singer ko 1 Sammy Mandell, New York	
1930 14 Nov	Tony Canzoneri ko 1 Al Singer, New York	
1931 10 Sep	Tony Canzoneri pts 15 Jack Kid Berg, New York	
1932 4 Nov	Tony Canzoneri pts 15 Billy Petrolle, New York	
1933 23 June	Barney Ross pts 10 Tony Canzoneri, Chicago	
1933 12 Sep	Barney Ross pts 15 Tony Canzoneri, New York	
1935 10 May	Tony Canzoneri pts 15 Lou Ambers, New York	
1935 4 Oct	Tony Canzoneri pts 15 Al Roth, New York	
1936 3 Sep	Lou Ambers pts 15 Tony Canzoneri, New York	
1937 7 May	Lou Ambers pts 15 Tony Canzoneri, New York	
1937 23 Sep	Lou Ambers pts 15 Pedro Montanez, New York	
1938 17 Aug	Henry Armstrong pts 15 Lou Ambers, New York	
1939 22 Aug	Lou Ambers pts 15 Henry Armstrong, New York	
1940 10 May	Lew Jenkins rsf 3 Lou Ambers, New York	
1940 22 Nov	Lew Jenkins ko 2 Pete Lello, New York	
1941 19 Dec	Sammy Angott pts 15 Lew Jenkins, New York	
1942 15 May	Sammy Angott pts 15 Allie Stolz, New York	
1942 18 Dec	Beau Jack ko 3 Tippy Larkin, New York (NY only)	
1943 27 Oct	Sammy Angott pts 15 Slugger White, Hollywood (NBA only)	
1944 3 Mar	Bob Montgomery pts 15 Beau Jack, New York (NY only)	

1945 18 Apr	Ike Williams ko 2 Juan Zarita, Mexico City (NBA only)
1947 4 Aug	Ike Williams ko 6 Bob Montgomery, Philadelphia
1948 25 May	Ike Williams pts 15 Enrique Bolanos, Los Angeles
1948 12 July	Ike Williams ko 6 Beau Jack, Philadelphia
1948 23 Sep	Ike Williams ko 10 Jesse Flores, New York
1949 21 July	Ike Williams ko 4 Enrique Bolanos, Los Angeles
1949 5 Dec	Ike Williams pts 15 Freddie Dawson, Philadelphia
1951 25 May	James Carter rsf 14 Ike Williams, New York
1951 14 Nov	James Carter pts 15 Art Aragon, Los Angeles
1952 1 Apl	James Carter pts 15 Lauro Salas, Los Angeles
1952 14 May	Lauro Salas pts 15 James Carter, Los Angeles
1952 15 Oct	James Carter pts 15 Lauro Salas, Chicago
1953 24 Apl	James Carter rsf 4 Tommy Collins, Boston
1953 12 June	James Carter rsf 13 George Araujo, New York
1953 11 Nov	James Carter ko 5 Armand Savoie, Montreal
1954 5 Mar	Paddy de Marco pts 15 James Carter, New York
1954 17 Nov	James Carter rsf 15 Paddy de Marco, San Francisco
1955 29 June	Wallace Bud Smith pts 15 James Carter, Boston
1955 19 Oct	Wallace Bud Smith pts 15 James Carter, Cincinnati
1956 24 Aug	Joe Brown pts 15 Wallace Bud Smith, New Orleans
1957 13 Feb	Joe Brown rsf 10 Wallace Bud Smith, Miami Beach
1957 19 June	Joe Brown rsf 15 Orlando Zuluata, Denver
1957 4 Dec	Joe Brown rsf 11 Joey Lopes, Chicago
1958 7 May	Joe Brown rsf 8 Ralph Dupas, Houston
1958 23 July	Joe Brown pts 15 Kenny Lane, Houston
1959 11 Feb	Joe Brown pts 15 Johnny Busso, Houston
1959 3 June	Joe Brown rsf 8 Paolo Rosi, Washington, DC
1959 2 Dec	Joe Brown rsf 5 Dave Charnley, Houston
1960 28 Oct	Joe Brown pts 15 Cisco Andrade, Los Angeles
1961 18 Apl	Joe Brown pts 15 Dave Charnley, London, Eng.
1961 28 Oct	Joe Brown pts 15 Bert Somodio, Quezon City, Manila
1962 21 Apl	Carlos Ortiz pts 15 Joe Brown, Las Vegas
1962 3 Dec	Carlos Ortiz ko 5 Taruo Kosaka, Tokyo
1962 7 Apl	Carlos Ortiz rsf 13 Doug Vaillant, San Juan
1964 15 Feb	Carlos Ortiz rsf 14 Flash Elorde, Manila
1964 11 Apl	Carlos Ortiz pts 15 Kenny Lane, San Juan
1965 10 Apl	Ismael Laguna pts 15 Carlos Ortiz, Panama City
1965 13 Nov	Carlos Ortiz pts 15 Ismael Laguna, San Juan
1966 20 June	Carlos Ortiz rsf 12 Johnny Bizzarro, Pittsburgh
1966 22 Oct	Carlos Ortiz rsf 5 Sugar Ramos, Mexico City
1966 28 Nov	Carlos Ortiz ko 14 Flash Elorde, New York
1967 1 July	Carlos Ortiz rsf 4 Sugar Ramos, San Juan
1967 16 Aug	Carlos Ortiz pts 15 Ismael Laguna, New York
1968 29 June	Carlos Teo Cruz pts 15 Carlos Ortiz, Santo Domingo, Dominica
1968 27 Sep	Carlos Teo Cruz pts 15 Mando Ramos, Los Angeles
1969 18 Feb	Mando Ramos rsf 11 Carlos Teo Cruz, Los Angeles
1969 4 Oct	Mando Ramos ko 6 Yoshio Numata, Los Angeles
1970 3 Mar	Ismael Laguna ret 9 Mando Ramos, Los Angeles
1970 7 June	Ismael Laguna rsf 13 Ishimatsu Suzuki, Panama City
1970 26 Sep	Ken Buchanan pts 15 Ismael Laguna, San Juan (WBA only)
1971 12 Feb	Ken Buchanan pts 15 Ruben Navarro, Los Angeles
1971 13 Sep	Ken Buchanan pts 15 Ismael Laguna, New York (WBA only)
1972 26 June	Roberto Duran rsf 13 Ken Buchanan, New York (WBA only)
1972 28 June	Mando Ramos pts 15 Pedro Carrasco, Madrid (WBC only)
1972 15 Sep	Chango Carmona rsf 8 Mando Ramos, Los Angeles (WBC only)
1972 10 Nov	Rodolfo Gonzales ret 12 Chango Carmona, Los Angeles (WBC only)
1973 20 Jan	Roberto Duran ko 5 Jimmy Robertson, Panama City (WBA only)
1973 17 Mar	Rodolfo Gonzales rsf 9 Ruben Navarro, Los Angeles (WBC only)
1973 8 Sep	Roberto Duran rsf 10 Ishimatsu Suzuki, Panama City (WBA only)
1973 27 Oct	Rodolfo Gonzales rsf 10 Antonio Puddu, Los Angeles (WBC

1974 16 Mar	Roberto Duran ko 11 Esteban de Jesus, Panama City (WBA only)
1974 11 Apl	Ishimatsu Suzuki ko 8 Rodolfo Gonzales, Tokyo (WBC only)
1974 12 Sep	Ishimatsu Suzuki dr 15 Arturo Pineda, Nagoya (WBC only)
1974 28 Nov	Ishimatsu Suzuki ko Rodolfo Gonzales, Osaka (WBC only)
1974 21 Dec	Roberto Duran rsf 1 Masataka Takayama, Costa Rica (WBA only)
1975 27 Feb	Ishimatsu Suzuki pts 15 Ken Buchanan, Tokyo (WBC only)
1975 1 Mar	Roberto Duran ko 14 Ray Lampkin, Panama City (WBA only)
1975 5 June	Ishimatsu Suzuki pts 15 Arturo Pineda, Osaka (WBC)
1975 4 Dec	Ishimatsu Suzuki ko 14 Alvaro Rojas, Tokio (WBC)
1975 20 Dec	Roberto Duran ko 15 Leoncio Ortiz, San Juan (WBA)
1976 8 May	Esteban de Jesus pts 15 Ishimatsu Suzuki, San Juan (WBC)
1976 23 May	Roberto Duran ko 14 Lou Bizzaro, Erie (WBA)
1976 11 Sep	Esteban de Jesus ko 7 Hector Julio Medina, Bayamon (WBC)
1976 15 Oct	Roberto Duran ko 1 Alvaro Rojas, Hollywood, Fla (WBA)
1977 29 Jan	Roberto Duran ko 13 Vilomar Fernandez, Miami Beach (WBA)
1977 12 Feb	Esteban de Jesus rsf 6 Buzzsaw Yamabe, San Juan (WBC)
1977 25 June	Esteban de Jesus ko 11 Vicente Saldivar, San Juan (WBC)
1977 17 Sep	Roberto Duran pts 15 Edwin Viruet, Philadelphia (WBA)
1978 21 Jan	Roberto Duran ko 12 Esteban de Jesus, Las Vegas
1979 17 Apl	Jim Watt rsf 12 Alfredo Pitalua, Glasgow (WBC)
1979 16 June	Ernesto Espana ko 13 Claude Noel, San Juan (WBA)
1979 4 Aug	Ernesto Espana rsf 9 Johnny Lira, Chicago (WBA)
1979 3 Nov	Jim Watt rsf 9 Roberto Vasquez, Glasgow (WBC)
1980 2 Mar	Hilmer Kenty rsf 9 Ernesto Espana, Detroit (WBA)
1980 14 Mar	Jim Watt rsf 4 Charlie Nash, Glasgow (WBC)
1980 7 June	Jim Watt pts 15 Howard Davis Jnr, Glasgow (WBC)
1980 2 Aug	Hilmer Kenty rsf 9 Young Oh Ho, Detroit (WBA)
1980 20 Sep	Hilmer Kenty rsf 4 Ernesto Espana, San Juan (WBA)
1980 1 Nov	Jim Watt rsf 12 Sean O'Grady, Glasgow (WBC)
1980 8 Nov	Hilmer Kenty pts 15 Vilomar Fernandez, Detroit (WBA)
1981 12 Apl	Sean O'Grady pts 15 Hilmer Kenty, Atlantic City (WBA)
1981 20 June	Alexis Arguello pts 15 Jim Watt, London (WBC)
1981 12 Sep	Claude Noel pts 15 Rodolfo Gonzalez, Atlantic City (WBA)
1981 3 Oct	Alexis Arguello rsf 14 Ray Mancini, Atlantic City (WBC)
1981 21 Nov	Alexis Arguello ko 7 Roberto Elizondo, Las Vegas (WBC)
1981 5 Dec	Arturo Frias ko 8 Claude Noel, Las Vegas (WBA)
1982 30 Jan	Arturo Frias tec dec 9 Ernesto Espana, Los Angeles (WBA)
1982 13 Feb	Alexis Arguello rsf 6 James Busceme, Beaumont (WBC)

Junior-welterweight

1926 21 Sep	Mushy Callahan pts 10 Pinkie Mitchell, Vernon, Cal.
1930 18 Feb	Jack Kid Berg ko 10 Mushy Callahan, London, Eng.
1931 24 Apl	Tony Canzoneri ko 3 Jack Kid Berg, Chicago
1931 13 July	Tony Canzoneri pts 10 Cecil Payne, Los Angeles
1931 29 Oct	Tony Canzoneri pts 10 Phillie Griffin, Newark, NJ
1931 20 Nov	Tony Canzoneri pts 15 Kid Chocolate, New York
1932 18 Jan	Johnny Jadick pts 10 Tony Canzoneri, Philadelphia
1932 18 July	Johnny Jadick pts 10 Tony Canzoneri, Philadelphia
1933 20 Feb	Battling Shaw pts 10 Johnny Jadick, New Orleans
1933 21 May	Tony Canzoneri pts 10 Battling Shaw, New Orleans
1933 23 June	Barney Ross pts 10 Tony Canzoneri, Chicago
1933 17 Nov	Barney Ross pts 10 Sammy Fuller, Chicago
1934 7 Feb	Barney Ross pts 12 Pete Nebo, Kansas City
1934 5 Mar	Barney Ross dr Frankie Klick, San Francisco
1934 10 Dec	Barney Ross pts 12 Bobby Pacho, Cleveland
1935 28 Jan	Barney Ross pts 10 Frankie Klick, Miami
1935 9 Apl	Barney Ross pts 12 Henry Woods, Seattle
1946 29 Apl	Tippy Larkin pts 12 Willie Joyce, Boston
1946 13 Sep	Tippy Larkin pts 12 Willie Joyce, New york
1959 12 June	Carlos Ortiz rsf 2 Kenny Lane, New York
1960 4 Feb	Carlos Ortiz ko 10 Battling Torres, Los Angeles
1960 15 June	Carlos Ortiz pts 15 Duilio Loi, San Francisco
1960 1 Sep	Duilio Loi pts 15 Carlos Ortiz, Milan
1961 10 May	Duilio Loi pts 15 Carlos Ortiz, Milan
1961 21 Oct	Duilio Loi dr 15 Eddie Perkins, Milan

1962 14 Sep	Eddie Perkins pts 15 Duilio Loi, Milan
1962 15 Dec	Duilio Loi pts 15 Eddie Perkins, Milan
1963 15 June	Eddie Perkins pts 15 Roberto Cruz, Manila
1964 4 Jan	Eddie Perkins rsf 13 Yoshinori Takahashi, Tokyo
1964 18 Apl	Eddie Perkins pts 15 Bunny Grant, Kingston, Jam.
1965 18 Jan	Carlos Hernandez pts 15 Eddie Perkins, Caracas
1965 15 May	Carlos Hernandez rsf 4 Mario Rossito, Maracaibo
1965 10 July	Carlos Hernandez ko 3 Percy Hayles, Kingston, Jam.
1966 29 Apl	Sandro Lopopolo pts 15 Carlos Hernandez, Rome
1966 21 Oct	Sandro Lopopolo ret 7 Vicente Rivas, Rome
1967 30 Apl	Paul Fuji ret 2 Sandro Lopopolo, Tokyo
1967 16 Nov	Paul Fuji ko 4 Willie Quatuor, Tokyo (WBA only)
1968 12 Dec	Nicolino Loche ret 9 Paul Fuji, Tokyo (WBA only)
1968 14 Dec	Pedro Adigue pts 15 Adolph Pruitt, Manila (WBC only)
1969 4 May	Nicolino Loche pts 15 Carlos Hernandez, Buenos Aires (WBA only)
1969 12 Oct	Nicolino Loche pts 15 Joao Henrique, Buenos Aires (WBA only)
1970 31 Jan	Bruno Arcari pts 15 Pedro Adigue, Rome (WBC only)
1970 16 May	Nicolino Loche pts 15 Adolph Pruitt, Buenos Aires (WBA only)
1970 10 July	Bruno Arcari dis 6 Rene Roque, Lignano Sabbiadoro (WBC only)
1970 30 Oct	Bruno Arcari ko 3 Raimundo Dias, Genoa (WBC only)
1971 6 Mar	Bruno Arcari pts 15 Joao Henrique, Rome (WBC only)
1971 3 Apl	Nicolino Loche pts 15 Domingo Barrera Corpas, Buenos Aires (WBA only)
1971 26 June	Bruno Arcari rsf 9 Enrique Jana, Palermo (WBC only)
1971 9 Oct	Bruno Arcari ko 10 Domingo Barrera Corpas, Genoa (WBC only)
1971 12 Dec	Nicolino Loche pts 15 Antonio Cervantes, Buenos Aires (WBA only)
1972 10 Mar	Alfonso Frazer pts 15 Nicolino Loche, Panama City (WBA only)
1972 10 June	Bruno Arcari ko 12 Joao Henrique, Genoa (WBC only)
1972 29 Oct	Antonio Cervantes ko 10 Alfonso Frazer, Panama City (WBA only)
1972 2 Dec	Bruno Arcari pts 15 Everaldo Costa Azevedo, Turin (WBC only)
1973 15 Feb	Antonio Cervantes pts 15 Jose Marquez, San Juan, PR (WBA only)
1973 17 Mar	Antonio Cervantes ret 9 Nicolino Loche, Maracay, Ven. (WBA only)
1973 19 May	Antonio Cervantes rsf 5 Alfonso Frazer, Panama City (WBA only)
1973 8 Sep	Antonio Cervantes rsf 5 Carlos Maria Gimenez, Bogota (WBA only)
1973 1 Nov	Bruno Arcari ko 5 Jorgen Hansen, Copenhagen (WBC only)
1973 5 Dec	Antonio Cervantes pts 15 Lion Furuyama, Panama City (WBA only)
1974 16 Feb	Bruno Arcari dis 8 Antonio Ortiz, Turin (WBC only)
1974 2 Mar	Antonio Cervantes ko 6 Chang-Kil Lee, Cartagena (WBA only)
1974 27 July	Antonio Cervantes ko 2 Victor Ortiz, Cartagena (WBA only)
1974 21 Sep	Perrico Fernandez pts 15 Lion Furuyama, Rome (WBC only)
1974 26 Oct	Antonio Cervantes ko 8 Yasuaki Kadota, Tokyo (WBA only)
1975 20 Apl	Perrico Fernandez ko 9 Joao Henrique, Barcelona (WBC)
1975 17 May	Antonio Cervantes pts 15 Esteban de Jesus, Panama City (WBA)
1975 15 July	Saensak Mangsurin ret 8 Perrico Fernandez, Bangkok (WBC)
1975 15 Nov	Antonio Cervantes ret 7 Hector Thompson, Panama City (WBA)
1976 25 Jan	Saensak Mangsurin pts 15 Lion Furuyama, Tokio (WBC)
1976 6 Mar	Wilfredo Benitez pts 15 Antonio Cervantes, San Juan (WBA)
1976 31 May	Wilfredo Benitez pts 15 Emiliano Villa, San Juan (WBA)
1976 30 June	Miguel Velasquez dis 4 Saensak Mangsurin, Madrid (WBC)
1976 16 Oct	Wilfredo Benitez rsf 3 Tony Petronelli, San Juan (WBA)
1976 29 Oct	Saensak Mangsurin rsf 2 Miguel Velasquez, Segovia (WBC)

1977 15 Jan	Saensak Mangsurin rsf 15 Monroe Brooks, Chiang Mai (WBC)
1977 2 Apl	Saensak Mangsurin ko 6 Guts Ishimatsu, Tokio (WBC)
1977 17 June	Saensak Mangsurin pts 15 Perrico Fernandez, Madrid (WBC)
1977 25 June	Antonio Cervantes rsf 5 Carlos Maria Gimenez, Maracaibo (WBA)
1977 20 Aug	Saensak Mangsurin rsf 6 Mike Everett, Roi-et (WBC)
1977 22 Oct	Saensak Mangsurin pts 15 Saoul Mamby, Bangkok (WBC)
1977 5 Nov	Antonio Cervantes pts 15 Adriano Marrero, Maracay (WBA)
1977 30 Dec	Saensak Mangsurin rsf 13 Jo Kimpwani, Chantaburi (WBC)
1978 8 Apl	Saensak Mangsurin ko 13 Francisco Moreno, Hat Yai (WBC)
1978 29 Apl	Antonio Cervantes ko 6 Tongta Kiatvayupak, Udon Thani (WBA)
1978 26 Aug	Antonio Cervantes rsf 9 Norman Sekgapane, Mmabatho (WBA)
1978 30 Dec	Kim Sang-Hyun ko 13 Saensak Mangsurin, Seoul (WBC)
1979 18 Jan	Antonio Cervantes pts 15 Miguel Montilla, New York (WBA)
1979 1 June	Kim Sang-Hyun pts 15 Fitzroy Giusippa, Seoul (WBC)
1979 25 Aug	Antonio Cervantes pts 15 Kim Kwang Min, Seoul (WBA)
1979 3 Oct	Kim Sang-Hyun ko 11 Masahiro Yohia, Tokio (WBC)
1980 23 Feb	Saoul Mamby rsf 14 Kim Sang-Hyun, Seoul (WBC)
1980 29 Mar	Antonio Cervantes rsf 7 Miguel Montilla, Cartagena (WBA)
1980 7 July	Saoul Mamby rsf 13 Esteban de Jesus, Bloomington (WBC)
1980 2 Aug	Aaron Pryor ko 4 Antonio Cervantes, Cincinnati (WBA)
1980 2 Oct	Saoul Mamby rsf 5 Termite Watkins, Las Vegas (WBC)
1980 22 Nov	Aaron Pryor rsf 6 Gaetan Hart, Cincinnati (WBA)
1981 12 June	Saoul Mamby pts 15 Jo Kimpwani, Detroit (WBC)
1981 27 June	Aaron Pryor rsf 2 Lennox Blackmore, Las Vegas (WBA)
1981 29 Aug	Saoul Mamby pts 15 Thomas Americo, Djakarta (WBC)
1981 14 Nov	Aaron Pryor rsf 7 Dujuan Johnson, Cleveland (WBA)
1981 19 Dec	Saoul Mamby pts 15 Obisia Nwankpa, Lagos (WBC)
1982 21 Mar	Aaron Pryor rsf 12 Miguel Montilla, Atlantic City (WBA)

Welterweight

1892 14 Dec	Mysterious Billy Smith ko 14 Danny Needham, San Francisco
1893 17 Apl	Mysterious Billy Smith ko 2 Tom Williams, Coney Island, NY
1894 26 July	Tommy Ryan pts 20 Mysterious Billy Smith, Minneapolis
1895 27 May	Tommy Ryan dr 18 Mysterious Billy Smith, Coney Island
1896 2 Mar	Kid McCoy ko 15 Tommy Ryan, Maspeth, LI
1898 25 Aug	Mysterious Billy Smith pts 25 Matty Matthews, New York
1898 7 Oct	Mysterious Billy Smith pts 25 Charley McKeever, New York
1898 6 Dec	Mysterious Billy Smith pts 20 Joe Walcott, New York
1899 30 June	Mysterious Billy Smith dr 20 Charley McKeever, New York
1900 15 Jan	Rube Ferns dis 21 Mysterious Billy Smith, Buffalo, NY
1900 16 Oct	Matty Matthews pts 15 Rube Ferns, Detroit
1901 29 Apl	Matty Matthews pts 20 Tom Couhig, Louisville, Ky.
1901 24 May	Rube Ferns ko 10 Matty Matthews, Toronto
1901 23 Sep	Rube Ferns ko 9 Frank Erne, Fort Erie
1901 18 Dec	Joe Walcott ko 5 Rube Ferns, Fort Erie
1902 23 June	Joe Walcott pts 15 Tommy West, London, Eng.
1904 30 Apl	Dixie Kid dis 20 Joe Walcott, San Francisco
1904 12 May	Dixie Kid dr 20 Joe Walcott, San Francisco
1906 16 Oct	Honey Mellody pts 15 Joe Walcott, Chelsea, Mass.
1907 23 Apl	Mike Twin Sullivan pts 20 Honey Mellody, Los Angeles
1915 31 Aug	Ted Kid Lewis pts 12 Jack Britton, Boston
1915 27 Sep	Ted Kid Lewis pts 12 Jack Britton, Boston
1916 24 Apl	Jack Britton pts 20 Ted Kid Lewis, New Orleans
1917 25 June	Ted Kid Lewis pts 20 Jack Britton, Dayton, Ohio
1917 4 July	Ted Kid Lewis no-dec. 15 Johnny Griffiths, Akron
1917 31 Aug	Ted Kid Lewis ko 1 Albert Badcud, New York
1918 17 May	Ted Kid Lewis pts 20 Johnny Tillman, Denver
1918 4 July	Ted Kid Lewis no-dec. 20 Johnny Griffiths, Akron
1919 17 Mar	Jack Britton ko 9 Ted Kid Lewis, Canton, Ohio
1919 5 May	Jack Britton no-dec. 10 Johnny Griffiths, Buffalo, NY
1922 17 Feb	Jack Britton dr 15 Dave Shade, New York
1922 26 June	Jack Britton dis 13 Benny Leonard, New York
1922 1 Nov	Mickey Walker pts 15 Jack Britton, New York
1924 2 June	Mickey Walker pts 10 Lew Tendler, Philadelphia
1925 21 Sep	Mickey Walker pts 15 Dave Shade, New York
1926 20 May	Pete Latzo pts 10 Mickey Walker, Scranton, Pa.
1926 29 June	Pete Latzo ko 5 Willie Harmon, Newark, NJ

1926	9 July	Pete Latzo dis 4 George Levine, New York
1927	3 June	Joe Dundee pts 15 Pete Latzo, New York
1929	25 July	Jackie Fields dis 2 Joe Dundee, Detroit
1930	9 May	Young Jack Thompson pts 15 Jackie Fields, Detroit
1930	5 Sep	Tommy Freeman pts 15 Young Jack Thompson, Cleveland
1931	9 Jan	Tommy Freeman pts 10 Pete August, Hot Springs
1931	26 Jan	Tommy Freeman pts 10 Eddie Murdock, Oklahoma City
1931	5 Feb	Tommy Freeman ko 5 Duke Trammel, Memphis
1931	9 Feb	Tommy Freeman ko 5 Al Kober, New Orleans
1931	1 Mar	Tommy Freeman pts 10 Alfredo Gaona, Mexico City
1931	14 Apl	Young Jack Thompson ko 12 Tommy Freeman, Cleveland
1931	23 Oct	Lou Brouillard pts 15 Young Jack Thompson, Boston
1932	28 Jan	Jackie Fields pts 10 Lou Brouillard, Chicago
1933	22 Feb	Young Corbett III pts 10 Jackie Fields, San Francisco
1933	29 May	Jimmy McLarnin ko 1 Young Corbett III, Los Angeles
1934	28 May	Barney Ross pts 15 Jimmy McLarnin, Long Island, NY
1934	17 Sep	Jimmy McLarnin pts 15 Barney Ross, New York
1935	28 May	Barney Ross pts 15 Jimmy McLarnin, New York
1936	27 Nov	Barney Ross pts 15 Izzy Janazzo, New York
1937	23 Sep	Barney Ross pts 15 Ceferino Garcia, New York
1938	31 May	Henry Armstrong pts 15 Barney Ross, Long Island, NY
1938	25 Nov	Henry Armstrong pts 15 Ceferino Garcia, New York
1938	5 Dec	Henry Armstrong ko 3 Al Manfredo, Cleveland
1939	10 Jan	Henry Armstrong pts 10 Baby Arizmendi, Los Angeles
1939	4 Mar	Henry Armstrong ko 4 Bobby Pacho, Havana
1939	16 Mar	Henry Armstrong ko 1 Lew Feldman, St. Louis
1939	31 Mar	Henry Armstrong ko 12 Davey Day, New York
1939	25 May	Henry Armstrong pts 15 Ernie Roderick, London, Eng.
1939	9 Oct	Henry Armstrong ko 4 Al Manfrado, Des Moines
1939	13 Oct	Henry Armstrong ko 2 Howard Scott, Minneapolis
1939	20 Oct	Henry Armstrong ko 3 Ritchie Fontaine, Seattle
1939	24 Oct	Henry Armstrong pts 10 Jimmy Garrison, Los Angeles
1939	30 Oct	Henry Armstrong ko 4 Bobby Pacho, Denver
1939	11 Dec	Henry Armstrong ko 7 Jimmy Garrison, Cleveland
1940	4 Jan	Henry Armstrong ko 5 Joe Ghnouly, St. Louis
1940	24 Jan	Henry Armstrong ko 9 Pedro Montanez, New York
1940	26 Apl	Henry Armstrong ko 7 Paul Junior, Boston
1940	24 May	Henry Armstrong ko 5 Ralph Zanelli, Boston
1940	21 June	Henry Armstrong ko 3 Paul Junior, Portland, Me.
1940	17 July	Henry Armstrong ko 6 Lew Jenkins, New York
1940	23 Sep	Henry Armstrong ko 4 Phil Furr, Washington, DC
1940	4 Oct	Fritzie Zivic pts 15 Henry Armstrong, New York
1941	17 Jan	Fritzie Zivic rsf 12 Henry Armstrong, New York
1941	29 July	Freddie Red Cochrane pts 15 Fritzie Zivic, Newark, NJ
1946	1 Feb	Marty Servo ko 4 Freddie Red Cochrane, New York
1945	20 Dec	Sugar Ray Robinson pts 15 Tommy Bell, New York
1947	24 June	Sugar Ray Robinson ko 8 Jimmy Doyle, Cleveland
1947	19 Dec	Sugar Ray Robinson ko 6 Chuck Taylor, Detroit
1948	28 June	Sugar Ray Robinson pts 15 Bernard Docusen, Chicago
1949	11 July	Sugar Ray Robinson pts 15 Kid Gavilan, Philadelphia
1950	9 Aug	Sugar Ray Robinson pts 15 Charley Fusari, Jersey City
1951	14 Mar	Johnny Bratton pts 15 Charley Fusari, Chicago (NBA only)
1951	18 May	Kid Gavilan pts 15 Johnny Bratton, New York
1951	29 Aug	Kid Gavilan pts 15 Billy Graham, New York
1952	4 Feb	Kid Gavilan pts 15 Bobby Dykes, Miami
1952	7 July	Kid Gavilan rsf 11 Gil Turner, Philadelphia
1952	5 Oct	Kid Gavilan pts 15 Billy Graham, Havana
1953	11 Feb	Kid Gavilan rsf 10 Chuck Davey, Chicago
1953	18 Sep	Kid Gavilan pts 15 Carmen Basilio, Syracuse, NY
1953	13 Nov	Kid Gavilan pts 15 Johnny Bratton, Chicago
1954	20 Oct	Johnny Saxton pts 15 Kid Gavilan, Philadelphia
1955	1 Apl	Tony de Marco rsf 14 Johnny Saxton, Boston
1955	10 June	Carmen Basilio rsf 12 Tony de Marco, Syracuse
1955	30 Nov	Carmen Basilio rsf 12 Tony de Marco, Boston
1956	14 Mar	Johnny Saxton pts 15 Carmen Basilio, Chicago
1956	12 Sep	Carmen Basilio rsf 9 Johnny Saxton, Syracuse

1957	22 Feb	Carmen Basilio ko 2 Johnny Saxton, Cleveland
1958	6 June	Virgil Akins rsf 4 Vince Martinez, St. Louis
1958	5 Dec	Don Jordan pts 15 Virgil Akins, Los Angeles
1959	24 Apl	Don Jordan pts 15 Virgil Akins, St. Louis
1959	10 July	Don Jordan pts 15 Denny Moyer, Portland, Ore.
1960	27 May	Benny Paret pts 15 Don Jordan, Las Vegas
1960	10 Dec	Benny Paret pts 15 Federico Thompson, New York
1961	1 Apl	Emile Griffith ko 13 Benny Paret, Miami Beach
1961	3 June	Emile Griffith rsf 12 Gaspar Ortega, Los Angeles
1961	30 Sep	Benny Paret pts 15 Emile Griffith, New York
1962	24 Mar	Emile Griffith rsf 12 Benny Paret, New York
1962	13 July	Emile Griffith pts 15 Ralph Dupas, Las Vegas
1962	8 Dec	Emile Griffith rsf 9 Jorge Fernandez, Las Vegas
1963	21 Mar	Luis Rodriguez pts 15 Emile Griffith, Los Angeles
1963	8 June	Emile Griffith pts 15 Luis Rodriguez, New York
1964	12 June	Emile Griffith pts 15 Luis Rodriguez, Las Vegas
1964	22 Sep	Emile Griffith pts 15 Brian Curvis, London, Eng.
1965	30 Mar	Emile Griffith pts 15 Jose Stable, New York
1965	10 Dec	Emile Griffith pts 15 Manuel Gonzales, New York
1966	28 Nov	Curtis Cokes pts 15 Jean Josselin, Dallas
1967	19 May	Curtis Cokes rsf 10 Francois Pavilla, Dallas
1967	2 Oct	Curtis Cokes rsf 8 Charley Shipes, Oakland, Cal.
1968	16 Apl	Curtis Cokes rsf 5 Willie Ludick, Dallas
1968	21 Oct	Curtis Cokes pts 15 Ramon La Cruz, New Orleans
1969	18 Apl	Jose Napoles rsf 13 Curtis Cokes, Los Angeles
1969	29 June	Jose Napoles ret 10 Curtis Cokes, Mexico City
1969	12 Oct	Jose Napoles pts 15 Emile Griffith, Los Angeles
1970	15 Feb	Jose Napoles rsf 15 Ernie Lopez, Los Angeles
1970	3 Dec	Billy Backus rsf 4 Jose Napoles, Syracuse, NY
1971	4 June	Jose Napoles rsf 8 Billy Backus, Los Angeles
1971	14 Dec	Jose Napoles pts 15 Hedgmon Lewis, Los Angeles
1972	28 Mar	Jose Napoles ko 7 Ralph Charles, London, Eng.
1972	10 June	Jose Napoles rsf 2 Adolph Pruitt, Monterrey
1973	28 Feb	Jose Napoles ko 7 Ernie Lopez, Los Angeles
1973	23 June	Jose Napoles pts 15 Roger Menetrey, Grenoble
1973	22 Sep	Jose Napoles pts 15 Clyde Gray, Toronto
1974	3 Aug	Jose Napoles rsf 9 Hedgmon Lewis, Mexico City
1974	14 Dec	Jose Napoles ko 3 Horacio Saldano, Mexico City
1975	29 Mar	Jose Napoles tec. dec. 12 Armando Muniz, Acapulco
1975	28 June	Angel Espada pts 15 Clyde Gray, San Juan (WBA)
1975	12 July	Jose Napoles pts 15 Armando Muniz, Mexico City (WBC)
1975	11 Oct	Angel Espada pts 15 Johnny Gant, San Juan (WBA)
1975	6 Dec	John H Stracey rsf 6 Jose Napoles, Mexico City (WBC)
1976	20 Mar	John H Stracey rsf 10 Hedgemon Lewis, London (WBC)
1976	22 June	Carlos Palomino rsf 12 John H Stracey, London (WBC)
1976	28 July	Jose Cuevas rsf 2 Angel Espada, Mexicali (WBA)
1976	27 Oct	Jose Cuevas ko 6 Shoji Tsujimoto, Kanazawa (WBA)
1977	22 Jan	Carlos Palomino rsf 15 Armando Muniz, Los Angeles (WBC)
1977	12 Mar	Jose Cuevas ko 2 Miguel Angel Campanino, Mexico City (WBA)
1977	14 June	Carlos Palomino ko 11 Dave Green, London (WBC)
1977	6 Aug	Jose Cuevas ko 2 Clyde Gray, Los Angeles (WBA)
1977	12 Sep	Carlos Palomino pts 15 Everaldo Costa Azevedo, Los Angeles (WBC)
1977	19 Nov	Jose Cuevas rsf 11 Angel Espada, San Juan (WBA)
1977	10 Dec	Carlos Palomino ko 13 Jose Palacios, Los Angeles (WBC)
1978	11 Feb	Carlos Palomino ko 7 Ryu Sorimachi, Las Vegas (WBC)
1978	4 Mar	Jose Cuevas rsf 9 Harold Weston, Los Angeles (WBA)
1978	18 Mar	Carlos Palomino rsf 9 Minoun Mohatar, Las Vegas (WBC)
1978	20 May	Jose Cuevas rsf 1 Billy Backus, Los Angeles (WBA)
1978	27 May	Carlos Palomino pts 15 Armando Muniz, Los Angeles (WBC)
1978	9 Sep	Jose Cuevas rsf 2 Pete Ranzany, Sacramento (WBA)
1979	14 Jan	Wilfredo Benitez pts 15 Carlos Palomino, San Juan (WBC)
1979	29 Jan	Jose Cuevas rsf 2 Scott Clark, Los Angeles (WBA)
1979	25 Mar	Wilfredo Benitez pts 15 Harold Weston, San Juan (WBC)
1979	30 July	Jose Cuevas pts 15 Randy Shields, Chicago (WBA)
1979	30 Nov	Sugar Ray Leonard rsf 15 Wilfredo Benitez, Las Vegas (WBC)

1979	8 Dec	Jose Cuevas rsf 10 Angel Espada, Los Angeles (WBA)
1980	31 Mar	Sugar Ray Leonard ko 4 Dave Green, Landover (WBC)
1980	6 Apl	Jose Cuevas ko 5 Harold Volbrecht, Houston (WBA)
1980	20 June	Roberto Duran pts 15 Sugar Ray Leonard, Montreal (WBC)
1980	2 Aug	Thomas Hearns rsf 2 Jose Cuevas, Detroit (WBA)
1980	25 Nov	Sugar Ray Leonard ret 8 Roberto Duran, New Orleans (WBC)
1980	6 Dec	Thomas Hearns ko 6 Luis Primera, Detroit (WBA)
1981	28 Mar	Sugar Ray Leonard rsf 10 Larry Bonds, Syracuse (WBC)
1981	25 Apl	Thomas Hearns rsf 12 Randy Shields, Phoenix (WBA)
1981	25 June	Thomas Hearns rsf 4 Pablo Baez, Houston (WBA)
1981	16 Sep	Sugar Ray Leonard rsf 14 Thomas Hearns, Las Vegas
1982	15 Feb	Sugar Ray Leonard rsf 3 Bruce Finch, Reno

Junior-middleweight

1962	20 Oct	Danny Moyer pts 15 Joey Giambra, Portland, Ore. (WBA only)
1963	19 Feb	Danny Moyer pts 15 Stan Harrington, Honolulu
1963	29 Apl	Ralph Dupas pts 15 Danny Moyer, New Orleans
1963	17 June	Ralph Dupas pts 15 Danny Moyer, Baltimore
1963	7 Sep	Sandro Mazzhingi ko 9 Ralph Dupas, Milan
1963	2 Dec	Sandro Mazzhingi rsf 13 Ralph Dupas, Sydney
1964	3 Oct	Sandro Mazzhingi rsf 12 Tony Montano, Genoa
1964	11 Dec	Sandro Mazzhingi pts 15 Fortunato Manca, Rome
1965	18 June	Nino Benvenuti ko 6 Sandro Mazzhingi, Milan
1964	17 Dec	Nino Benvenuti pts 15 Sandro Mazzhingi, Rome
1966	25 June	Kim Ki-Soo pts 15 Nino Benvenuti, Seoul, Korea
1966	17 Dec	Kim Ki-Soo pts 15 Stan Harrington, Seoul
1967	3 Oct	Kim Ki-Soo pts 15 Freddie Little, Seoul
1968	26 May	Sandro Mazzhingi pts 15 Kim Ki-Soo, Milan
1968	25 Oct	Sandro Mazzhingi no-contest 8 Freddie Little, Rome
1969	17 Mar	Freddie Little pts 15 Stan Hayward, Las Vegas
1969	9 Sep	Freddie Little ko 2 Hisao Minami, Osaka
1970	20 Mar	Freddie Little pts 15 Gerhard Piaskowy, Berlin
1970	9 July	Carmelo Bossi pts 15 Freddie Little, Monza
1971	29 Apl	Carmelo Bossi dr 15 Jose Hernandez, Madrid
1971	31 Oct	Koichi Wajima pts 15 Carmelo Bossi, Tokyo
1972	7 May	Koichi Wajima ret 1 Domenico Tiberia, Fukuoka
1972	3 Oct	Koichi Wajima ko 3 Matt Donovan, Tokyo
1973	9 Jan	Koichi Wajima dr 15 Miguel de Oliveira, Tokyo
1973	20 Apl	Koichi Wajima pts 15 Ryu Sorimachi, Osaka
1973	14 Aug	Koichi Wajima ret 12 Silvano Bertini, Sapporo
1974	5 Feb	Koichi Wajima pts 15 Miguel de Oliveira, Tokyo
1974	4 June	Oscar Albarado ko 15 Koichi Wajima, Tokyo
1974	8 Oct	Oscar Albarado rsf 7 Ryu Sorimachi, Tokyo
1975	21 Jan	Koichi Wajima pts 15 Oscar Albarado, Tokyo
1975	7 May	Miguel de Oliveira pts 15 Jose Duran, Monte Carlo (WBC)
1975	7 June	Jae do Yuh ko 7 Koichi Wajima, Kitakyushu (WBA)
1975	11 Nov	Jae do Yuh rsf 6 Masahiro Misako, Shizuoaka (WBA)
1975	13 Nov	Elisha Obed ret 10 Miguel de Oliveira, Paris (WBC)
1976	16 Feb	Koichi Wajima ko 15 Jae do Yuh, Tokyo (WBA)
1976	28 Feb	Elisha Obed ko 2 Tony Gardner, Nassau (WBC)
1976	24 Apl	Elisha Obed pts 15 Sea Robinson, Abidjan (WBC)
1976	18 May	Jose Duran ko 14 Koichi Wajima, Tokyo (WBA)
1976	18 June	Eckhard Dagge ret 10 Elisha Obed, Berlin (WBC)
1976	18 Sep	Eckhard Dagge pts 15 Emile Griffith, Berlin (WBC)
1976	8 Oct	Miguel Angel Castellini pts 15 Jose Duran, Madrid (WBA)
1977	6 Mar	Eddie Gazo pts 15 Miguel Angel Castellini, Managua (WBA)
1977	15 Mar	Eckhard Dagge dr 15 Maurice Hope, Berlin (WBC)
1977	7 June	Eddie Gazo ret 11 Koichi Wajima, Tokyo (WBA)
1977	6 Aug	Rocky Mattioli ko 5 Eckhard Dagge, Berlin (WBC)
1977	13 Sep	Eddie Gazo pts 15 Kenji Shibata, Tokyo (WBA)
1977	18 Dec	Eddie Gazo pts 15 Yim Jae-Kun, Inchon (WBA)
1978	11 Mar	Rocky Mattioli ko 7 Elisha Obed, Melbourne (WBC)
1978	14 May	Rocky Mattioli rsf 5 Jose Duran, Pescara (WBC)
1978	9 Aug	Masashi Kudo pts 15 Eddie Gazo, Akita (WBA)
1978	13 Dec	Masashi Kudo pts 15 Ho Joo, Osaka (WBA)
1979	4 Mar	Maurice Hope ret 8 Rocky Mattioli, San Remo (WBC)
1979	14 Mar	Masashi Kudo pts 15 Manuel Gonzalez, Tokyo (WBA)

1979	23 June	Masashi Kudo rsf 12 Manuel Gonzalez, Tokio (WBA)
1979	25 Sep	Maurice Hope rsf 7 Mike Baker, London (WBC)
1979	24 Oct	Ayub Kalule pts 15 Masashi Kudo, Akita (WBA)
1979	6 Dec	Ayub Kalule pts 15 Steve Gregory, Copenhagen (WBA)
1980	17 Apl	Ayub Kalule ret 11 Emiliano Villa, Copenhagen (WBA)
1980	12 June	Ayub Kalule pts 15 Marijan Benes, Randers (WBA)
1980	12 July	Maurice Hope rsf 11 Rocky Mattioli, London (WBC)
1980	6 Sep	Ayub Kalule pts 15 Bushy Bester, Aarhus (WBA)
1980	26 Nov	Maurice Hope pts 15 Carlos Herrera, London (WBC)
1981	23 May	Wilfredo Benitez ko 12 Maurice Hope, Las Vegas (WBC)
1981	23 June	Sugar Ray Leonard rsf 9 Ayub Kalule, Houston (WBA)
1981	7 Nov	Tadashi Mihara pts 15 Rocky Fratto, Rochester (WBA)
1981	14 Nov	Wilfredo Benitez pts 15 Carlos Santos, Las Vegas (WBC)
1982	30 Jan	Wilfredo Benitez pts 15 Roberto Duran, Las Vegas (WBC)
1982	2 Feb	Davey Moore rsf 6 Tadashi Mihara, Tokyo (WBA)

Middleweight

1891	14 Jan	Bob Fitzsimmons ko 13 Nonpareil Jack Dempsey, New Orleans
1894	26 Sep	Bob Fitzsimmons ko 2 Dan Creedon, New Orleans
1898	25 Feb	Tommy Ryan pts 18 George Green, San Francisco
1898	24 Oct	Tommy Ryan pts 20 Jack Bonner, Coney Island, NY
1899	18 Sep	Tommy Ryan pts 10 Frank Craig, Coney Island
1901	4 Mar	Tommy Ryan ko 17 Tommy West, Louisville, Ky.
1902	15 Sep	Tommy Ryan ko 6 Kid Carter, Fort Erie
1907	2 Sep	Stanley Ketchel ko 32 Joe Thomas, San Francisco
1908	22 Feb	Stanley Ketchel ko 1 Mike Twin Sullivan, Colma, Cal.
1908	31 July	Stanley Ketchel ko 3 Hugo Kell, San Francisco
1908	18 Aug	Stanley Ketchel ko 2 Joe Thomas, San Francisco
1908	7 Sep	Billy Papke ko 12 Stanley Ketchel, Los Angeles
1908	26 Nov	Stanley Ketchel ko 11 Billy Papke, San Francisco
1909	5 July	Stanley Ketchel pts 20 Billy Papke, Colma
1910	19 Mar	Billy Papke ko 3 Willie Lewis, Paris, Fra.
1911	11 Feb	Cyclone Johnny Thompson pts 20 Billy Papke, Sydney
1912	29 June	Billy Papke pts 16 Marcel Moreau, Paris
1912	23 Oct	Billy Papke dis 17 Georges Carpentier, Paris
1912	4 Dec	Billy Papke ko 7 George Bernard, Paris
1913	5 Mar	Frank Klaus dis 15 Billy Papke, Paris
1913	11 Oct	George Chip ko 6 Frank Klaus, Pittsburgh
1913	23 Dec	George Chip ko 5 Frank Klaus, Pittsburgh
1914	6 Apl	Al McCoy ko 1 George Chip, Brooklyn
1917	14 Nov	Mike O'Dowd ko 6 Al McCoy, Brooklyn
1919	17 July	Mike O'Dowd ko 3 Al McCoy, St Paul, Minn.
1920	6 May	Johnny Wilson pts 12 Mike O'Dowd, Boston
1921	17 Jan	Johnny Wilson no-dec. 10 George Chip, Pittsburgh
1921	17 Mar	Johnny Wilson pts 15 Mike O'Dowd, New York
1921	5 Sep	Johnny Wilson no-dec. 12 Bryan Downey, Jersey City
1923	31 Aug	Harry Greb pts 15 Johnny Wilson, New York
1923	3 Dec	Harry Greb pts 10 Bryan Downey, Pittsburgh
1924	18 Jan	Harry Greb pts 15 Johnny Wilson, New York
1924	24 Mar	Harry Greb ko 12 Fay Kaiser, Baltimore
1924	26 June	Harry Greb pts 15 Ted Moore, New York
1925	2 July	Harry Greb pts 15 Mickey Walker, New York
1925	13 Nov	Harry Greb pts 15 Tony Marullo, New Orleans
1926	26 Feb	Tiger Flowers pts 15 Harry Greb, New York
1926	19 Aug	Tiger Flowers pts 15 Harry Greb, New York
1926	3 Dec	Mickey Walker pts 10 Tiger Flowers, Chicago
1927	30 June	Mickey Walker ko 10 Tommy Milligan, London, Eng.
1928	21 June	Mickey Walker pts 10 Ace Hudkins, Chicago
1929	29 Oct	Mickey Walker pts 10 Ace Hudkins, Los Angeles
1931	25 Aug	Gorilla Jones pts 10 Tiger Thomas, Milwaukee (NBA only)
1932	11 June	Marcel Thil dis 11 Gorilla Jones, Paris (NBA & Eur)
1932	4 July	Marcel Thil pts 15 Len Harvey, London, Eng.
1933	2 Oct	Marcel Thil pts 15 Kid Tunero, Paris
1934	26 Feb	Marcel Thil Pts 15 Ignacio Ara, Paris
1934	15 Oct	Marcel Thil dr 15 Carmelo Candel, Paris
1935	2 June	Marcel Thil pts 15 Ignacio Ara, Madrid

Two middleweight champions:
Carmen Basilio in his winning
fight with Sugar Ray Robinson,
23 September 1957

1935 28 June	Marcel Thil pts 10 Carmelo Candel, Paris
1936 20 Jan	Marcel Thil dis 4 Lou Brouillard, Paris
1937 15 Feb	Marcel Thil dis 6 Lou Brouillard, Paris
1937 1 Jan	Freddie Steele pts 10 Gorilla Jones, Milwaukee (NBA only)
1938 26 July	Al Hostak ko 1 Freddie Steele, Seattle (NBA only)
1940 19 July	Tony Zale ko 13 Al Hostak, Seattle (NBA only)
1941 28 Nov	Tony Zale pts 15 Georgie Abrams, New York
1946 27 Sep	Tony Zale ko 6 Rocky Graziano, New York
1947 16 July	Rocky Graziano rsf 6 Tony Zale, Chicago
1948 10 June	Tony Zale ko 3 Rocky Graziano, Newark, NJ
1948 21 Sep	Marcel Cerdan rsf 12 Tony Zale, Jersey City
1949 16 June	Jake La Motta ret 10 Marcel Cerdan, Detroit
1950 12 July	Jake La Motta pts 15 Tiberio Mitri, New York
1950 13 Sep	Jake La Motta ko 15 Laurent Dauthuille, Detroit
1951 14 Feb	Sugar Ray Robinson rsf 13 Jake La Motta, Chicago
1951 10 July	Randolph Turpin pts 15 Sugar Ray Robinson, London, Eng.
1951 12 Sep	Sugar Ray Robinson rsf 10 Randolph Turpin, New York
1952 13 Mar	Sugar Ray Robinson pts 15 Carl Olson, San Francisco
1952 16 Apl	Sugar Ray Robinson ko 3 Rocky Graziano, Chicago
1953 21 Oct	Carl Olson pts 15 Randolph Turpin, New York
1954 2 Apl	Carl Olson pts 15 Kid Gavilan, Chicago
1954 20 Aug	Carl Olson pts 15 Rocky Castellani, San Francisco
1954 15 Dec	Carl Olson rsf 11 Pierre Langlois, San Francisco
1955 9 Dec	Sugar Ray Robinson ko 2 Carl Olson, Chicago
1956 18 May	Sugar Ray Robinson ko 4 Carl Olson, Los Angeles
1957 2 Jan	Gene Fullmer pts 15 Sugar Ray Robinson, New York
1957 1 May	Sugar Ray Robinson ko 5 Gene Fullmer, Chicago
1957 23 Sep	Carmen Basilio pts 15 Sugar Ray Robinson, New York
1958 25 Mar	Sugar Ray Robinson pts 15 Carmen Basilio, Chicago
1960 22 Jan	Paul Pender pts 15 Sugar Ray Robinson, Boston
1960 10 June	Paul Pender pts 15 Sugar Ray Robinson, Boston
1961 14 Jan	Paul Pender rsf 7 Terry Downes, Boston
1961 22 Apl	Paul Pender pts 15 Carmen Basilio, Boston
1961 11 July	Terry Downes ret 9 Paul Pender, London, Eng.
1962 7 Apl	Paul Pender pts 15 Terry Downes, Boston
1962 23 Oct	Dick Tiger pts 15 Gene Fullmer, San Francisco (WBA only)
1963 23 Feb	Dick Tiger dr 15 Gene Fullmer, Las Vegas
1963 10 Aug	Dick Tiger ret 7 Gene Fullmer, Ibadan, Nigeria
1963 7 Dec	Joey Giardello pts 15 Dick Tiger, Atlantic City
1964 14 Dec	Joey Giardello pts 15 Rubin Carter, Philadelphia
1965 21 Oct	Dick Tiger pts 15 Joey Giardello, New York
1966 25 Apl	Emile Griffith pts 15 Dick Tiger, New York
1966 13 July	Emile Griffith pts 15 Joey Archer, New York
1967 23 Jan	Emile Griffith pts 15 Joey Archer, New York
1967 17 Apl	Nino Benvenuti pts 15 Emile Griffith, New York
1967 29 Sep	Emile Griffith pts 15 Nino Benvenuti, New York
1968 4 Mar	Nino Benvenuti pts 15 Emile Griffith, New York
1968 14 Dec	Nino Benvenuti pts 15 Don Fullmer, San Remo
1969 4 Oct	Nino Benvenuti dis 7 Fraser Scott, Naples
1969 22 Nov	Nino Benvenuti ko 11 Luis Rodriguez, Rome
1970 23 May	Nino Benvenuti ko 8 Tom Bethea, Umag, Yugo.
1970 7 Nov	Carlos Monzon ko 12 Nino Benvenuti, Rome
1971 9 May	Carlos Monzon ret 3 Nino Benvenuti, Monte Carlo
1971 25 Sep	Carlos Monzon rsf 14 Emile Griffiths, Buenos Aires
1972 4 Mar	Carlos Monson rsf 5 Denny Moyer, Rome
1972 17 June	Carlos Monzon ret 12 Jean Claude Bouttier, Paris
1972 19 Aug	Carlos Monzon rsf 5 Tom Bogs, Copenhagen
1972 11 Nov	Carlos Monzon pts 15 Benny Briscoe, Buenos Aires
1973 2 June	Carlos Monzon pts 15 Emile Griffith, Monte Carlo
1973 29 Sep	Carlos Monzon pts 15 Jean Claude Bouttier, Paris
1974 9 Feb	Carlos Monzon ret 6 Jose Napoles, Paris
1974 25 May	Rodrigo Valdez rsf 7 Bennie Briscoe, Monaco (WBC only)
1974 5 Oct	Carlos Monzon ko 7 Tony Mundine, Buenos Aires (WBA only)
1974 30 Nov	Rodrigo Valdez ko 11 Gratien Tonna, Paris (WBC only)
1975 31 May	Rodrigo Valdez rsf 8 Ramon Mendez, Cali (WBC)
1975 30 June	Carlos Monzon rsf 10 Tony Licata, New York (WBA)
1975 16 Aug	Rodrigo Valdez pts 15 Rudy Robles, Cartagena (WBC)
1975 13 Dec	Carlos Monzon ko 5 Gratien Tonna, Paris (WBA)
1976 28 Mar	Rodrigo Valdez ret 4 Max Cohen, Paris (WBC)
1976 26 June	Carlos Monzon pts 15 Rodrigo Valdez, Monte Carlo
1977 30 July	Carlos Monzon pts 15 Rodrigo Valdez, Monte Carlo
1977 5 Nov	Rodrigo Valdez pts 15 Bennie Briscoe, Campione d'Italia
1978 22 Apl	Hugo Corro pts 15 Rodrigo Valdez, San Remo
1978 5 Aug	Hugo Corro pts 15 Ronnie Harris, Buenos Aires
1978 11 Nov	Hugo Corro pts 15 Rodrigo Valdez, Buenos Airies
1979 30 June	Vito Antuofermo pts 15 Hugo Corro, Monte Carlo
1979 30 Nov	Vito Antuofermo dr 15 Marvin Hagler, Las Vegas
1980 16 Mar	Alan Minter pts 15 Vito Antuofermo, Las Vegas
1980 28 June	Alan Minter ret 8 Vito Antuofermo, London
1980 27 Sep	Marvin Hagler rsf 3 Alan Minter, London
1981 17 Jan	Marvin Hagler rsf 8 Fulgencio Obelmeijas, Boston
1981 13 June	Marvin Hagler ret 4 Vito Antuofermo, Boston
1981 3 Oct	Marvin Hagler rsf 11 Mustapha Hamsho, Rosemont
1982 7 Mar	Marvin Hagler rsf 1 William Lee, Atlantic City

Light-heavyweight

1903 22 Apl	Jack Root pts 10 Kid McCoy, Detroit
1903 4 July	George Gardner ko 12 Jack Root, Buffalo, NY
1903 25 Nov	Bob Fitzsimmons pts 20 George Gardner, San Francisco
1905 20 Dec	Philadelphia Jack O'Brien ko 13 Bob Fitzsimmons, San Francisco
1914 28 Apl	Jack Dillon pts 10 Al Norton, Kansas City
1916 25 Apl	Jack Dillon pts 15 Battling Levinsky, Kansas City
1916 24 Oct	Battling Levinsky pts 12 Jack Dillon, Boston
1920 12 Oct	Georges Carpentier ko 4 Battling Levinsky, Jersey City
1922 11 May	Georges Carpentier ko 1 Ted Kid Lewis, London, Eng.
1922 24 Sep	Battling Siki ko 6 Georges Carpentier, Paris
1923 17 Mar	Mike McTigue pts 20 Battling Siki, Dublin
1925 30 May	Paul Berlenbach pts 15 Mike McTigue, New York
1926 16 July	Jack Delaney pts 15 Paul Berlenbach, Brooklyn
1927 7 Oct	Tommy Loughran pts 15 Mike McTigue, New York
1927 12 Dec	Tommy Loughran pts 15 Jimmy Slattery, New York
1928 6 Jan	Tommy Loughran pts 15 Leo Lomski, New York
1929 8 Mar	Tommy Loughran pts 10 Mickey Walker, Chicago
1929 18 July	Tommy Loughran pts 15 James J. Braddock, New York
1930 10 Feb	Jimmy Slattery pts 15 Lou Scozza, Buffalo, NY (New York only)
1930 25 June	Maxie Rosenbloom pts 15 Jimmy Slattery, Buffalo (New York only)
1932 14 July	Maxie Rosenbloom pts 15 Lou Scozza, Buffalo
1933 22 Feb	Maxie Rosenbloom pts 10 Al Stillman, St. Louis
1933 10 Mar	Maxie Rosenbloom pts 10 Ad Heuser, New York
1933 24 Mar	Maxie Rosenbloom ko 4 Bob Godwin, New York
1933 3 Nov	Maxie Rosenbloom pts 15 Mickey Walker, New York
1934 5 Feb	Maxie Rosenbloom dr 15 Joe Knight, Miami
1934 16 Nov	Bob Olin pts 15 Maxie Rosenbloom, New York
1935 31 Oct	John Henry Lewis pts 15 Bob Olin, St. Louis
1936 13 Mar	John Henry Lewis pts 15 Jock McAvoy, New York
1936 9 Nov	John Henry Lewis pts 15 Len Harvey, London, Eng.
1937 3 June	John Henry Lewis ko 8 Bob Olin, St. Louis
1938 25 Apl	John Henry Lewis ko 4 Emilio Martinez, Minneapolis
1938 28 Oct	John Henry Lewis pts 15 Al Gainer, New Haven
1939 3 Feb	Melio Bettina rsf 9 Tiger Jack Fox, New York (New York only)
1939 25 Sep	Billy Conn pts 15 Melio Bettina, New York
1939 17 Nov	Billy Conn pts 15 Gus Lesnevich, New York
1940 5 June	Billy Conn pts 15 Gus Lesnevich, Detroit
1941 13 Jan	Anton Christoforidis pts 15 Melio Bettina, Cleveland (NBA only)
1941 22 May	Gus Lesnevich pts 15 Anton Christoforidis, New York (NBA only)
1941 26 Aug	Gus Lesnevich pts 15 Tami Mauriello, New York

1941 14 Nov	Gus Lesnevich pts 15 Tami Mauriello, New York
1946 14 May	Gus Lesnevich rsf 10 Freddie Mills, London, Eng.
1947 28 Feb	Gus Lesnevich ko 10 Billy Fox, New York
1948 5 Mar	Gus Lesnevich ko 1 Billy Fox, New York
1948 26 July	Freddie Mills pts 15 Gus Lesnevich, London, Eng.
1950 24 Jan	Joey Maxim ko 10 Freddie Mills, London, Eng.
1951 22 Aug	Joey Maxim pts 15 Bob Murphy, New York
1952 25 June	Joey Maxim ret 13 Sugar Ray Robinson, New York
1952 17 Dec	Archie Moore pts 15 Joey Maxim, St. Louis
1953 24 June	Archie Moore pts 15 Joey Maxim, Ogden, Utah
1954 27 Jan	Archie Moore pts 15 Joey Maxim, Miami
1954 11 Aug	Archie Moore rsf 14 Harold Johnson, New York
1955 22 June	Archie Moore ko 3 Carl Olson, New York
1956 5 June	Archie Moore rsf 10 Yolande Pompey, London, Eng.
1957 20 Sep	Archie Moore rsf 7 Tony Anthony, Los Angeles
1958 10 Dec	Archie Moore ko 11 Yvon Durelle, Montreal
1959 12 Aug	Archie Moore ko 3 Yvon Durelle, Montreal
1961 10 June	Archie Moore pts 15 Giulio Rinaldi, New York
1962 12 May	Harold Johnson pts 15 Doug Jones, Philadelphia
1962 23 June	Harold Johnson pts 15 Gustav Scholz, Berlin
1963 1 June	Willie Pastrano pts 15 Harold Johnson, Las Vegas
1964 10 Apl	Willie Pastrano rsf 5 Gregorio Peralta, New Orleans
1964 30 Nov	Willie Pastrano rsf 11 Terry Downes, Manchester, Eng.
1965 30 Mar	Jose Torres rsf 9 Willie Pastrano, New York
1966 21 May	Jose Torres pts 15 Wayne Thornton, Long Island, NY
1966 15 Aug	Jose Torres pts 15 Eddie Cotton, Las Vegas
1966 15 Oct	Jose Torres ko 2 Chic Calderwood, San Juan
1966 16 Dec	Dick Tiger pts 15 Jose Torres, New York
1967 16 May	Dick Tiger pts 15 Jose Torres, New York
1967 17 Nov	Dick Tiger rsf 12 Roger Rouse, Las Vegas
1968 24 May	Bob Foster ko 4 Dick Tiger, New York
1969 22 Jan	Bob Foster ko 1 Frankie de Paula, New York
1969 24 May	Bob Foster rsf 4 Andy Kendall, West Springfield, Mass.
1970 4 Apl	Bob Foster rsf 3 Roger Rouse, Missoula
1970 27 June	Bob Foster ko 10 Mark Tessman, Baltimore
1971 2 Mar	Bob Foster ko 4 Hal Carroll, Scranton, Pa.
1971 24 Apl	Bob Foster pts 15 Ray Anderson, Tampa, Fla.
1971 30 Oct	Bob Foster rsf 8 Tommy Hicks, Scranton
1971 16 Dec	Bob Foster rsf 3 Brian Kelly, Oklahoma City
1972 7 Apl	Bob Foster ko 2 Vicente Rondon, Miami Beach
1972 27 June	Bob Foster ko 4 Mike Quarry, Las Vegas
1972 26 Sep	Bob Foster ko 14 Chris Finnegan, London, Eng.
1973 21 Aug	Bob Foster pts 15 Pierre Fourie, Albuquerque
1973 1 Dec	Bob Foster pts 15 Pierre Fourie, Johannesburg
1974 17 June	Bob Foster dr 15 Jorge Ahumada, Albuquerque
1974 1 Oct	John Conteh pts 15 Jorge Ahumada, London, Eng. (WBC only)
1974 7 Dec	Victor Galindez ret 12 Len Hutchins, Buenos Aires (WBA only)
1975 11 Mar	John Conteh rsf 5 Lonnie Bennett, London, Eng. (WBC only)
1975 7 Apl	Victor Galindez pts 15 Pierre Fourie, Johannesburg (WBA only)
1975 30 June	Victor Galindez pts 15 Jorge Ahumada, New York (WBA)
1975 13 Sep	Victor Galindez pts 15 Pierre Fourie, Johannesburg (WBA)
1976 28 Mar	Victor Galindez ret 3 Harald Skog, Oslo (WBA)
1976 22 May	Victor Galindez ko 15 Richie Kates, Johannesburg (WBA)
1976 5 Oct	Victor Galindez pts 15 Kosie Smith, Johannesburg (WBA)
1976 9 Oct	John Conteh pts 15 Alvaro Lopez, Copenhagen (WBC)
1977 5 Mar	John Conteh rsf 3 Len Hutchins, Liverpool (WBC)
1977 21 May	Miguel Angel Cuello ko 9 Jesse Burnett, Monte Carlo (WBC)
1977 18 June	Victor Galindez pts 15 Richie Kates, Rome (WBA)
1977 17 Sep	Victor Galindez pts 15 Alvaro Lopez, Rome (WBA)
1977 19 Nov	Victor Galindez pts 15 Eddie Gregory, Turin (WBA)
1978 7 Jan	Mate Parlov ko 9 Miguel Angel Cuello, Milan (WBC)
1978 6 May	Victor Galindez pts 15 Alvaro Lopez, Viareggio (WBA)
1978 17 June	Mate Parlov pts 15 John Conteh, Belgarde (WBC)
1978 15 Sep	Mike Rossman rsf 13 Victor Galindez, New Orleans (WBA)
1978 2 Dec	Marvin Johnson rsf 10 Mate Parlov, Marsala (WBC)
1978 5 Dec	Mike Rossman rsf 6 Aldo Traversaro, Philadelphia (WBA)
1979 14 Apl	Victor Galindez ret 9 Mike Rossman, New Orleans (WBA)
1979 22 Apl	Matthew Franklin rsf 8 Marvin Johnson, Indianapolis (WBC)
1979 18 Aug	Matthew Saad Muhammad (formerly Franklin) pts 15 John Conteh, Atlantic City (WBC)
1979 30 Nov	Marvin Johnson ko 11 Victor Galindez, New Orleans (WBA)
1980 29 Mar	Matthew Saad Muhammad rsf 4 John Conteh, Atlantic City (WBC)
1980 31 Mar	Eddie Gregory rsf 11 Marvin Johnson, Knoxville (WBA)
1980 11 May	Matthew Saad Muhammad rsf 5 Louis Pergaud, Halifax (WBC)
1980 31 July	Matthew Saad Muhammad rsf 14 Alvaro Lopez, Great Gorge (WBC)
1980 20 July	Eddie Mustafa Muhammad (formerly Gregory) rsf 10 Jerry Martin, McAfee NJ (WBA)
1980 28 Nov	Matthew Saad Muhammad rsf 4 Lotte Mwale, San Diego (WBC)
1980 29 Nov	Eddie Mustafa Muhammad ret 3 Rudi Koopmans, Los Angeles (WBA)
1981 28 Feb	Matthew Saad Muhammad rsf 11 Vonzell Johnson, Atlantic City (WBC)
1981 25 Apl	Matthew Saad Muhammad ko 9 Murray Sutherland, Atlantic City (WBC)
1981 18 July	Mike Spinks pts 15 Eddie Mustafa Muhammad, Las Vegas (WBA)
1981 26 Sep	Matthew Saad Muhammad rsf 11 Jerry Martin, Atlantic City (WBC)
1981 7 Nov	Mike Spinks rsf 7 Vonzell Johnson, Atlantic City (WBA)
1981 19 Dec	Dwight Braxton rsf 10 Matthew Saad Muhammad, Atlantic City (WBA)
1982 13 Feb	Mike Spinks rsf 6 Mustapha Wassaja, Atlantic City (WBA)
1982 21 Mar	Dwight Braxton rsf 6 Jerry Martin, Las Vegas (WBC)

Cruiserweight (inaugurated 1979)

1979 8 Dec	Mate Parlov & Marvin Camel dr. 15, Split (WBC)
1980 31 Mar	Marvin Camel pts 15 Mate Parlov, Las Vegas (WBC)
1980 25 Nov	Carlos de Leon pts 15 Marvin Camel, New Orleans (WBC)
1982 13 Feb	Ossie Ocasio pts 15 Robbie Williams, Johannesburg (WBA)
1982 24 Feb	Carlos de Leon rsf 7 Marvin Camel, Atlantic City (WBC)

Heavyweight

*1882 7 Feb	John L. Sullivan ko 9 Paddy Ryan, Mississippi City
*1889 8 July	John L. Sullivan rsf 75 Jake Kilrain, Richburg, Miss.
1892 7 Sep	James J. Corbett ko 21 John L. Sullivan, New Orleans
1894 25 Jan	James J. Corbett ko 3 Charley Mitchell, Jacksonville, Fla.
1897 17 Mar	Bob Fitzsimmons ko 14 James J. Corbett, Carson City, Nev.
1899 9 June	James J. Jeffries ko 11 Bob Fitzsimmons, Coney Island, NY
1899 3 Nov	James J. Jeffries pts 25 Tom Sharkey, Coney Island
1900 11 May	James J. Jeffries ko 23 James J. Corbett, Coney Island
1901 15 Nov	James J. Jeffries ret 5 Gus Ruhlin, San Francisco
1902 25 July	James J. Jeffries ko 8 Bob Fitzsimmons, San Francisco
1903 14 Aug	James J. Jeffries ko 10 James J. Corbett, San Francisco
1904 25 Aug	James J. Jeffries ko 2 Jack Munroe, San Francisco
1905 3 July	Marvin Hart rsf 12 Jack Root, Reno, Nev.
1906 23 Feb	Tommy Burns pts 20 Marvin Hart, Los Angeles
1906 2 Oct	Tommy Burns ko 15 Jim Flynn, Los Angeles
1906 28 Nov	Tommy Burns dr 20 Philadelphia Jack O'Brien, Los Angeles
1907 8 May	Tommy Burns pts 20 Philadelphia Jack O'Brien, Los Angeles
1907 4 July	Tommy Burns ko 1 Bill Squires, Colma, Cal.
1907 2 Dec	Tommy Burns ko 10 Gunner Moir, London, Eng.
1908 10 Feb	Tommy Burns ko 4 Jack Palmer, London, Eng.
1908 17 Mar	Tommy Burns ko 1 Jem Roche, Dublin
1908 18 Apl	Tommy Burns ko 5 Jewey Smith, Paris
1908 13 June	Tommy Burns ko 8 Bill Squires, Paris
1908 24 Aug	Tommy Burns ko 13 Bill Squires, Sydney
1908 2 Sep	Tommy Burns ko 6 Bill Lang, Melbourne
1908 26 Dec	Jack Johnson rsf 14 Tommy Burns, Sydney
1909 16 Oct	Jack Johnson ko 12 Stanley Ketchel, Colma, Cal.

1910 4 July	Jack Johnson rsf 15 James J. Jeffries, Reno, Nev.
1912 4 July	Jack Johnson rsf 9 Jim Flynn, Las Vegas, N.M.
1913 28 Nov	Jack Johnson ko 2 Andre Spoul, Paris
1913 19 Dec	Jack Johnson dr 10 Jim Johnson, Paris
1914 27 June	Jack Johnson pts 20 Frank Moran, Paris
1915 5 Apl	Jess Willard ko 26 Jack Johnson, Havana
1916 25 Mar	Jess Willard no-dec. 10 Frank Moran, New York
1919 4 July	Jack Dempsey ret 3 Jess Willard, Toledo, Ohio
1920 6 Sep	Jack Dempsey ko 3 Billy Miske, Benton Harbor, Mich.
1920 14 Dec	Jack Dempsey ko12 Bill Brennan, New York
1921 2 July	Jack Dempsey ko 4 Georges Carpentier, Jersey City
1923 4 July	Jack Dempsey pts 15 Tommy Gibbons, Shelby, Mont.
1923 14 Sep	Jack Dempsey ko 2 Luis Firpo, New York
1926 23 Sep	Gene Tunney pts 10 Jack Dempsey, Philadelphia
1927 22 Sep	Gene Tunney pts 10 Jack Dempsey, Chicago
1928 26 July	Gene Tunney rsf 11 Tom Heeney, New York
1930 12 June	Max Schmeling dis 4 Jack Sharkey, New York
1931 3 July	Max Schmeling rsf 15 Young Stribling, Cleveland
1932 21 June	Jack Sharkey pts 15 Max Schmeling, Long Island, NY
1933 29 June	Primo Carnera ko 6 Jack Sharkey, Long Island
1933 22 Oct	Primo Carnera pts 15 Paolino Uzcudun, Rome, Italy
1934 1 Mar	Primo Carnera pts 15 Tommy Loughran, Miami
1934 14 June	Max Baer ko 11 Primo Carnera, Long Island
1935 13 June	James J. Braddock pts 15 Max Baer, Long Island
1937 22 June	Joe Louis ko 8 James J. Braddock, Chicago
1937 30 Aug	Joe Louis pts 15 Tommy Farr, New York
1938 23 Feb	Joe Louis ko 3 Nathan Mann, New York
1938 1 Apl	Joe Louis ko 5 Harry Thomas, Chicago
1938 22 June	Joe Louis ko 1 Max Schmeling, New York
1939 25 Jan	Joe Louis rsf 1 John Henry Lewis, New York
1939 17 Apl	Joe Louis ko 1 Jack Roper, Los Angeles
1939 28 June	Joe Louis rsf 4 Tony Galento, New York
1939 20 Sep	Joe Louis ko 11 Bob Pastor, Detroit
1940 9 Feb	Joe Louis pts 15 Arturo Godoy, New York
1940 29 Mar	Joe Louis ko 2 Johnny Paychek, New York
1940 20 June	Joe Louis ko 8 Arturo Godoy, New York
1940 16 Dec	Joe Louis ret 6 Al McCoy, Boston
1941 31 Jan	Joe Louis ko 5 Red Burman, New York
1941 17 Feb	Joe Louis ko 2 Gus Dorazio, Philadelphia
1941 21 Mar	Joe Louis ko 13 Abe Simon, Detroit
1941 8 Apl	Joe Louis ko 9 Tony Musto, St. Louis
1941 23 May	Joe Louis dis 7 Buddy Baer, Washington, DC
1941 18 June	Joe Louis ko 13 Billy Conn, New York
1941 29 Sep	Joe Louis rsf 6 Lou Nova, New York
1942 9 Jan	Joe Louis ko 1 Buddy Baer, New York
1942 27 Mar	Joe Louis ko 6 Abe Simon, New York
1946 19 June	Joe Louis ko 8 Billy Conn, New York
1946 18 Sep	Joe Louis ko 1 Tami Mauriello, New York
1947 5 Dec	Joe Louis pts 15 Jersey Joe Walcott, New York
1948 25 June	Joe Louis ko 11 Jersey Joe Walcott, New York
1949 22 June	Ezzard Charles pts 15 Jersey Joe Walcott, Chicago (NBA only)
1950 27 Sep	Ezzard Charles pts 15 Joe Louis, New York
1950 5 Dec	Ezzard Charles ko 11 Nick Barone, Cincinnati
1951 12 Jan	Ezzard Charles rsf 10 Lee Oma, New York
1951 7 Mar	Ezzard Charles pts 15 Jersey Joe Walcott, Detroit
1951 30 May	Ezzard Charles pts 15 Joey Maxim, Chicago
1951 18 July	Jersey Joe Walcott ko 7 Ezzard Charles, Pittsburgh
1952 5 June	Jersey Joe Walcott pts 15 Ezzard Charles, Philadelphia
1952 23 Sep	Rocky Marciano ko 13 Jersey Joe Walcott, Philadelphia
1953 15 May	Rocky Marciano ko 1 Jersey Joe Walcott, Chicago
1953 24 Sep	Rocky Marciano rsf 11 Roland La Starza, New York
1954 17 June	Rocky Marciano pts 15 Ezzard Charles, New York
1954 17 Sep	Rocky Marciano ko 8 Ezzard Charles, New York
1955 16 May	Rocky Marciano rsf 9 Don Cockell, San Francisco
1955 21 Sep	Rocky Marciano ko 9 Archie Moore, New York
1956 30 Nov	Floyd Patterson ko 5 Archie Moore, Chicago

1957 29 July	Floyd Patterson rsf 10 Tommy Jackson, New York
1957 22 Aug	Floyd Patterson ko 6 Pete Rademacher, Seattle
1958 18 Aug	Floyd Patterson ret 12 Roy Harris, Los Angeles
1959 1 May	Floyd Patterson ko 11 Brian London, Indianapolis
1959 26 June	Ingemar Johansson rsf 3 Floyd Patterson, New York
1960 20 June	Floyd Patterson ko 5 Ingemar Johansson, New York
1961 13 Mar	Floyd Patterson ko 6 Ingemar Johansson, Miami Beach
1961 4 Dec	Floyd Patterson ko 4 Tom McNeeley, Toronto
1962 25 Sep	Sonny Liston ko 1 Floyd Patterson, Chicago
1963 22 July	Sonny Liston ko 1 Floyd Patterson, Las Vegas, Nev.
1964 25 Feb	Muhammad Ali (Cassius Clay) ret 6 Sonny Liston, Miami Beach
1965 25 May	Muhammad Ali ko 1 Sonny Liston, Lewiston, Me.
1965 22 Nov	Muhammad Ali rsf 12 Floyd Patterson, Las Vegas
1966 29 Mar	Muhammad Ali pts 15 George Chuvalo, Toronto
1966 21 May	Muhammad Ali rsf 6 Henry Cooper, London, Eng.
1966 6 Aug	Muhammad Ali ko 3 Brian London, London, Eng.
1966 10 Sep	Muhammad Ali rsf 12 Karl Mildenberger, Frankfurt
1966 14 Nov	Muhammad Ali rsf 3 Cleveland Williams, Houston, Tex.
1967 6 Feb	Muhammad Ali pts 15 Ernie Terrell, Houston
1967 22 Mar	Muhammad Ali ko 7 Zora Folley, New York
1968 27 Apl	Jimmy Ellis pts 15 Jerry Quarry, Oakland, Cal. (WBA only)
1970 16 Feb	Joe Frazier ret 4 Jimmy Ellis, New York
1970 18 Nov	Joe Frazier ko 2 Bob Foster, Detroit
1971 8 Mar	Joe Frazier pts 15 Muhammad Ali, New York
1972 15 Jan	Joe Frazier rsf 4 Terry Daniels, New Orleans
1972 25 May	Joe Frazier rsf 4 Ron Stander, Omaha, Neb.
1973 22 Jan	George Foreman rsf 2 Joe Frazier, Kingston, Jam.
1973 1 Sep	George Foreman ko 1 Joe Roman, Tokyo
1974 26 Mar	George Foreman rsf 2 Ken Norton, Caracas (WBA only)
1974 30 Oct	Muhammad Ali ko 8 George Foreman, Kinshasa
1975 24 Mar	Muhammad Ali rsf 15 Chuck Wepner, Cleveland
1975 16 May	Muhammad Ali rsf 11 Ron Lyle, Las Vegas
1975 1 July	Muhammad Ali pts 15 Joe Bugner, Kuala Lumpur
1975 1 Oct	Muhammad Ali ret 14 Joe Frazier, Manila
1976 20 Feb	Muhammad Ali ko 5 Jean Pierre Coopman, San Juan (WBA)
1976 30 Apl	Muhammad Ali pts 15 Jimmy Young, Landover
1976 25 May	Muhammad Ali rsf 5 Richard Dunn, Munich
1976 28 Sep	Muhammad Ali pts 15 Ken Norton, New York
1977 16 May	Muhammad Ali pts 15 Alfredo Evangelista, Landover
1977 29 Sep	Muhammad Ali pts 15 Earnie Shavers, New York
1978 15 Feb	Leon Spinks pts 15 Muhammad Ali, Las Vegas
1978 9 June	Larry Holmes pts 15 Ken Norton, Las Vegas (WBC)
1978 15 Sep	Muhammad Ali pts 15 Leon Spinks, New Orleans (WBA)
1978 10 Nov	Larry Holmes ko 7 Alfredo Evangelista, Las Vegas (WBC)
1979 24 Mar	Larryu Holmes rsf 7 Ossie Ocasio, Las Vegas (WBC)
1979 22 June	Larry Holmes rsf 12 Mike Weaver, New York (WBC)
1979 28 Sep	Larry Holmes rsf 11 Earnie Shavers, Las Vegas (WBC)
1979 20 Oct	John Tate pts 15 Gerrie Coetzee, Pretoria (WBA)
1980 3 Feb	Larry Holmes ko 6 Lorenzo Zanon, Las Vegas (WBC)
1980 31 Mar	Larry Holmes rsf 8 Leroy James, Las Vegas (WBC)
1980 31 Mar	Mike Weaver ko 15 John Tate, Knoxville (WBA)
1980 7 July	Larry Holmes rsf 7 Scott Ledoux, Bloomington (WBC)
1980 2 Oct	Larry Holmes ret 10 Muhammad Ali, Las Vegas (WBC)
1980 25 Oct	Mike Weaver ko 13 Gerrie Coetzee, Sun City (WBA)
1981 11 Apl	Larry Holmes pts 15 Trevor Berbick, Las Vegas (WBC)
1981 12 June	Larry Holmes rsf 3 Leon Spinks, Detroit (WBC)
1981 3 Oct	Mike Weaver pts 15 James Tillis, Rosemont (WBA)
1981 6 Nov	Larry Holmes rsf 11 Renaldo Snipes, Pittsburgh (WBC)

Joe Louis against ex-champion
Primo Carnera. Louis stayed
heavyweight champion from
1937-1948

Olympic Champions

dna = data not available

NB: from 1904-48, losing semi-finalists boxed off for the bronze medal. Since 1952, both losing semi-finalists have received a bronze medal

Weights: Light-fly 48kg. (approx. 106lbs [7st.8lbs]).
Fly 51kg. (approx. 112lbs. [8st.])
Bantam 54kg. (approx. 119lbs [8st.7lbs])
Feather 57kg. (approx. 126lbs [9st.])
Light 60 kg. (approx. 132lbs [9st.6lbs])
Light-welter 63.5kg. (approx. 140lbs [10st.])
Welter 67kg. (approx. 148lbs [10st.8lbs])
Light-middle 71kg. (approx. 156lbs [11st.2lbs])
Middle 75kg. (approx. 165lbs [11st.11lbs])
Light-heavy 81kg. (approx. 179lbs [12st.11lbs])
Heavy over 81kg. (over 179lbs)

	Gold	Silver	Bronze
1904 (St Louis)			
Fly	George Finnegan (USA)	Miles Burke (USA)	dna
Bnt	O. L. Kirk (USA)	George Finnegan (USA)	dna
Fth	O. L. Kirk (USA)	Frank Haller (USA)	dna
Lgt	H. J. Spanger (USA)	James Eagan (USA)	R. Van Horn (USA)
Wlt	Albert Young (USA)	H. J. Spanger (USA)	Joseph Lydon (USA)
Mdl	Charles Mayer (USA)	Ben Spradley (USA)	dna
Hvy	Sam Berger (USA)	Charles Mayer (USA)	dna
1908 (London)			
Bnt	H. Thomas (GB)	J. Condon (GB)	W. Webb (GB)
Fth	Dick Gunn (GB)	C. Morris (GB)	H. Roddin (GB)
Lgt	Fred Grace (GB)	F. Spiller (GB)	H. Johnson (GB)
Mdl	John W. H. T. Douglas (GB)	Reggie Baker (Australasia)	W. Philo (GB)
Hvy	A. L. Oldman (GB)	S. Evans (GB)	F. Parks (GB)
1920 (Antwerp)			
Fly	Frankie Genaro (USA)	Anders Petersen (Den)	W. Cuthbertson (GB)
Bnt	Clarence Walker (S. Afr)	C. Graham (Can)	James McKenzie (GB)
Fth	Paul Fritsch (Fra)	Gauchet (Fra)	Edoardo Garzeno (Ita)
Lgt	Sam Mosberg (USA)	Gotfred Johanssen (Den)	Newton (Can)
Wlt	T. Schneider (Can)	Alex Ireland (GB)	Fred Colberg (USA)
Mdl	Harry Mallin (GB)	Prudhomme (Can)	Herzowitch (Can)
L-h	Eddie Eagan (USA)	Sverre Sorsdal (Nor)	H. Frank (GB)
Hvy	R. R. Rawson (GB)	Soren Petersen (Den)	Elvere (Fra)
1924 (Paris)			
Fly	Fidel La Barba (USA)	James McKenzie (GB)	Ray Fee (USA)
Bnt	Willie Smith (S. Afr)	Salvatore Tripoli (USA)	Jean Ces (Fra)
Fth	Jackie Fields (USA)	Joe Salas (USA)	Pedro Quartucci (Arg)
Lgt	Hans Neilsen (Den)	Alfredo Copello (Arg)	Freddie Boylstein (USA)
Wlt	Jean Delarge (Bel)	Hector Mendez (Arg)	Doug Lewis (Can)
Mdl	Harry Mallin (GB)	John Elliott (GB)	Joseph Beecken (Bel)
L-h	Harry Mitchell (GB)	Thyge Petersen (Den)	Sverre Sorsdal (Nor)
Hvy	Otto von Porat (Nor)	Soren Petersen (Den)	Alfredo Porzio (Arg)

Fred Grace (Great Britain) lightweight gold medallist at the 1908 Olympics

	Gold	Silver	Bronze

1928 (Amsterdam)

	Gold	Silver	Bronze
Fly	Antal Kocsis (Hun)	Armand Apell (Fra)	Carlo Cavagnoli (Ita)
Bnt	Vittorio Tamagnini (Ita)	John Daley (USA)	Harry Isaacs (S. Afr)
Fth	L. van Klaveren (Neth)	Victor Peralta (Arg)	Harold Devine (USA)
Lgt	Carlo Orlandi (Ita)	Stephen Halaiko (USA)	Gunnar Berggren (Swe)
Wlt	Ed Morgan (NZ)	Paul Landini (Arg)	Ray Smillie (Can)
Mdl	Piero Toscani (Ita)	Jan Hermanek (Cze)	Leonard Steyaert (Bel)
L-h	Victorio Avendano (Arg)	Ernst Pistulla (Ger)	Karel Miljon (Neth)
Hvy	A. Rodriguez Durado (Arg)	Nils Ramm (Swe)	Michael Michaelsen (Den)

1932 (Los Angeles)

	Gold	Silver	Bronze
Fly	Istvan Enakes (Hun)	Francisco Cabanas (Mex)	Lou Salica (USA)
Bnt	Horace Gwynne (Can)	Hans Ziglarski (Ger)	Jose Villanueva (Phi)
Fth	Carmelo Robledo (Arg)	Josef Schleinkofer (Ger)	Carl Carlsson (Swe)
Lgt	Laurie Stevens (S. Afr)	Thure Ahlquist (Swe)	Nathan Bor (USA)
Wlt	Eddie Flynn (USA)	Erich Campe (Ger)	Bruno Ahlberg (Fin)
Mdl	Carmen Barth (USA)	Amado Azar (Arg)	Ernest Pierce (S. Afr)
L-h	David Carstens (S. Afr)	Gino Rossi (Ita)	Peter Jorgensen (Den)
Hvy	Alberto Lovell (Arg)	Luigi Rovati (Ita)	Freddie Feary (USA)

1936 (Berlin)

	Gold	Silver	Bronze
Fly	Willie Kaiser (Ger)	Gavino Matta (Ita)	Louis Laurie (USA)
Bnt	Ulderico Sergo (Ita)	Jackie Wilson (USA)	Fidel Ortiz (Mex)
Fth	Oscar Casanova (Arg)	Charles Catterall (S. Afr)	Joseph Miner (Ger)
Lgt	Imre Harangi (Hun)	Nikolai Stepulov (Est)	Erik Agren (Swe)
Wlt	Sten Suvio (Fin)	Michael Murach (Ger)	Gerhard Petersen (Den)
Mdl	Jean Despeaux (Fra)	Henry Tiller (Nor)	Raul Villareal (Arg)
L-h	Roger Michelot (Fra)	Richard Voigt (Ger)	Francisco Risiglione (Arg)
Hvy	Herbert Runge (Ger)	Guillermo Lovell (Arg)	Erling Nilsen (Nor)

1948 (London)

	Gold	Silver	Bronze
Fly	Pascual Perez (Arg)	Spartaco Bandinelli (Ita)	Soo Ann Han (Kor)
Bnt	Tibor Csik (Hun)	Giovanni Zuddas (Ita)	Juan Venegas (P.R.)
Fth	Ernesto Formenti (Ita)	Denis Shepperd (S. Afr)	Aleksey Antkiewicz (Pol)
Lgt	Gerald Dreyer (S. Afr)	Joseph Vissers (Bel)	Svend Wad (Den)
Wlt	Julius Torma (Cze)	Horace Herring (USA)	Alessandro Ottavio (Ita)
Mdl	Laszlo Papp (Hun)	Johnny Wright (GB)	Ivano Fontana (Ita)
L-h	George Hunter (S. Afr)	Don Scott (GB)	M. Cia (Arg)
Hvy	Rafael Iglesias (Arg)	Gunnar Nilsson (Swe)	Johnny Arthur (S. Afr)

1952 (Helsinki)

	Gold	Silver	Bronze
Fly	Nata Brooke (USA)	Edgar Basel (Ger)	Anatolij Bulakov (USSR)
			Willie Toweel (S. Afr)
Bnt	Pentti Hamalainen (Fin)	John McNally (Ire)	Gennadij Garbuzov (USSR)
			Joon Ho Kang (Kor)
Fth	Jan Zachara (Cze)	Sergio Caprari (Ita)	Joseph Vantaja (Fra)
			Len Leisching (S. Afr)
Lgt	Aureliano Bolognesi (Ita)	Aleksey Antkiewicz (Pol)	Gheorge Fiat (Rum)
			Erkki Pakkanen (Fin)
L-w	Charles Adkins (USA)	Viktor Mednov (USSR)	Erkki Malenius (Fin)
			Bruno Visintin (Ita)
Wlt	Zygmunt Chychla (Pol)	Sergei Scherbakov (USSR)	Victor Jorgensen (Den)
			Gunther Heidmann (Ger)
L-m	Laszlo Papp (Hun)	Theunis van Schalkwyk (S. Afr)	Boris Tischin (USSR)
			Eladio Herrera (Arg)
Mdl	Floyd Patterson (USA)	Vasile Tita (Rum)	Boris Nikolov (Bul)
			Stig Sjolin (Swe)
L-h	Norvel Lee (USA)	Antonio Pacenza (Arg)	Anatolij Perov (USSR)
			Harry Siljander (Fin)
Hvy	Ed Sanders (USA)	No award: I. Johansson (Swe) disq.	Andries Nieman (S. Afr)
			Ilkka Koski (Fin)

1956 (Melbourne)

	Gold	Silver	Bronze
Fly	Terry Spinks (GB)	Mircea Dobrescu (Rum)	Rene Libber (Fra)
			Johnny Caldwell (Ire)

	Gold	Silver	Bronze		Gold	Silver

	Gold	Silver	Bronze
Bnt	Wolfgang Behrendt (Ger)	Soon Chun Song (Kor)	Freddie Gilroy (Ire)
Fth	Vladimir Safronov (USSR)	Tommy Nicholls (GB)	Claudio Barrientos (Chile)
Lgt	Dick McTaggart (GB)	Harry Kurschat (Ger)	Henryk Niedzwiedzki (Pol)
L-w	Vladimir Jengibarian (USSR)	Franco Nanci (Ita)	Pentti Hamalainen (Fin)
Wlt	Nicolas Linca (Rum)	Freddie Teidt (Ire)	Tony Byrne (Ire)
L-m	Laszlo Papp (Hun)	Jose Torres (USA)	Anatolij Laguetko (USSR)
Mdl	Gennadij Schatkow (USSR)	Ramon Tapia (Chile)	Henry Louoscher (S. Afr)
L-h	James Boyd (USA)	Gheorge Negrea (Rum)	Constantin Dumitrescu (Rum)
Hvy	Pete Rademacher (USA)	Lev Mukhin (USSR)	Kevin Hogarth (Aus)

Additional bronze names: Nicky Gargano (GB), Zbigniew Pietrzykowski (Pol), John McCormack (GB), Gilbert Chapron (Fra), Victor Zalazar (Arg), Romualdas Murauskas (USSR), Carlos Lucas (Chile), Dan Bekker (S. Afr), Giacomo Bozzano (Ita)

1960 (Rome)

	Gold	Silver	Bronze
Fly	Gyula Torok (Hun)	Sergei Sivko (USSR)	Kiyoshi Tanabe (Jap)
Bnt	Oleg Grigoriev (USSR)	Primo Zamparini (Ita)	Abdel Elguindi (UAR)
Fth	Francesco Musso (Ita)	Jerzy Adamski (Pol)	Bruno Bendig (Pol)
Lgt	Kazimierz Pazdzior (Pol)	Sandro Lopopolo (Ita)	Ollie Taylor (Aus)
L-w	Bohumil Nemecek (Cze)	Clement Quartey (Gha)	William Meyers (S. Afr)
Wlt	Nino Benevenuti (Ita)	Yuri Radonyak (USSR)	Jorma Limmonen (Fin)
L-m	Wilbert McClure (USA)	Carmelo Bossi (Ita)	Dick McTaggart (GB)
Mdl	Eddie Crook (USA)	Tadeusz Walasek (Pol)	Alberto Laudonio (Arg)
L-h	Cassius Clay (USA)	Zbig. Pietrzykowski (Pol)	Quincy Daniels (USA)
Hvy	Franco de Piccoli (Ita)	Dan Bekker (S. Afr)	Marian Kasprzyk (Pol)

Additional bronze names: Leszek Drogosz (Pol), Jim Lloyd (GB), Boris Lagutin (USSR), Willie Fisher (GB), Ion Monea (Rum), Evgenij Feofanov (USSR), Tony Madigan (Aus), Giulio Saraudi (Ita), Josef Nemec (Cze), Gunter Siegmund (Ger)

1964 (Tokyo)

	Gold	Silver	Bronze
Fly	Fernando Atzori (Ita)	Artur Oleck (Pol)	Bob Carmody (USA)
Bnt	Takao Sakurai (Jap)	Shin Cho Chung (Kor)	Stanislav Sorokin (USSR)
Fth	Stanislav Stepashkin (USSR)	Anthony Villanueva (Phi)	Juan F. Mendoza (Mex)
Lgt	Jozef Grudzien (Pol)	Vilikton Barranikov (USSR)	Washington Rodriguez (Uru)
L-w	Jerzy Kulei (Pol)	Evgenij Frolov (USSR)	Charles Brown (USA)
Wlt	Marian Kasprzyk (Pol)	Ricardas Tamulis (USSR)	Heinz Schulz (Ger)
L-m	Boris Lagutin (USSR)	Joseph Gonzales (Fra)	Ronnie Harris (USA)
Mdl	Valerij Popenchenko (USSR)	Emil Schultz (Ger)	Jim McCourt (Ire)
L-h	Cosimo Pinto (Ita)	Alexei Kiselov (USSR)	Eddie Blay (Gha)
Hvy	Joe Frazier (USA)	Hans Huber (Ger)	Habib Galhia (Tun)

Additional bronze names: Pertti Purhonen (Fin), Silvano Bertini (Ita), Nojim Maiyegun (Nigeria), Jozef Grzesiak (Pol), Franco Valle (Ita), Tadeusz Walasak (Pol), Alexander Nicolov (Bul), Zbig. Pietrzykowski (Pol), Bepi Ros (Ita), Vadim Yemelyanov (USSR)

1968 (Mexico City)

	Gold	Silver
L-f	Francisco Rodriguez (Ven)	Yong-Ju Jee (Kor)
Fly	Ricardo Delgado (Mex)	Artur Olech (Pol)
Bnt	Valerij Sokolov (USSR)	Eridadi Mukwanga (Uga)
Fth	Antonio Roldan (Mex)	Albert Robinson (USA)
Lgt	Ronnie Harris (USA)	Jozef Grudzien (Pol)
L-w	Jerzy Kulei (Pol)	Enriqua Regueiferos (Cu)
Wlt	Manfred Wolhe (E. Ger)	Jo Bessala (Camerun)
L-m	Boris Lagutin (USSR)	Rolando Garbey (Cub)
Mdl	Chris Finnegan (GB)	Alexei Kiselov (USSR)
L-h	Dan Pozniak (USSR)	Ion Monea (Rum)
Hvy	George Foreman (USA)	Ionas Chepulis (USSR)

1972 (Munich)

	Gold	Silver
L-f	Gyorgy Gedo (Hun)	U Gil Kim (N. Kor)
Fly	Gheorgi Kostadinov (Bul)	Leo Rwabwogo (Uga)
Bnt	Orlando Martinez (Cub)	Alfonso Zamora (Mex)
Fth	Boris Kousnetsov (USSR)	Philip Waruinge (Ken)
Lgt	Jan Szczopanski (Pol)	Laszlo Orban (Hun)
L-w	Ray Seales (USA)	Anghal Anghalov (Bul)
Wlt	Emilio Correa (Cub)	Janos Kajdi (Hun)
L-m	Dieter Kottysch (W. Ger)	Wieslaw Rudkowski (Po)
Mdl	Viatcheslav Lemeschev (USSR)	Reima Virtanen (Fin)
L-h	Mate Parlov (Yug)	Gilberto Carrillo (Cub)
Hvy	Teofilio Stevenson (Cub)	Ion Alexe (Rum)

Bronze		Gold	Silver	Bronze

1976 (Montreal)

Bronze		Gold	Silver	Bronze
Harlan Marbley (USA)	L-f	Jorge Hernandez (Cub)	Byong Uk Li (N Kor)	Payao Pooltarat (Thai)
Hubert Skrzypczek (Pol)				Orlando Maldonado (P.R.)
Servilio de Oliveira (Bra)	Fly	Leo Randolph (USA)	Ramon Duvalon (Cub)	David Torosyan (USSR)
Leo Rwabwogo (Uga)				Leszek Blazynski (Pol)
Eiji Morioka (Jap)	Bnt	Yong Jo Gu (N Kor)	Charles Mooney (USA)	Pat Cowdell (GB)
Soon-Kill Chang (Kor)				Victor Rybakov (USSR)
Philip Waruinga (Ken)	Fth	Angel Herrera (Cub)	Richard Nowakowski (EG)	Leszek Kosedowski (Pol)
Ivan Michailov (Bul)				Juan Paredes (Mex)
Calistrat Cutov (Rum)	Lgt	Howard Davis (USA)	Simion Cutov (Rum)	Vasily Solomin (USSR)
Zvonimir Vujin (Yug)				Ace Rusevski (Yug)
Arto Nilsson (Fin)	L-w	Ray Leonard (USA)	Andres Aldama (Cub)	Vladimir Kolev (Bul)
James Wallington (USA)				Kazimierz Szczerba (Pol)
Vladimir Musalimov (USSR)	Wlt	Jochen Bachfeld (EG)	Pedro Gammaro (Ven)	Reinhard Skricek (WG)
Mario Giulotti (Arg)				Victor Zilberman (Rum)
John Baldwin (USA)	L-m	Jerzy Rybicki (Pol)	Tadija Kacar (Yug)	Victor Savchenko (USSR)
Gunter Meier (W. Ger)				Rolando Garbey (Cub)
Agustin Zaragoza (Mex)	Mdl	Michael Spinks (USA)	Rufat Riskiev (USSR)	Alec Nastac (Rum)
Al Jones (USA)				Luis Martinez (Cub)
Georgi Stankov (Bul)	L-h	Leon Spinks)USA)	Sixto Soria (Cub)	Costica Dafinoiu (Rum)
Stanislav Dragan (Pol)				Janusz Gortat (Pol)
Giorgio Bambini (Ita)	Hvy	Teofilio Stevenson (Cub)	Mircea Simon (Rum)	John Tate (USA)
Joaquin Rocha (Mex)				Clarence Hill (Bermuda)

1980 (Moscow)

Bronze		Gold	Silver	Bronze
Ralph Evans (GB)	L-f	Shamil Sabirov (USSR)	Hipolito Ramos (Cub)	Ismail Moustafov (Bul)
Enrique Rodriguez (Spa)				Byong Uk Li (N Kor)
Leszek Blazynski (Pol)	Fly	Petar Lessov (Bul)	Victor Miroschnichenko (USSR)	Janos Varadi (Hun)
Doug Rodriguez (Cub)				Hugh Russell (Ire)
George Turpin (GB)	Bnt	Juan Hernandez (Cub)	Jose Pinango (Ven)	Michael Anthony (Guy)
Ricardo Carreras (USA)				Dumitru Cipere (Rum)
Clemente Rojas (Col)	Fth	Rudi Fink (EG)	Adolfo Horta (Cub)	Krzystof Kosedowski (Pol)
Andras Botos (Hun)				Victor Rybakov (USSR)
Sam Mbogwa (Ken)	Lgt	Angel Herrera (Cub)	Victor Demianenko (USSR)	Richard Nowakowski (EG)
Alfonso Perez (Col)				Kazimierz Adach (Pol)
Zvonimir Vujin (Yug)	L-w	Patrizio Oliva (Ita)	Serik Konakbaev (USSR)	Tony Willis (GB)
Issaka Dabore (Niger)				Jose Aguilar (Cub)
Dick Murunga (Ken)	Wlt	Andres Aldama (Cub)	John Mugabi (Uga)	Karl-Heinz Kruger (EG)
Jesse Valdez (USA)				Kazimierz Szczerba (Pol)
Alan Minter (GB)	L-m	Armando Martinez (Cub)	Alexandrei Koshkin (USSR)	Detlef Kastner (EG)
Peter Tiepold (E. Ger)				Jan Franek (Cze)
Prince Amartey (Gha)	Mdl	Jose Gomez (Cub)	Victor Savchenko (USSR)	Valentin Silaghi (Rum)
Marvin Johnson (USA)				Jerzy Rybicki (Pol)
Isaac Ikhuoria (Nigeria)	L-h	Slobodan Kacar (Yug)	Pavel Skrzecz (Pol)	Herbert Bauch (EG)
Janusz Gortat (Pol)				Ricardo Rojas (Cub)
Peter Hussing (W. Ger)	Hvy	Teofilio Stevenson (Cub)	Pyotr Zaev (USSR)	Istvan Levai (Hun)
Hasse Thomsen (Swe)				Jurgen Fanghanel (EG)

Index

Page references in italic refer to illustrations